BREATHING

D1405163

MOVEMENT

EXPLORATION

Barbara Sellers-Young

Illustrations by
Joel Robert Smith

&

Photos by
Neil Michaels

APPLAUSE
NEW YORK • LONDON

This book is dedicated to
Kimberly and Berri
who have enriched my life beyond words.

CONTENTS

EXPLORATIONS

Part One: Awareness

1. Body Sensing: Exploration, Breath, and Imagery

2. Dynamic Alignment

3. Energy, Metaphor, Action

Part Two: Application

4. Mask, Myth, and Archetype

5. Performing Identity: Creating Character

ILLUSTRATIONS AND PHOTOS

FOREWORD

Breathing, Movement, Exploration is aimed at helping actors, actors in training, teachers of acting, and students of drama, to understand better how to use their entire bodies effectively on the stage. There are few books that take the actor through a program which develops body consciousness, and this may be the first to bring together traditions from both eastern and western cultures into such a guide. Barbara Sellers-Young has immediate experience of a wide range of cultural practices and is uniquely positioned to make this commentary. Thus, this book is both timely and necessary.

Breathing, Movement, Exploration can be read as a course of work that takes one along a sequence of techniques to develop acting skills from body awareness to textual application. The book combines background information with exercises that are always beneficial, practical, to the point and clearly explained. In addition there are many illuminating illustrations to aid the user. The techniques are drawn from western sources such as Feldenkrais, Alexander, Laban and Stanislavski, as well as eastern concepts of breath and energy. Sellers-Young translates eastern techniques both by finding analogous western concepts and by making accessible practices that are quite different from Western practices. What is useful about the combination is not only the holistic vision it offers, but the way that it strengthens specific acting skills used in the development of mask and character. Sellers-Young uses the phrase 'Feel, fuse and follow', which summarizes her approach: feel internal awareness of the body, fuse with it by applying the combined practices she explores, and follow the body energy/trajectory of this awareness.

Students of drama always receive instruction in movement, but often it is discipline-specific and based on one particular teaching method such as that developed by Laban. These discipline-specific systems of movement were often developed for other walks of life, and a joy this course of learning provides is that it takes what is useful from these disciplines and develops them for the stage; a grammar of movement if you like. For this reason *Breathing, Movement, Exploration* is especially helpful to teachers of general acting courses, and to those wanting to integrate a broadly based and cross-cultural approach to movement and drama. Professional actors and directors are usually under constraints of time, space and resources. This book can help them by prompting them to strategies that they may have forgotten, or introducing them to new ways of working.

Because the commentary takes the reader through a detailed exploration, it is not necessary to have prior knowledge about the various traditions on which it draws, although of course, previous experience can be used to build them further. Even more helpful, is the detail of this guide; anyone training or working in the profession can work on it at home, developing techniques on their own. The commentary is direct, clear and takes the reader step-by-step through each exercise, and students' testaments are used throughout the text, allowing an acute perception of the way that the course has been received, and the potential in her approach. The clarity with which Sellers-Young moves from basic concepts about movement into their application in the understanding and development of mask and character, also makes the commentary a valuable source for related professions and disciplines. Students, teachers and researchers in, for example, literature, anthropology, media and cultural studies, will find it accessible and illuminating, as will the general reader with an interest in how an actor works and how the performance of identity can be probed.

Peter Lichtenfels
Manchester Metropolitan University, England

ACKNOWLEDGMENTS

The ideas and exercises in this book have been the basis for classes, workshops, and presentations in the United States and elsewhere. I want to thank the organizers of the conferences and panels for providing me with the opportunity to explore this material with them. I particularly want to thank Niamh Dowling and Janelle Reinelt for making it possible for me to share this work with students at Manchester Metropolitan University and the International College at Beijing. I also want to express my deep appreciation to all the students in the MFA Acting program at Davis, but particularly my faithful teaching assistants: John Leonard, Tom Gough, Ari Kreith, Adrienne Southard, Jennifer King, Yawar Charlie, Shawn Dorazio, and Jeremy Southard. Thanks also to other students in the program who shared with me their personal response to the text: Carla Spindt, Deborah Adams, Mark Philpot, Kate Hall, Kristina Goodnight, Caroyln Burgoyne, Dionne Poindexter, Hannah Rahilly, and Robert Wilson. David Williams was a careful editor as well as helping me to understand how a historian looks at acting. Sondra Reid, Linda Rentner and Shona McCarthy provided solid editorial assistance. Ninette Medovoy, Emma Katleba, and Socorro Figueroa supported the writing and editing process in ways too numerous to detail, but were always much appreciated.

There are many others whose ideas and support were pivotal to the evolution of this text. Special thanks to Robert Barton; his approach to actor training is the foundation for this text. Sarah Pia Anderson, as a director, demonstrated unique and powerful ways to work with actors. Janet Descutner introduced me to the arts of Asia and Larry Kominz and Jonah Saltz supported my 'on site' education in them. James Kapp opened my being to the vast possibilities of the martial arts. My Nihon Buyô teachers, Fujima Kanriye and Hanayagi Jutemai, have been consistent models of teaching excellence. My colleague Karen Shimakawa has helped me to understand the complex relationship between the body and the text. Bobbie Saltzman's insights on the relationship between acting and life are an integral part of this text. Elizabeth Carlin-Metz and Peter Lichtenfels provided invaluable and thoughtful observations at all stages of the text's evolution. It would not be what it is without their knowledge and insight.

I also want to extend my thanks to Gail Finney, my adopted sister, who has consistently encouraged my personal and intellectual growth. I also wish to thank those friends who through their willingness to share their thoughts on life and performance have shaped this project: Terra Pressler, Susan Bowie, Jeanne Bader, Christina Forakis, Susan McFadden, Kathy Drake, Judith Ryan, Kathleen Whelan, Kate Davy, Terri Lundgren, Rachel Edelson, Louise Pare, and Jan Brierley. Particular thanks to Geri LaDuke, who in her wisdom and compassion has helped me to understand living as a combination of faith and trust. This text was made possible by the enormous emotional support and life lessons provided over the years by my daughters, Kimberly and Berri.

Elaborations of the text's theoretical framework have appeared in *Theatre Topics* and *Theatre Research International* ("Somatic Processes: Convergence of Theory and Practice," *Theatre Topics* 8/2 (September 1998) 173-187; "Technique and the Embodied Actor," *Theatre Research International* 24/1 (Spring 1999) 89-102.) My thanks to the editorial staff of both journals for their thoughtful comments which significantly contributed to the development of the conceptual framework of this text.

INTRODUCTION

Programs for creative human change need to be based on a clear perception of each individual's psychophysical uniqueness.

Michael Murphy

Acting is an act of the imagination that takes place in front of an audience. Learning to free your imagination is an act of self-cultivation that combines states of heightened bodily awareness with a method for applying this awareness to the task of creating a performance. Thus, the concept of action, both in the development of awareness and in its application, is a fundamental principle of acting. Our guide to understanding both awareness and application is the Russian performance theorist, Constantin Stanislavski. As Stanislavski points out in *Creating a Character*, life is a series of actions that start the moment one leaves the mother's womb. The first action of life is an intake of breath. From this moment, individual lives are a series of actions that are responses to the environment. Unique and individual sensory modes–eyes, ears, nose, tongue, skin receptors, and internal sensing devises–take in information from the environment, process it, and stage a response. This three-fold process– perception, contemplation, and response or action–is not only the foundation of individual lives, it is also the fundamental component of theatre. As Stanislavski suggests, theatre is the revelation of a character's life through a set of *staged actions*. An actor's creation of a stage persona through use of his/her imagination is a process of discovery of a character's actions. The goal of this book is to help you to accomplish this. Therefore, the material in the text consistently unites three somatic or body/mind processes that are associated with action and acting: *an attitude of exploration, the awareness of breath*, and *the unifying power of imagery*.

The creative process, from initial idea through final product, is a *state of ongoing somatic exploration* in which you as a sensing and feeling being discover, investigate, and sometimes rehearse a set of actions in relationship to your environment. This approach to actor training unites internal (psychological) and external (kinesthetic) aspects of your creative process. It assumes: (1) When you alter an aspect of your muscle or skeletal system, the nervous system, including the brain and, therefore, your imagination, is affected; (2) The inverse is also true; the nervous system, including the brain, therefore the imagination through imagery, influences your body's reaction. Thus, an attitude of exploration immerses you in an experience of self as a perceptual being who has the capacity to explore internal and external aspects of self in the evolution of new actions. Consequently, the approach to training provided here helps you to increase your awareness of the somatic interplay between your mind and body, between your imagination and physical life.

With an *attitude of exploration*, you will learn increased awareness of the basic structures of the self–bones, muscles, nerves, skin–to the complexity of creating and maintaining a state of dynamic alignment with its associated states of a released, relaxed, and open attitude toward your work. Other explorations use *breath and imagery* to explore masks, the physical life of a character, and a text. Breath is also used to expand your awareness and thus enlarge your self-image. Combined with sound, breath and energy help to unite your body with a character's emotional life. *Imagery and metaphor* are used throughout the text to increase focus and concentration, improve alignment, define characters, and explore a text.

Often we will work with these three processes–exploration, breath, imagery–as separate somatic processes to increase your level of awareness or to develop such skills as concentration or listening. While each process may be approached individually, all three are in constant interaction with each other. This text is also linked by a method of concentration that I call *feel, fuse,* and *follow.* This is a physical technique that unites breath with physical states. The technique is applied throughout the text–from your experience of the breath, the expansion of your awareness, your exploration of dynamic alignment, and your investigation of imagery and energy to the creation of character and, finally, to your interaction with others and a script.

The text is divided into two sections, *Awareness* and *Application.* The goal of the first section, Awareness, is to increase your cognizance of the basic structure of your body, including breath, dynamic alignment, energy, and expressiveness. It is divided into three chapters: "Body Sensing," "Dynamic Alignment," and "Energy, Metaphor, Action." Chapter one, "Body Sensing," provides a foundation for understanding the basic mechanisms of your body. Incorporating material from eastern and western theories of the self, the material is divided into explanations of the basic somatic processes and explorations that encourage you to increase somatic skills related to dynamic alignment–relaxation, focus, and concentration. The second chapter, "Dynamic Alignment," combines an intellectual understanding of the movement potential of specific body parts, such as the pelvis and the spine, with the use of imagery. Images are used throughout to help correct common muscular holding patterns, such as pronation of the feet, locked knees, hyper-extended back, and forward head. The final chapter in this section, "Energy, Metaphor, Action," integrates the concept of physical action with your emotional and physical awareness through the study of the movement theories of Rudolf Laban. His approach to the body helps you to identify and expand upon your personal action style.

The objective of the second section, *Application*, is to explore ways of using your increased awareness. Chapter 4, "Mask, Myth, and Archetype," provides a set of mask explorations, beginning with self mask exercises and ending with archetypal masks. Each mask helps you to discover skills that are important ingredients in performance. Some explorations use an actual mask; other exercises concentrate on using the idea of the mask to help you create a character. Chapter 5, "Performing Identity: Creating a Character," furnishes a method for integrating three aspects of your creative identity–you as an individual, your process of creation, and your integration of self and process in the evolution of a character. As such, it blends text analysis and the physical embodiment of a character through points of exploration that focus on breath, imagery, character's journey, space, time, ensemble, and audience.

Each chapter of the book provides opportunities for you to elaborate and expand upon your experience through a journal. The journal is considered an important tool as it provides a consistent reference point for you in the ongoing expansion of self-awareness and creativity. The progress of your awareness of specific physical traits and habits, as well as your relationship to your cultural heritage, may be documented in the journal. You can keep track of emotional responses evoked by individual explorations and trace your progress in the use and refinement of breath and imagery. The entire journal can be referred to in the ongoing process of developing a character. Each chapter ends with a checklist of ideas developed in the chapter. Use this checklist as a beginning point to recall what you have learned, but personalize it with your own observations.

Finally, this book is based on a belief that we are all works in progress who are the result of complex personal histories. Accordingly, I believe that the way to achieve creative potential is not through make, force, push, and coerce, but through allow, accept, embrace, and enjoy. Besides adapting explorations from somatic therapist Moshe Feldenkrais, kinesiologist Lulu Sweigaard, and movement theorist Rudolph Laban, I have devised open-ended explorations which I believe will engage you in a process of discovery. Thus, the explorations in each section, *Awareness* and *Application*, combine a set of body-focused tasks and related questions that encourage you to expand your awareness of the body (first section) and methods of using self in application to a score or text (second section). They have been written to stimulate you to consider the topic of a particular exploration from a variety of viewpoints. Students or teachers should read through the exploration twice. The first reading gives you a general impression of the exploration. During the second reading, use a marker to highlight those sections which are for you the salient points. Use the highlighted sections as an experiential guide for the exploration. This approach to the explorations will personalize your experience with the material. Teachers using this text can individualize the explorations to meet the needs of a particular group of students as well as use the explorations as a guide from which to create their own.

This text provides a method of self-development that enhances various stages of actor training, from beginning classes to scene study. The first two chapters, "Body Sensing" and "Dynamic Alignment", are designed to complement exercises in relaxed readiness or body awareness offered in beginning acting classes. The Laban explorations in Chapter three and mask explorations in Chapter four provide methods to evolve and analyze characters that can accompany classes focused on characterization. The final chapter uses Stanislavski's conceptual framework to provide a process of combining previous explorations with text analysis and thus can be used in conjunction with classes in scene study. Nevertheless, you may discover in your individual work with this text that the material on mask precedes rather than follows the work with Laban. I would encourage you to use the text in the order you feel will help you to develop your creative potential.

The following is a list of terms that have evolved from theories of the body and of Stanislavski's approach to acting. I have placed them at the beginning rather than in a glossary at the end of the text to give you an opportunity to familiarize yourself with them.

Vocabulary of the Body:

Archetypes: Carl Jung conceived of personality as a confluence of the body with culture. The result of which was a set of personae (archetypes) that could be found in all cultural groups. Archetype or sets of archetypes derived from the myths and stories of one's childhood can influence an actor's physical choices. Actors can also use archetypes as images to create a role.

Associative memory: The mind's ability to create imaginative leaps between various experience. This is often revealed in phrases or images during periods of exploration. These phrases and images can be used to increase awareness or as the basis for exploring a text.

Awareness: There are several different forms of awareness that encompass self, self as actor, and actor in relationship to community. First, there is a level of self understanding that acknowledges physical and mental habits. Next there is an awareness of the process and related performance techniques you use as an actor to create characters. Finally, there is the awareness of how to work and communicate with colleagues. Each of these constantly interacts with the other.

Body/mind or Soma: This term refers to the unified integration of the entire self, including muscle or kinesthetic awareness, sensory awareness, psychophysical images and vocal awareness. Somatic training encourages the integration of the entire self, allowing the associative, intuitive, creative self to flow with the impulses of the moment.

Body Attitude: The physical or external representation of your internal experience or body image.

Breath: This includes internal and external respiration and the kinesthetic awareness of each.

Constructive Rest: A position of the body in which the major muscle groups of the body are at rest in relationship to each other.

Dynamic Alignment: Dynamic alignment is the constant adjustment of your body's bony and muscular systems in relationship to each other.

Energy: This is the movement of the electrical energy that takes place in the body due to constant changes in the neuro-muscular system or the relationship between breath and energy. You can achieve an awareness of the energy flowing through your body by first becoming aware of the breath flowing through your entire body as you focus on a task or an intention. Asian body disciplines refer to this as *chi*.

Exploration: The attitude of exploration encompasses a mode of inquiry; a period of questioning followed by a moment of decision. While there is an element of improvisation in every moment of our day, we are generally not actively engaged in exploration. A conscious placement of yourself in this attitude increases your level of awareness and provides you with a means of expanding your creative choices. Some acting texts refer to this as openness.

Imagery: Imagery is the mental-sensory picture you use in visualization. Images can be based on actual lived experience as in sensory imagery, imaginative creations based on the script and metaphoric representations of nature such as a withered oak tree, a billowy cloud, on a yellow daisy. You can use well-placed images to develop a character's physical life.

Imagination: The imagination is the source of new images that emerge through the integration of mind and body.

Internal Landscape: Your kinesthetic experience of your body developed through the increased awareness of your body's sensory system.

Intuition: Intuition refers to the release of the creative self in the development of the dramatic moment. The active component of intuition is impulse.

Neutral: A active state of consciousness from which the actor approaches his/her work.

Personal Movement Signature: An individual's physical style that is the result of a person's gender, family, education, and other aspects of their social and cultural background.

Self Monologue: We each have an internal monologue or a conversation that is our attempt to integrate past experience with the present moment. Noting this monologue in the form of a journal can help one understand how you conceive of your relationship to yourself, your process, and your method of creating a character.

Sounding: Sounding is an aspect of sensory imagery. It is the energy created by the unification of thought/intention, breath and your vocal chords. The energy of sound is used to increase kinesthetic and emotional awareness and is part of working with a text.

Text: A text can refer to a script, a piece of poetry, or a movement score.

Visualization: Visualization is an act of mental intention. Thus, it is a process by which we use our imaginations to create new states of being. With an appropriate image, you can use the visualization technique to change your alignment, develop the life of a character and prepare for a performance.

Stanislavski's Terms:

The definitions of the terms listed are stated from the standpoint of the character. It is, however, the actor, in collaboration with the director, who makes decisions about what the character thinks, wants, and feels.

Actions: These are playable verbs or actions that an actor uses to reveal the character's desire to create a reaction in the other characters in the scene. It combines the internal desires of the character with the actual physical vocabulary of the character. These are sometimes written as a score and referred to as an action score.

Beats: This is the division of a script into separate segments evolved around a specific task. Usually, these beats or phrases of the script are determined by directors and actors during early rehearsals.

Given Circumstances: These are the who, when, and where of a particular script. It includes information on occupation, age, gender, ethnicity and national identity of characters as well as historical time period and location.

Intention/Objective: This is what a character wants to happen at a given moment of time. The character's intention can change over the course of the script. A super-objective or intention is the character's primary goal within the world of the play.

Internal Monologue: This is what the character is thinking in reference to what is taking place within the scene. It is experienced as a set of images that are related to the character's past experience. This is often the basis for the sub-text of a scene.

Obstacle: These are the aspects of the character's personality, the environment, or the situation that work to prevent a character from succeeding in his/her intentions. The goal of the actor is to discover methods for the character to overcome the obstacles in a scene.

World of the Play: This is the establishment of where the action of the play takes place. This includes the specific location or environment, the related social structures and status hierarchies, religious beliefs, physical style, and other aspects of the play's context.

PART ONE

AWARENESS

Awareness is the primary creative tool of a performing artist. The many aspects of this awareness are similar to the knowledge a painter must have of color, form, and the texture of a paint brush, and the many possibilities inherent in each. At the outset, there is awareness of self and your modes of perception and related energy states that are a result of your physical and psychological being. The primary goal of the chapters included in this section is to increase your awareness and related perceptual capabilities. This primary goal implies a development of your understanding of the somatic processes—breath, exploration, and imagery—and your ability to use them to relax within the moment, concentrate on a task, and observe and analyze the physical life of yourself and others. From this awareness, you develop an ability to use self–akin to a painter's use of form, color, and brush—as a creative vehicle for performance.

Top: *Cloud Nine* Directed by Sarah Pia Anderson, Jon Jackson as Joshua

Middle: *The Rover* Directed by Sarah Pia Anderson, from right to left Craig Swogger as Belville, Jona Newhall as Willmore, Maceo Oliver as Frederick

Bottom: *Cloud Nine* Directed by Sarah Pia Anderson, Nancy Stone as Edward

CHAPTER ONE

BODY SENSING:
BREATH, EXPLORATION, AND IMAGERY

An actor's tool is himself, but his use of himself informs all the things of his mind and body; his observations, his struggles, his nightmares, his prison, his patterns, himself as a citizen of his times and his society.

Joseph Chaikin

THREE BODY PROCESSES

Actor training in the United States has, since the establishment of the American Laboratory Theatre in 1923, been dominated by the Freudian-based approaches of Russian director Constantin Stanislavski. This system is often referred to as "psychological realism "and is documented in his four books: *An Actor Prepares* (1936), *Building a Character* (1949), *My Life in Art* (1956), and *Creating A Role* (1961). In *Creating a Role*, Stanislavski situated elements of his training method, including text analysis and improvisation, around the concept of physical action, which he defined as containing inner and outer aspects: "In every physical action, unless it is purely mechanical, there is concealed some inner action, some feelings. This is how the two levels of life in a part (dramatic role) are created, the inner and the outer. They are intertwined. A common purpose brings them together and reinforces the unbreakable bond."[1] According to Stanislavski, any play or film is a dramatic unfolding of physical actions that are the revelation of a character's inner reactions to an external situation. This approach to movement training integrates Stanislavski's concept of physical action with core concepts from Asian physical disciplines and western conceptions of the body to provide you with an approach to the creative process that unites internal and external aspects of yourself

---

[1]Constantin Stanislavski, *Creating a Role*, trans. Elizabeth Reynolds Hapgood (New York: Routedge/Theatre Arts Books, 1989), 228.

or what Peter Brook refers to as the body's subtle energies:

> Acting begins with a tiny movement so slight it is almost
> invisible … I make a proposition to an actor's imagination
> such as "She is leaving you." At this moment a subtle move-
> ment occurs deep in anyone, but in most non-actors the
> movement is too slight to manifest itself in any way; the actor
> is a more sensitive instrument and in him the tremors detect-
> ed.[2]

Your ability to access this subtle tremor is the result of increased
awareness of internal energy states. This book outlines a journey of
discovering these internal states and their related impulses. It evolves
in a series of explorations that combines information from a variety of
approaches to self-awareness and applies them to the craft of performance.

The beginning of this journey is an understanding of the interaction between two aspects of your soma or body/mind—your structural
self, or actual physical system, and your imaginal self, or the images of
the world you have stored in memory. The integration of the structural
and imaginal systems through interaction with your environment creates your somatic or energy state and body attitude. By modeling the
behavior of others, for example, you learned to walk, talk, and wear the
situationally appropriate social mask. Whether by yourself or in a
group, your awareness is generally limited to the momentary joy or
frustration you felt at the success or failure of some social interaction.
If it was successful, you repeated the physical style and associated tac-
tics that brought success; if it was not successful, you tried to discover
a new behavior pattern. The new behavior pattern creates a new self-
image and related body attitude. This replication of experience creates
a generalized self-image and energy state that you adjust as necessary
to accommodate different social situations.

The majority of people are not aware of the relationship
between these two systems. One aim of performance training, however, is to make conscious the unconscious aspects of behavior.
Experience teaches us that bringing unconscious acts to the realm of

---

[2]Peter Brook, *The Empty Space* (London: Pelican, 1972), 122-123.

conscious behavior helps you to initiate change from a standpoint of choice rather than the nebulous method of trial and error. This expanded knowledge allows you to engage new patterns to enhance your creative potential. Three body processes help guide these new levels of awareness—*an attitude of exploration, the experience of breath,* and *the unifying power of imagery.*

An Attitude of Exploration

Anthropologist Mary Catherine Bateson points out that life is an improvisation.[3] Each of us may attempt to plan the next moment from the previous one, but we have no certain knowledge that our perceptions and related actions will fulfill our desires. We constantly have to respond to changing circumstances by creating new strategies based on new perceptions. Focusing your attention on the sensory attributes of any task as an exploration immerses you in a dialogue with self and the environment that includes modes of attention, methods of inquiry, and application of information. Thus, an attitude of exploration relies on your ability to take in, at any moment, new information through your sensory modalities (eyes, ears, nose, tongue, and skin) and to process this information with that taken in simultaneously through the proprioceptor or sensing devices located in the skin, muscles, joints, and inner ear. This combination of sense information is examined or explored by the memory in order to take action.

Exploration thus encourages you, through the three-part process of attention, investigation, and application, to examine, probe, research, analyze, and study aspects of self. Exploration, practiced as a process, also helps you to stay focused on the present moment; not on what did or did not work in the previous moment or on what might work in the next. This is a somatic state, referred to in the martial arts as "open attention," in which your senses are attuned to both yourself and to other people and the environment.[4] Attributes of exploration or open attention, identified as a flow state by psychologist Mihaly Csikszentmihalyi, are immediate feedback, focus or one-pointedness of mind, appropriate challenge, loss of self-consciousness, and an altered

---

[3] Mary Catherine Bateson, *Peripherl Visions* (New York: Harper, 1994), 1-15.

[4] A discussion of this state is in Wendy Palmer, *The Intuitive Body* (Berkeley, CA: North Atlantic Books, 1994), 87-96.

sense of time.[5] In a flow state, the exploration itself becomes "autotelic," worth doing for its own sake. Committing to the process of exploration, you dedicate yourself to the awareness necessary for using yourself as an instrument of creation.

Some explorations within the text will seem easy while others will present a challenge. Clive Barker encourages actors to realize, "Methods of self-exploration have to be found, and, at the core of these, is the process of creative transformation, which is at the root of acting."[6] Besides opening up new avenues for your imagination, focused exploration takes you into the realm in which you become your own teacher. In becoming your own teacher, you are making a commitment to the potential of your unique artistic expression.

One method of introducing yourself to exploration as a process of attention, investigation, and application is to concentrate on a single part of the body. Place yourself into an exploratory state by softening the focus of your eyes (slightly close your eyelids) and allow the breath to drop into your belly.

1. Now, bring your visual and kinesthetic attention to your hands.
2. Begin to notice the shape of the hands. How are the fingers, thumbs, and palms relating to each other?
3. Start to open and close the hands in a simple, grasping motion. Transfer your attention to the fingers. How do they move individually and together? What motions are the fingers capable of achieving? Individually? As a unit?
4. Move your attention to the thumbs. What motions are unique to the thumb? How do the thumbs integrate with the palms and fingers?
5. Bring your attention to your wrists. How does the action in your wrists influence either thumb?
6. Now come back to an investigation of the entire hand. What is your current awareness of your hand as a unit? As a section of individual parts? Of the possible articulation of the hands?
7. Look for an object to pick up—a pencil, cup, book, plant, shoe, etc. Pick up the object with attention on the palm. The fingers. The thumb. The wrist. The entire hand.

---

[5]Mihaly Csikszentmihalyi, *Flow* (New YOrk: harper Row, 1990).
[6]Clive Barker, *Theatre Games* (London: Methuen, 1977), 110.

8. What are all the ways you could pick up the object?
9. How does attention to each individual part inform your kinetic understanding of the whole?

Within the sample exploration, you undertook the act of exploration from a relaxed mode of attention or flow state, but with a specific task. You discovered new levels of awareness as a result of the task and applied this new information to a different task. Trained to explore and maintain "open attention," you will bring increased creative potential to the rehearsal. This form of attention is also inherently dramatic as you are constantly in a state of invention, a form of improvisation. For this reason, I refer to the exercises in this text as explorations. The use of the verb; explore; as a noun; exploration; is to remind you that you are engaged in an ongoing process of increased awareness, discovery, and application; a process that is not limited to a series of exercises or a definite time period. Instead, your somatic knowledge and related artistry is constantly folding back on itself as new discoveries create new levels of awareness that can be applied to new performance challenges.

To aid you in this, many of the explorations in the text are divided into two sections—bold and ordinary type face. The bold face sections give you the outline of the exploration. The ordinary type face provides additional methods of exploring the text. First read and follow the instructions in the bold face sections. Use the ordinary type face to expand your experience.

One method of documenting your increased understanding of self and craft is to keep a journal. Each exploration in this text has a related journal entry that asks you to answer specific questions or visually illustrate your experience. These questions are a guide to expand your level of awareness by focusing on aspects of the exploration you might not otherwiseconsider. However, you do not need to limit the journal entry to the precise questions or to the exploration. You can expand on the journal questions of a particular exploration. You can also incorporate experience outside of this text; for example, observations of actors you see on stage, television, film or your experiences in a rehearsal.

The journal is a dialogue with yourself that also serves as a memory aide. In describing or explaining your experience, you add another layer of meaning by connecting kinetic experience with language. You also create a document you can reflect upon later both as a means to remember what you did and to note working patterns. Thus, the journal serves to help you to refine your craft.

The Experience of Breath

The following statements by student actors outline the transformative power of breath, from its power to create a unity of experience to its links to emotional states.

> *When I think of breathing, of "being" with my entire body, it is as if every inch of my body is a membrane through which I can take in air and therefore energy, I realize a more integrated sense of self—that it is not just my brain with an attached body, but rather that my body is my "brain." It is all connected if I allow it to be.*[7]

> *Breathing and my heartbeat are the two symbiotic clocks that are the fundamental music of the body. Not only do they set the pace, but also mood, thought, timing, and every other biological function within me. Generally the hot moods, excitement and anger, encourage a faster-paced breathing, not quite shallow but not completely deep either. They incite the body to action of some kind and thus the breath follows, prepared for that action whether it is fighting, running, or sex. Cool moods, sadness, grief, depression, have a slower-paced breathing; these bring the body to stillness or death.*[8]

Breath is, after all, the essence of life. While we can live for periods of time without food or water, we will die instantly if we cannot breathe. Clinically, breath is functionally defined as it is related to the respiratory system: Oxygen is inhaled and carbon dioxide is exhaled. Many authors have demonstrated, however, that although respiration is involuntary, it is influenced by an individual's mental/emotional state.[9] Yogic and Taoist traditions have long known (and western biofeedback researchers have recently discovered) that

---

[7]Cynthia Winston, Personal communication, September, 1997.

[8]Anonymous actor, Personal communication, November 1997.

[9]Sheila Haas, for example, as discussed in J.E. Loehr and P.J. Mclaughlin, *Mentally Tough* (New York: M. Evans and Company, 1986), 153-154.

conscious control of the breath influences somatic states. Breath explorations are used in the beginning stages of self-repatterning in many body therapies. Judith Leibowitz, a practitioner of Alexander technique, adds observing breath patterns to Alexander's directions to "let the neck be free, to let my head go forward and up, to let my torso lengthen and widen, to let my legs release away from my torso, and let my shoulders widen."[10]

Breath, as Susanna Bloch's research has demonstrated, is also tied to an actor's emotional life. Her research in the effector patterns of the six basic emotions (joy, sadness, tenderness, fear, anger, and sensuality) suggests that performers with the ability to control breath patterns and individual muscle groups can be taught to replicate these six states:

> Indeed, we have determined that each basic emotion can be evoked by a particular configuration composed of: 1) a breathing pattern, characterized by amplitude and frequency modulation; 2) a muscular activation characterized by a set of contracting and/or relaxing groups of muscles, defined by a particular posture; 3) a facial expression or mimicry characterized by the activation of different facial muscle patterns.[11]

When the multiple possibilities of breath are explored, it becomes an element to which one can constantly return and still focus on other information. Breath is an element of learning to relax, center, and explore alignment. The experience of internal respiration becomes your starting point to allow a state of mental quiet, often referred to as neutral, and thus influences your potential to become a conduit for a character. With breath as the starting point, you will become aware of your individual emotional states and the emotional states of a character. Breath is the beginning of communicating the goals and desires of a character. Breath can also be integrated with imagery to create and manipulate energy. The placement, use, and mastery of the breath also allows you to unite the two technical approaches to acting–internal and external, or psychological and physical.

---

[10]Judith Leibowitz and Bill Connington, *The Alexander Technique* (New York: Harper and Row, 190), 135.

[11]Susana Bloch, Pedro Orthous, and Guy Santibanez "Effector Patterns of Basic Emotions: A Psychophysiological Method for Training Actors, "*Journal of Social Biological Structure*, (10, 1987), 3.

Inasmuch as breath is automatic, we rarely notice it. Take a moment, close your eyes and place your attention on your breath. Answer the following questions:

1. Can you distinguish the inhalation from the exhalation?

2. Where do you feel the inhalation in your body? Chest? Ribs? Belly? Pelvis? Feet? Hands? Head?

3. Where do you feel the exhalation leaving your body? Chest? Ribs? Belly? Pelvis? Feet? Hands? Head?

4. What do you note about the phrasing or tempo of the breath? Fast? Slow? Medium? Where do you feel the inhalation and exhalation if you change the tempo?

5. Do you experience an emotional change when you change the tempo of the breath? Do these emotions seem to be centered in one part of the body more than another?

6. Now open your eyes and ask the same set of questions. Are your answers the same or different?

In this sample breath exploration, there was introduced a set of questions concerning breath placement, emotional association with, and phrasing that will be returned to again and again throughout the text. You also had an opportunity to work with your eyes closed that focused you inward on your internal landscape and with your eyes open that focused you outward on the external environment. Ultimately, "open attention" combines internal and external focus. Thus, many explorations in this text will ask you to begin with an internal focus and maintain this internal connection as you interact with the environment.

The Power of Imagery

Actor Lisa Maxine intuitively remarked that "imagery is a proactive way to influence our reality by visualizing the desired result/situation and investing energy into that image. It gradually becomes you and your reality."[12] Imagery is the nervous system's unifying process. Information from your eyes, ears, nose, skin, tongue, and the proprioceptive system is stored in the brain as images. These images come

---

[12]Lisa Maxine, Personal communication, October 1997.

from a range of sources–from family, school, church, and community. In contemporary society, among the primary distributors of images are the media—books, newspapers, magazines, television, films, and the Internet. As Mark Johnson has indicated, these images become for the individual coded metaphors that represent experience.[13]

There is evidence of people using imagery and related visualization techniques dating from 60,000 to 10,000 B.C. In 200 B.C., Hindu scholar Patanjali recorded centuries of yogic exercises in the Yoga Sutra. He described visualization as consisting of three parts: "*dharana*, the focusing of attention on one place, either inside or outside the body; *dhyana*, the continued focus of attention aided by supportive suggestions; and *samadhi*, the union between the object and the person concentrating upon it."[14] Through a three-part process of focus, suggestion, and unification on a particular image, you create deep levels of awareness. You can use this three-part method to elevate alignment problems, expand your expressive range, create physical characters, discover the emotional life of a character, and control your energy states. Director Elizabeth Carlin-Metz points out, "This is the process actor's engage that convinces the audience that they can actually see what the actor is imaginatively seeing."[15]

Energy

The unifying power of images can be combined with a state of exploration and an awareness of internal respiration to create new energy states. Thus, energy is defined as a combination the three somatic processes–exploration, breath and imagery. While we often consider only external respiration, actual breathing involves an internal respiration process that takes place as oxygen replaces carbon dioxide on a cellular level. Breathing is therefore one of the body's processes that connects the internal landscape with external communication. In Asian physical disciplines, including yoga and t'ai chi, students are taught how to focus their intention through the self by becoming aware of internal respiration. One often-repeated phrase is: 'Mind follows

---

[13] Mark Johnson, *The Mind in the Body* (Chicago: University of Chicago Press, 1987).

[14] Mike Samuels and Nancy Samuels, *Seeing with the Mind's Eye* (New York: Random House, 1975), 22.

[15] Elizabeth Carlin-Metz, Personal Communication, September 2000.

attention and attention follows breath and breath generates energy.' Another way of phrasing this would be, 'Images from the mind create attention. This attention integrates with the breath and the body's systems to create energy.' In China this internal energy is referred to as chi; in Japan, it is ki. This is an invisible, silent, and formless life force that combines the respiratory process with the sensory-motor system's ability to attend to and develop sensory images.[16] The combination of breath, metaphoric imagery, and the act of exploration unifies your sensory, memory, and respiratory systems. In Asian somatic terms, the image you hold follows the breath and moves throughout your body.

A method that combines exploration, breath, and imagery is a technique referred to by martial arts instructor James Kapp as *feel, fuse,* and *follow*.[17] Inspired by this technique, the following exploration focuses your sensory and mental systems on a task. Perform this exercise alone or in a class where a number of objects have been brought in and randomly spread around the room.

1. Pick up an object. If the object has a standard use, ignore that information and "discover" it as new. Begin to feel the size, shape, and texture of it.
2. While touching the object itself, become aware of your breath moving through your body and out your hand.
3. Extend the feeling of breath into the object, allowing the breath to fuse with your experience of touching it.
4. As your hand becomes comfortable with the object, follow the impulse to manipulate or use the object derived from that fusion.
5. Try not to plan the action at all, but rather allow it to evolve from the experience of feeling, fusing and following your internal impulses to explore.
6. Whenever possible, explore other ways of discovering objects, beyond touch. For example, you might employ eyes, ears, and nose, substituting see, hear, and smell as the opening guide word instead of feel. Allow each sensory system to increase your awareness of another. You can actually learn to listen to your muscles, hear through your feet and smell with your skin.

In using the feel, fuse, and follow technique, you are engaging the three

---

[16]Yasuo Yuasa, *The Body: Toward an Eastern Mind-Body Theory*, trans. by Shigenori Nagatomo and Thomas Kasulis (New York: SUNY Press, 1987).

[17] James Kapp, Personal Communication, June 1995.

stages of a physical action–perception, contemplation, and response or action. This technique will be adapted in various ways to enhance your experience of breath, to explore dynamic alignment, to create a physical character, and to investigate a text.

BODY ATTITUDE

A *gesture* is a movement of any body part, including all parts of your torso, head, and limbs. In contrast, a *posture* is the position of your body when not moving. Postures and gestures are physical actions we use to navigate our environment. Each time we enter a room, sit in a chair, walk through a building, greet a friend, get in and out of bed, brush our teeth, and perform other daily tasks we make postural and gestural choices. Many people refer to this combination of posture and gesture as *body attitude*. In Figure 1, each individual displays a different body attitude that is a combination of three separate but interacting selves.

The first is the *essential self*. This is your individual mode of sensory perception that influences how you perceive information, process it, and, consequently, interact with your environment. It includes the combined functioning of all your body's systems, from the pattern of your eyes, nose, and mouth to your height and weight and includes special talents, such as a melodic vocal instrument, an ear for dialects, or a feel for rhythm. Your individual perceptive modalities are what make you unique.

Second is your *habitual self*. This body attitude includes elements of your ways of thinking and behaving that have evolved in response to your environment. This self is the result of your enculturation into a community. It includes learning to walk, ride a bicycle, play a sport, and interact with family. It also includes childhood stories and associated heroes or heroines who have become part of your psyche and consequently your imagination. Individual body attitudes have been influenced by such cultural icons as Elvis Presley and Marilyn Monroe and cartoon figures like Mighty Mouse.

Your *social mask* is a combination of habits, cultural norms, and rules you learned from your family and social group, incorporating from them a view of yourself as a distinct individual with a specific

Figure 1: Body Attitude

Actors Dionne Poindexter, Carolyne Burgoyne, Rob Wilson and
Hannah Rahilly demonstrate different Body Attitudes.

gender, ethnic background, and sexual orientation. It is your "body image," the image you have of yourself interacting in the world. Over a lifetime you have learned many social masks that you put on, take off, and replace, depending on the occasion. Each time you engage in a situation, whether with another individual or a group, you are acting from your current integration of your essential self, habitual body attitude, and social mask.

Applied to a variety of situations, your body attitude and related postural and gestural language encompass your past, your current state of being, and your vision of what you anticipate for your future. These habits of behavior are your methods of survival. This postural or movement vocabulary is also, for the most part, unconscious. A goal of this text is to assist you in bringing the unconscious part of self into conscious reality. Once conscious, it can be transformed as needed to help improve breath awareness, resonance, centering, grounding, and expressiveness–all of which result in an expanded imagination. Personal analysis is a way to identify those physical patterns and their environmental and imagistic sources. Once identified, old patterns can be inhibited. The goal of the following observation exercise is to increase your awareness of your personal preferences and to increase your observational skills in general.

```
┌─────────────────────────────────────────────┐
│      Exploration 1: Personal Inventory       │
└─────────────────────────────────────────────┘
```

In this exploration, you will be analyzing either your own movement or that of a fellow actor. Any of this information can be shared with others as written information or as part of a group discussion. The following are questions to help you with the observation. While comprehensive, this chart does not cover all possible questions. Challenge yourself to add to it. If you choose to assess another individual, eventually assess yourself as a journal assignment. When assessing yourself, note which answers you had immediately and which ones you had to consider or even ask others for the answer.

Phase One: SELF AT REST

Standing

Where do you place your weight when standing? On one foot? Both feet?

What is the physical center of your body? Pelvis? Upper Torso? Head?

Where is the emotional center of your body? Is it the same place as your physical center?

Is there a part of your body that is more active or dominant than others parts, even when the body is at rest? This distinction can be established by noticing which body parts you use in accomplishing different tasks. For example: When you sit down, do you cross your right or left leg? When you get up from the floor, do you use the right or left arm to help you up?

Sitting

What is your relationship to the object on which you are sitting? Do you appear to be released or resistant? Which parts of your body seem to resist the object on which you are sitting? Do you sit on any part of yourself?

Is the body crossed in one or more places? How tightly crossed?

How much space do you take when you sit?

Do you create angles or a set of curves? Are these created by the spine? The appendages? What is the angle of the head? Are you curving your head or angling it in more than one direction?

Expression

What is the typical look on your face?

How would you describe it?

What range of facial expression do you notice?

Do you make eye contact with others? Is this eye contact direct or indirect?

Do you open your eyes wider or have a tendency to narrow them when you make eye contact? Do your eyebrows move at all and, if so, when?

Do you have other facial habits, such as pursing your lips or raising your eyebrows?

What is the phrasing of a typical expression? Fast? Medium? Slow?

Are you easy to read or somewhat poker-faced?

Phase Two: SELF IN MOTION

Walking

Is your pace while walking generally fast, slow, medium?

How constant is the tempo? Is it fairly predictable or can it change radically?

Do you punctuate or stress with any part of the body as you walk?

How regular or varied are you? What are the phrase or phrases of movement being repeated over and over?

Do you land with your full weight on the ground or glide, making only minimal contact?

What is your relationship to gravity? Do you indulge it by being pulled into it or do you resist in it by lifting yourself away from it?

When leaning on something, do you make full contact or partial? Is the contact flat or curved?

Do you prepare to move by shifting your weight, adjusting clothing, swaying slightly, or do you initiate the movement internally?

When you stop, is there a recovery period of similar realignments? Or is there a feeling that you stop internally?

Do you reach out with your hands to touch furniture before you sit, lean on walls or corners as you go round them, grab railings or stairways?

How would you define the general pattern of your gestures? Fluid, smooth, effortless, or jerky and labored?

From where do you initiate a change of direction or speed? From your feet and legs? From your torso? From your pelvis? From your head?

Basic Gesture Patterns

When you talk, do you use large or small amounts of space with your arms and hands?

Does your use of space change with types of conversations? With different people? Different situations?

Would you say that you change gestures a lot? Infrequently? Almost never?

Would you describe your gesture language as predictable?

Do you have props you play with such as your hair, pencil, articles of clothing?

Does one set of gestures often lead to another set of gestures?

What part of your body is highlighted by your gesture language? Your head? The center of your torso? The full length of your body?

Phase Three: SELF AND OTHER

What is the difference between your public and your private demeanor?

External Boundaries

What if any actual physical contact with others is involved in either situation?

What kind of an invader and receiver are you? How likely are you to initiate physical contact? Are you good at maintaining your own boundaries? At reading the intentions of others? What parts of people do you feel comfortable touching? What parts uncomfortable? What parts are you comfortable having other people touch?

Internal Boundaries

What is the relationship between your physical and emotional life?

How does your body reflect the receipt of good or bad news?

Can others tell what kind of day you are having?

Cultural Boundaries

Does everyone guess where you were born even if they don't hear you speak? Do people know you are from the city or the country without having to ask?

Is your ancestry obvious? Do you share a set of moves with other people whose parents were of the same nationality, religion, or any other dominant affiliation?

Psychological Boundaries

Do you send out the information that you have been told for years not to assert yourself in groups lest you be thought of as overbearing? Or do you signal that you have been taught to push, shove, shout, get seen, grab attention–whatever it takes to get what you deserve? How evident in your behavior are the rewarded and punished behaviors that were part of your home, school, or church?

Phase Four: SELF AND IMAGE

Can others tell your special skills and favorite activities? A dancer, athlete, pianist, body builder, scholar? Have you picked up all of the trademarks, along with the love of the activity? Do people get your age right or wrong? Do you fall into a traditional masculine/feminine image? An androgynous mix? Neutral or ambiguous? How flexible and changeable is this image?

Phase Five: SELF AS METAPHOR

If you were to describe yourself metaphorically, what would it be?

What kind of tree? (quiet oak, tall-standing pine, or?)

What kind of flower? (gentle daisy, bright red rose, or?)

What kind of car? (sports car, station wagon, or?)

What kind of building? (log cabin, skyscraper, or?)

What item in a house? (cooking pan, electric clock, or?)

What kind of community? (rural, urban, or?)

What kind of rock? (small, smooth stone, piece of lava, or?)

Journal: As you explored the personal inventory questions, either in relation to yourself or to another person, what did you discover about yourself? What part of the style of the other person was easy? Difficult? How has your image of yourself been modified by the assignment? Are you more aware of your patterns in relation to self and others than you were previously? What alternatives might you consider? Draw a picture of yourself.

STRESS, BODY ATTITUDE, AND AWARENESS

As long as you have this physical tenseness you cannot even think about delicate shadings of feeling or the spiritual life of your part. . . .Therefore, at times of great stress it is especially necessary to achieve a complete freeing of the muscles. In fact, in the high moments of a part the tendency to relax should become more normal than the tendency to contraction.

Constantin Stanislavski

Stress is a primary influence on your body attitude. Maintenance of a stress-free body is part of a daily discipline that is not limited to the rehearsal studio, but is part of each waking moment. This commitment to the discipline of developing a stress-free approach to your work ultimately creates a new set of habits that complement your acting process.

One advantage of body listening is the awareness it can bring to the influence of stress. A goal of awareness is to permit us to move free from unnecessary tension and with an expanded sense of our being, yet each of us has areas where we carry tension. This contracted state of the muscles allows less blood and nerve flow, thus inflaming nerves and instigating pain. The degree of tension, or muscle-holding, creates an imbalance in the mechanical functioning of the system. The sources of tension do not develop overnight; they are the result of mental and physical habits related to present and past environments. Changing these habits requires a commitment to move beyond self-imposed limits.

It is easy to go to a massage therapist and leave feeling a temporary release of physical and mental tension. Maintaining a released, relaxed body, however, requires consistent daily practice that includes breathing, stretching, strengthening, and grounding exercises. A variety of techniques help to create this body, from those included in this text to methods of meditation, positive visualization, and such Eastern tech-

niques as chi gong, t'ai chi, and aikido. Anyone who wants to stay physically and mentally healthy needs to consider incorporating a variety of
strategies.

One often-asked question is: Since I am so used to a specific way of
orienting myself in my environment, how do I know when a muscle is
being released and I am moving with less tension? The change can
either be dramatic, with the sudden release of a long-held muscle, or it
can occur in small stages over time. Most people will experience both
sudden releases and slow, small reorganizations. The most surprising
can be those in which there is a sudden or unanticipated change. The
effects from these changes can include nausea, disorientation, fear,
weeping, exhaustion, flashbacks, and hallucinations. It is possible to
reduce tension without these effects, however. The intensity of one's
experience is associated with the reason for the area of tension. Bodily
stress associated with some highly emotional experience is more likely
to create a sudden and intense release of tension than stress related to
a habit picked up from being raised within a certain family or geographical area. Sally Fitt explains:

> Understanding that these effects [responses to tension
> release] are common helps to neutralize the fear produced by
> the particular response. Anyone who works extensively with
> relaxation techniques is familiar with these effects and is usu-
> ally not frightened by them. We learn to accept that, in the
> past, the body dealt with some pain by locking it up in ten-
> sion. Reducing the tension allows access to the pain of the
> past, if the person wishes to deal with it, or sometimes even if
> the person does not wish to deal with it.[18]

General muscle soreness or momentary muscle spasms that might
be slightly painful can also occur as a contracted muscle releases to a
more relaxed state. Muscle soreness can be the result of many factors–failure to warm up and cool down the body before and after stren-
uous exercise, poor mechanical use of the body, stress on the body
related to lifestyle or overuse of specific muscle groups. Typically,
soreness is the result of an accumulation of toxins in the muscle

---

[18]Sally Sevey Fitt, *Dance Kinesiology* (New York: Schrimer Books, 1988), 294.

tissue. This waste, known as lactic acid, is caused by oxygen depriva tion related to some physiological phenomenon, but it can also be related to constant anxiety, which can only increase muscle tension as local circulation decreases. Scientists have discovered that injecting lactic acid into the bloodstream will lead to "anxiety attacks in a neu- rotic subject, and even produce all the symptoms of anxiety in a healthy one. So, once again, we find a mental state and a chemical reaction reinforcing one another, reciprocally increasing until serious local or system-wide imbalances, even damages, occur."[19] The situation per- petuates itself in a vicious cycle. Greater anxiety produces more lactic acid, more tense or sore muscles, and more anxiety.

Thus, there is an obvious relationship between stress and injury. Actors who are in a state of stress are more likely to injure themselves in physically aggressive scenes than those who are in a state of relaxed readiness. Hans Seyle points out:

> The stress producing factors–technically called stressors–are varied and different, yet they all elicit essentially the same bio- logical stress response. From the point of view of its stress producing or stressor activity, it is immaterial whether the agent or situation we face is pleasant or unpleasant; all that counts is the intensity of the demand for readjustment or adaptation ... Stress is not merely nervous tension or some- thing to be avoided.[20]

Seyle points out that stress can be either positive or negative. Positive stress exists when we feel in control of the situation and believe we can influence what is taking place. The experience is a challenge rather than a threat; you approach the situation with a combination of com- mitment and curiosity. By contrast, negative stress occurs in a situation with overtones of a demand or threat. Your experience is then one of alienation, frustration, or hopelessness; you are a victim of circum- stances, unable to influence what is taking place in your life.

How do you cope with negative stress? People who effectively deal with stress have developed a variety of coping mechanisms. One

---

[19]Deane Juhan, *Job's Body* (New York: Station Hill Press, 1987), 320-321.
[20]Robert Cooper, *Health and Fitness Excellence* (Massachusetts: Houghton Mifflin Co., 1989), 17.

of these mechanisms, called "transformational" by Joan Borysenko, director of the Mind/Body Clinic at Harvard Medical School, refers to transforming the moment, emphasizing a positive approach to stress management:

> Committed people who believe they are in control and expect situations to be challenging are likely to react to stressful events by increasing their interaction with them–exploring, controlling, and learning from them. This attitude transforms the event into something less stressful by placing it in a broader frame of reference that revolves around continued personal growth and understanding.[21]

Some people cope with stress regressively by avoiding interactions with stressful situations. They believe they are powerless to control their lives, and generally they are afraid of change. But, as we have seen, stress can be viewed as an opportunity to learn to live with change. Take a moment and practice the following. Note how your body transforms with each step. The combination can help to alleviate any stressful situation.

1. **Connecting with your breath.** Become aware that you are breathing and focus on the breath and sending it through your body.
2. **Changing imagery.** First, fully acknowledge your current circumstances. Then shift your thoughts away from problems, thinking not about what you do not want, but about what you want. Then take action by creating an image of what you want to have happen. Develop complete sensory-rich images that for you are empowering.
3. **Moving the body.** Get up, walk, and unstress by moving. Activity automatically helps to raise your mood. Make a quick assessment: What part of your body needs attention right now? Choose a physical activity according to that need and shift your visual focus to that activity.
4. **Replenishing of nutrients.** Have a drink of water. Eat a small snack that experience has taught gives you energy. Foods for

---

[21]Cooper, 17.

increased mental alertness are low in fat and include a small

amount of protein-rich food. These promote faster thinking, greater energy, increased attention to detail, and quicker response time. Foods for increased calmness are low in fat and protein but high in complex carbohydrates.

These suggestions can be combined with increased states of awareness. Take a walk outside while eating a small snack and looking at the view. Stop a moment to look at an inspiring section of a book or your journal while you eat a small snack, and follow that up with a specific muscle-releasing exercise. Have a cup of whatever liquid helps to rejuvenate you while you are taking a moment to reflect, and note muscular activity. Go for a short walk, normalizing your breathing with your movement. You can, with practice, train yourself to look for solutions instead of getting locked on problems and to focus on what you can control rather than what you cannot. Ultimately, you learn to pause and listen with an open mind instead of reacting. This practice helps you to evolve a personal philosophy that replaces anxiety and anger with a resolve to think clearly and approach people honestly.

Learning to live with stress will help prevent injury because you will have ascertained how to work with your body and not against it, and you will have been specific about the physical approach and will have listened to your body's signals. Despite the excellent care you give yourself, you are still going to experience muscle soreness and injury at times. These are separate but related phenomena. Muscle soreness is caused by extended use of the muscle, sometimes, but not always, associated with lactic acid build-up. One method of relieving tension is through use of the breath.

Journal: Describe your experience of the steps of relaxation. Be specific with regard to your body. For example, do not limit your description to, "I felt better when I connected to my breath." Instead, describe specific body parts and how they felt. For example, "my shoulders released and melted away from my ears." Or, "my stomach quit doing flip-flops and begin to feel like a calm pond." Which of the steps seemed an extension of your daily life? Which seemed distinctly different from what you normally do in stressful situations? How would you integrate the steps as part of the daily conduct of your life?

BODY LISTENING

The more we are aware of our bodies, the less likely it is that negative influences of stress will have a long term impact on our bodies. Body listening is a practice that uses the technique of exploration to listen toor sense the internal landscape of the body–that is, body sensing. By body sensing I mean the act of observing the internal landscape and related breath and energy states, together with their external manifestations, as physical actions or postures and gestures, and the use of these observations.

Body listening is the ability to be aware of what Asian body disciplines call the "teacher within," not necessarily a specific teacher but what some people refer to as an internal guide. Here I use the phrase metaphorically to mean listening to the various parts of the self as if they had something to teach you. By listening, you are asking the question, "What can I learn through awareness of my nervous system, muscles, skin, and bony structure?" The attitude with which you approach body listening strongly influences what you are doing. Being able to listen and be aware of your current state allows you to respond more directly and effectively. For example, knowing where you feel stiff allows you to engage in exercises that will release that part of your body.

Body listening also deepens your awareness of your internal emotional landscape in comparison to external action. Throughout the text, these aspects of self are often referred to as internal and external focus and awareness. Internal focus/awareness guides you to a deeper appreciation and understanding of your intuitive self. External focus/awareness, or the understanding of the impact of your actions on others, helps you to explore and to note other's reactions to potential choices that you as an actor make in the development of a character. When internal awareness is combined with external awareness, you have placed yourself at the center of Stanislavski's circles of concentration—from self, to interchange with another, to awareness of stage ensemble, and, finally, to incorporating the audience.[22]

---

[22]Jean Benedetti, *Stanislavski and the Actor* (New York: Routledge/Theatre Arts, 1998), 39-40.

An obstacle to becoming an effective body listener is the judgmental approach we bring to what we hear from our bodies. Our critical inner voices are often filled with such words as should, must, will, force, and discipline. As somatic therapist Moshe Feldenkrais phrases it:

> To learn we need time, attention, and discrimination; to discriminate we must sense. This means that in order to learn we must sharpen our powers of sensing, and if we try to do most things by sheer force we shall achieve precisely the opposite of what we need.[23]

The thoughts that arise during the explorations are an indication of the language incorporated into your construction of your body image. Include these thoughts in your journal as a means to evolve a clearer insight of the relationship between your body image and your essential self and social mask. Writing the thoughts down creates a personal distance that allows you to make decisions about what words or phrases you want to keep, because they expand your awareness, and what words or phrases you would like to eliminate, as they reduce your experience. For example, constant self-criticism of body parts, such as "My nose is too big for a woman" or "I am not tall enough to be a real man," do not expand our belief in your creative possibilities. The same can be said of critiques of methods of working such as "I should be able to do such and such," or "Why can't I work like so and so?" Once noted, the self-deprecating remarks can be replaced with words or phrases that appreciate your individual uniqueness and the progress you make each day as a creative artist.

A helpful tool in learning to overcome an overly critical inner audience involves re-framing the concept of discipline. Stephen Covey, author of *Seven Habits of Highly Effective People*, takes the term discipline, with its authoritarian overtones, and redefines it to mean becoming the disciple of your own life. This positive affirmation is employed by acting teacher Robert Benedetti, who advises his students:

> As you begin this journey, remember that one skill makes all others possible: discipline. Real discipline is not a matter of

---

[23]Moshe Feldenkrais, *Awareness Through Movement* (New York: Harper and Row, 1977), 58.

following someone else's rules; it is your acceptance of the responsibility for your own development through systematic effort. Discipline will come naturally if you can acknowledge the importance and seriousness of your work and the great need for it in the world.[24]

This definition encourages you to engage in a dialogue with your inner voice in order to allow, yield, surrender, accept, embrace, welcome, incorporate, and adopt the experiences and states of the moment while assimilating new ways of being. This act of exploration is a three-part process. First, you will want to immerse yourself in the experience from the viewpoint of "the first time." You are in a mode of inquiry, investigation, and search. Second, you will want to note the interaction between the physical and psychological aspects of the experience. The question you want to ask is, "What do I know about myself and my working process that I did not know before?" Finally, as you apply the new information to your method of working, you will want to try to avoid placing judgment on the quality of the experience. Instead, you can acknowledge all thoughts as information and return to exploring. Engaging in this process of body listening/exploration allows you to develop a new set of voices that nurture your development as you open your self to the possibilities offered by just saying "yes." MFA student David Garrett once remarked:

> I am constantly learning about myself as a moving person. I'm fine-tuning my mechanism and learning what its capabilities are. As I go forward, I am learning to trust my body as my friend and that it is up to the job of making me a well-rounded actor. I'm on my way and seeing the results.[25]

Exploration 2: Body Scan

The body scan increases the internal and external awareness necessary to maintain a state of flow. It also expands your ability to explore

---

[24]Robert Benedetti, *The Actor at Work*, 6th ed. (New Jersey: Simon and Simon, 1994), 9.
[25]David Garrett, Personal communication, 1991.

through increased awareness of the internal landscape of your body. It can be used at the beginning of all working sessions. You may discover, while you are concentrating on the body scan, that thoughts arise which take the focus away from your task. Without judging either yourself or the voices, allow them to dissolve as if they were stage fog and bring yourself back to the task of scanning your body.

1. **Lie on the floor on your back, legs long and arms at your side. Note your breath.**

2. **Starting either from your feet or head, investigate the external aspects of yourself.** Note your relationship to the floor. What parts of you are released into the floor and what parts are not? What is the connection between the floor and your feet, your ankles, thighs, hips, spine, shoulder blades, neck, back of the arms, hands? Do you have a sense of the shape you are creating as you lie there? If you were on a waterbed or soft sand and you got up, what shape would you see?

3. **Beginning with your feet and moving up through your legs, torso and out through your head and arms, move each body part and ask how it feels.** How do my feet feel, my ankle joints, my calves, knee, upper leg, hip joint, pelvis, spine, ribs, shoulder blades, head, arms, and hands feel today. Are they fluid? Stiff? Sore? Cranky? Tired? Bubbling with energy? Excited to move? Other possible words that might describe your experience of self.

4. **Expand the depth of the scan by concentrating on the internal space between body parts.** Can you feel the space between one body part and another? Can you feel the space between your shoulder blades? Can you feel the space between your hands and the sides of your body? Between your legs? From your inner thighs to your feet? Between your feet? Between your chin and your chest? Between your ears and your shoulders? Between your shoulders? Between your ribs? Between the vertebrae of your spine? Between your pelvic bones? Between the bones of your feet? Your hands? How does each one of those spaces feel?

5. **Now open your eyes and repeat the entire external and internal scan, first with your eyes in soft focus–not necessarily concentrating on any area of the room.** Note the experience.

6. **Now focus on some point on the ceiling above you—pointed**

focus—and repeat and note the difference from previous scans. Note the experience.

Journal: Describe the experience of your internal landscape in as much detail as possible, noting the difference between having the eyes closed, soft, and pointed focus.

BREATH AND AWARENESS

What voluntary breathing provokes is a spontaneous reappearance of life.
Antonin Artuad

Although often an unconscious act, breath is a means of increasing somatic awareness and reducing stress. Greeks considered the act of breathing to be *psyche pneuma*, a phrase that translates as a combination of soul, air, and spirit. Romans used *anima spiritus* to refer to breath and soul. The Japanese use the term *ki* for air and spirit, while in Sanskrit the term *prana* connotes the life force. The founder of Hakomi therapy, Joseph Heller, connects breath with spirit, creativity, and inspiration:

> But the simple act of breathing requires no special effort, and similarly no effort is required to become connected with spirit. The body is already an inspired organism, and every moment, from your first breath to your last, is an opportunity to breathe in life's joy and fullness. Inspiration not only includes both breath and spirit, then, but is actually the meeting point at which the two merge; and the unification that takes place in you takes place automatically, unconsciously, effortlessly, and inevitably.[26]

The placement of the breath can focus and calm your mind, relax muscles, release tension, and increase your awareness of subtle psychological and emotional states related to impulse.

The first phase of breathing, or external respiration, begins as oxygen-laden air moves through the structures of your respiratory system

---

[26]Joseph Heller, *Bodywise* (New York: Jeremy Tarcher, Co., 1986), 118.

via the nasal or mouth cavities, down the trachea (windpipe) to the bronchial tubes, lungs, and alveoli (air sacs). The lungs are housed inside the ribs. The primary muscle of respiration, the diaphragm, lies between the bottom of the lungs and the top of the abdominal cavity. Its central tendon connects it to the ribs and the lumbar region of the spine. As you breathe in, the diaphragm contracts, reaching downward toward your pelvic girdle. When you breathe out, the diaphragm releases upward. During inhalation, while the diaphragm is contracting, the muscles on the inner surface of the lungs expand, allowing the lungs to increase in size. Breathing out, or exhaling, is a reversal of this process. The diaphragm sets up a pump-like motion that creates a partial vacuum in the lungs that stimulates inhalation. Besides deepening the amount of oxygen available to the body, complete and deep use of the diaphragm provides a massage of the internal organs.

The second phase, or internal respiration, takes place as oxygen moves through the sacs in the lungs' lining into your bloodstream and to individual cells of the muscle system. During physical activity, carbon dioxide is produced in the cells of your musculature. This carbon dioxide is carried via your bloodstream back to your lungs, where it is exchanged for oxygen within the alveoli and expelled.

Like other body functions, respiration is responsive to changes in your activity. An intensive physical conditioning program, for example, increases the efficiency of the transport of oxygen. With increased levels of oxygen, longer periods of activity are possible. Longer periods of activity, in turn, expand the ability of muscles to respond, and these changes "make the body able to withstand the stress of continued exercise for longer periods of time."[27] When you are participating in a vigorous activity, your breathing tends to be faster and shallower, but while you are sleeping or relaxing it changes to a slower, deeper rhythm.

Most of us do not use our breath to its fullest capacity. We tend to breathe into the chest with an uneven, shallow rhythm, depriving ourselves of the relaxation and calm that would naturally accompany deep abdominal breathing. A relaxed breath can be developed by releasing the muscles of your abdomen and diaphragm, allowing your back to lengthen and your shoulders to relax. A tight diaphragm restricts your breathing capacity and consequently can block feelings. Some people

---

[27]Fitt, 256.

pull in their bellies or raise their shoulders when they inhale, instead of allowing the belly, followed by the chest, to expand. When practicing any of the breathing exercises that follow, pay attention to achieving a full inhalation, allowing your lungs to expel the stale air and considering the exhalation as a natural consequence of the inhalation. Put another way: allow the exhalation to be a release of all energy and inhalation to be a recreation of all energy. Said in yet another way: breathing out is letting go and breathing in is filling yourself with new sources of inspiration and information. Of course, a full breath also strengthens the abdominal muscles. Furthermore, as Charles Garfield has pointed out, "once you establish a habit of abdominal breathing, your heart will tend to decelerate. Mental concentration is increased and the ability to create mental imagery is greatly enhanced."[28]

Exploration 3: The Focused Breath

To improve your breathing, you need to become aware of your present breath pattern. This exercise will help you to begin to freely move your chest and belly when you breathe and bring you in touch with the motion of the diaphragm. It will also help to expand your breathing capacity by stretching and releasing the muscles integrated with the diaphragm.

There are four body positions from which you can investigate your breathing: lying, standing, sitting, and walking. We will begin with lying on your back and move through the other positions in subsequent explorations.

Part 1: Passive Breath:

1. **Lie down on your back and focus on your breathing.**
2. **Allow the breath to be your normal, passive breath.** This is your normal breath pattern. Should your breathing feel constricted, try yawning or sighing. Yawning and sighing are good ways to release holding patterns.

---

[28]Charles Garfield qtd in Robert K. Cooper, *Health and Fitness Excellence* (Boston: Hugh Mifflin Company, 1989), 115.

3. **Note the phrasing of the inhalation and exhalation including the slight pause between.**
4. **Give yourself the internal command to feel the breath as it moves through the passages of the mouth or nasal cavity and flows down the trachea to the lungs.** You can feel the breath touch the bottom of your lungs, thus placing pressure, like a gentle message, on your abdominal area.
5. **Be aware that in feeling the breath you are also fusing with it.**
6. **Begin to follow the breath's exhalation through the cells and internal pathways of your body.** Completing this exploration, you have used the breath and the technique of feel, fuse and follow to place yourself in a state of exploration.

Part 2: Diaphragmatic Breath:

The following will help you access the strength of your diaphragm.

1. **Concentrate your breathing into your belly, feeling it rise and fall, without moving your chest.** Put your hands on your chest to check that it remains relaxed. Continue breathing like this for a few minutes.
2. **Breathe only into your chest, feeling it swell and subside.** Place your hands on your belly this time, to see that it stays released. Which did you find easier? Do you tend to be a chest breather or a belly breather?
3. **Put your arms down by your sides and exhale, allowing the abdominal muscles to remain extended.** Repeat this several times.
4. **Reverse the movement, sucking in your belly and puffing/pressing out your chest after you exhale.** As before, repeat the in/out pattern and then relax, breathing normally.
5. **Combine the last two movements.** After exhaling, alternately press/puff out the belly, then the chest, in rapid succession. You can feel your diaphragm moving just under your ribs.
6. **Relax and then repeat, this time pumping faster.** Try putting one hand on your belly and one on your chest and feel how the belly, then the chest, swells as you inhale and subsides and releases as you exhale.
7. **Return to your normal breath pattern.**

Part 3: Active Breath:

Active breath is a manipulation of the breath to play with phrasing and placement as well as beginning to associate the breath with images and emotional experience.

1.   **Phrasing: Note the different phrases of the breath itself, how it reveals itself from the physical stillness at the end of the inhalation through the reverse process of exhalation.** Extend the length of inhalation. For example, you can count in for six and out for eight. This is a common phrase pattern for many people.
2.   **Placement: Breath only through the nose. Only through the mouth. In one and out the other.**
3.   **Send: Breath in and send the breath to different body parts.** To your feet. To your hands. To your head. Note pathways the breath moves through as it travels to the extremities of your body.
4.   **Images: If you could give the breath a color, what would it be?** Red? Yellow? Magenta? Green? Blue? Would the inhalation and the exhalation be the same color?
5.   **Emotions: What emotional states do you note with different phrasing, placement or images?** Joy? Sadness? Seduction? Tenderness? Fear? Anger?

Journal: When you complete the exercise, jot down phrases that represent your experience of your breath. Are there areas of the body where you generally feel the breath more than others? Did these areas change during the exploration? What were your discoveries exploring phrasing, placement, sending, and images.

Exploration 4: Body Breathing

A member of Peter Brook's company, Yoshi Oida, in *An Actor Adrift* describes his experience of learning to breathe, "At first, you breathe in through the mouth, and out the nose."[29] However, by focusing on the internal respiration process, you learn to breathe using the entire body. This exploration is an application of Oida's practice of self and breath.

---

[29] Yoshi Oida, *An Actor Adrift* (London: Methuen, 1993), 148.

In this exploration you are increasing the integration of your awareness of internal states related to breath/energy. This exploration can be repeated. Each repetition will increase the depth of your awareness.

1. **Lie down on your back and repeat the body scan from Exploration 2.**

2. **Note the breath and begin to bring it into your body beginning with your feet.** Breathe in through the feet and legs and out through the feet and legs. Expand this to include feet, legs, and pelvis. With the next breath, expand the felt awareness of the breath up the body to include the upper torso and shoulder area. With each exhalation, the breath continues to flow out your feet. With each inhalation, the breath moves from the soles of your feet and up through your legs, hips, and spine until it spills up and out of your head. On the exhalation, it reverses itself. Slowly expand your level of awareness of this internal respiration to include your entire body.

3. **Be aware of the breath moving up the legs and out the arms and head.** Experience the rhythm of the breath as an ongoing phrase in which the breath moves into the center of your being in the pelvic area and out again through the communicative extensions of your body; your arms, the palms of your hands, the bottoms of your feet, and your entire head, including your face.

4. **Become aware of breath's connection to your entire being.** Be aware of the breath that comes through the skin and the breath taken through the mouth and nasal passages.

5. **Breathe out and allow a soundless sigh to be expressed with the breath.** After experiencing the quality of this soundless sigh, allow more sound to be expressed with the breath.

6. **Send this sigh not only out your mouth but through your entire body.** If you are having a difficult time discovering a sigh, start with a yawn by lifting up your soft palate in the back of the throat. This starts the yawn reflex that often initiates a sigh.

7. **Note the phrasing of your breath/sound.**

8. **Become aware of the corresponding energy state of each area of your body.** What sensations do you experience as the breath/energy moves from your pelvis to your legs? What colors or sounds are attached to the energy related to this part of yourself? What colors or sounds do you sense as the breath moves

from your pelvis out through your arms? Out through your face and head? What colors or sounds do you sense evolving as the energy moves from the area of your sternum or upper rib cage and down through your legs? Out through your arms? Out through your face and head? What colors or sounds do you sense as the energy moves from the area of your throat and head out through your feet? Out through your arms? Out through your face?

9. **Keep exploring the energy through your felt sense of color or sound from different parts of your torso and through different parts of your communicative extensions. Slowly return to a focus on the act of breathing and release your concentration on the task.**

Journal: What colors or sounds seemed to be related to your experience of body breathing? Could you draw an image of your body filled with breath? This drawing does not have to be an anatomically correct. Instead, it represents your experience of the breath and related energy state.

Exploration 5: Breathing Methods

The following is a set of breathing methods that can be completed either sitting or standing. Sitting positions can be cross-legged or perched on a chair. Whatever the position, the spine is straight. If you are sitting on the floor, this position is made easier by placing a pillow under the back of the pelvis. When standing, place your feet shoulder-width apart with the feet slightly turned in. Your knees should be slightly released and bent directly over your toes.

Each of these breathing methods helps you learn to extend the sense of breath throughout your body. This felt sense of the breath resonating through you is analogous to a pebble that when dropped into a pool of water, creates waves throughout the pool. The breath is the pebble that redistributes the energy with each inhalation and exhalation. This movement through the body begins in the pelvic bowl behind the navel and continues simultaneously up the torso through the head and arms and out through the legs and feet.

Each method specifically focuses the breath on a particular task.

Hara or abdominal breathing integrates the breath into your entire pelvic cavity. It also helps you to become aware of your lower back. The breath of fire awakens the energy of the pelvic floor and thus deepens the breath into the body. The great circle breath trains you to send the breath through the body's energy channels; in this case, up the back of the body via the spine and down the front via the rib cage and abdomen.

Hara or Abdominal Breathing

Hara or Abdominal breathing is related to chi gong, the Chinese Taoist form that preceded t`ai chi. The breath techniques associated with it (Hara and Great Circle Breath) increase the flow of *chi*/energy through your body.

1. **Sit in a cross-legged position, focus your attention on a point just below your navel while breathing deeply into the lower abdomen.** Let your belly release as you inhale. Notice the breath being expanded into the depths of your belly in a spiral that starts behind the navel and circles inward.
2. **Exhale, drawing the belly in and letting the energy circulate behind the navel. Inhale, releasing the belly out.**
3. **After several breaths, take a breath in and hold it, and, as you do so, contract the muscles of your anal area, your abdomen (by contracting the muscles of the upper part of the abdominal wall), and the back of your throat (by contracting the muscles of the back of the throat), to lock the energy contained in the breath into your pelvic region.**
4. **After holding this for a specified count, slowly release the breath and the three contractions at the same time.**
5. **Repeat within the same phrasing framework several times before returning to a normal breath pattern.**

The Breath of Fire

Breath of fire is a technique adopted from yogic traditions. With practice, you will deepen your experience of the energy associated with your pelvic floor.

1. **Repeat a series of short, rapid breaths through the nose, creating a pumping sensation in the pelvic floor.** This is accom-

plished by contracting the muscles in the lower part of the abdomen and pelvic floor as you exhale. It should feel as if the breath is beating on the floor of the pelvis, which is pulsating or vibrating as if it were the head of a drum. If you cannot feel it in a seated position, try standing on your hands and knees–a position sometimes referred to as "all fours." This position uses the pull of gravity to help you feel the movement of the muscles. Once you feel you have achieved it, return to a seated position.

2. **Repeat a specified number of rapid breaths.** This can be as few as ten or as many as thirty or more. Follow these by an equal period of time in which you hold your breath. At the same time, tighten the locks of the muscles of your throat, solar plexus, and anus, turn your hands palm down on your knees, and close your eyes.

3. **At the end of each breathing cycle, exhale and release your eyes, hands, anus, throat, and solar plexus at the same time as you focus on the energy rushing up from the base of the spine.** You may not feel the energy moving up your spine the first time you practice this technique. The energy released in the movement is experienced with repeated practice.

4. **Repeat three or more times**. This breathing technique is intended to increase energy in the pelvic region and awaken the energy of the spine. As you release the locks, you will eventually feel a rush of energy from the base of your spine to the top of your head. The number of "breaths of fire" and corresponding periods of holding the breath can be increased or decreased depending on the person.

The Great Circle Breath

The Great Circle breath connects upper and lower body and helps to develop an experience of your body's spiral energy flow.

Begin by standing with feet the same width apart as your shoulders and slightly turned in from parallel. Release or slightly bend your knees. As you do this, make certain there is an equal bend at the knees and ankles, with the knees heading in the direction of your toes. You will probably feel a slight pull of the internal thigh muscles as your tail bone drops. The release of your tail bone downward will increase the bend in your knee. By assuming this position of the legs, you have created a circle of energy in your lower appendages that reaches from the left side to the right through the pelvis. Focus your breath and energy upon the floor through your feet, as if your legs were tree trunks and your feet the root structure of the tree that reaches into the earth. Now bring your hands in front of your sternum and rub your palms together, feeling the warmth of your palms as you do so. Reach your elbows to the side and allow your arms to form a circle that extends from the center of your back. The elbows should be slightly lifted. You have now created a circle with your arms in a horizontal direction that compliments the circle being made with your legs in a vertical direction. These two circles create a spiral effect in your energy system (Figure 2).

1. **Standing in this position, with the back straight and eyes focused on a site outside yourself, breathe into the lower abdomen, or *dantian*, and send the breath up through the great circle starting with the tail bone and moving up the back through the spine, or governing vessel.**

2. **After the breath has traversed the head, breathe in again into the lower abdomen, focusing on the breath moving down the front of the body, or conception vessel.**

3. **Continue to breathe, concentrating on the flow of the breath as it moves up the governing vessel in the back as you exhale and through the conception vessel in the front as you inhale.** In completing this circle, you have sent the breath in and around three points of energy, the lower dantian in your pelvis, middle dantian in your heart or sternum level, and upper dantian in your brain.

Journal: Describe your experience of each breathing technique. What parts of the body did each help you to connect with? Did any of the methods feel physically confrontational, in that you found it difficult to concentrate or found tiring to do? How would you combine these with other breath techniques?

Exploration 6: Walking and Breathing

---

1. **Begin walking around the room in a normal manner, chang-**

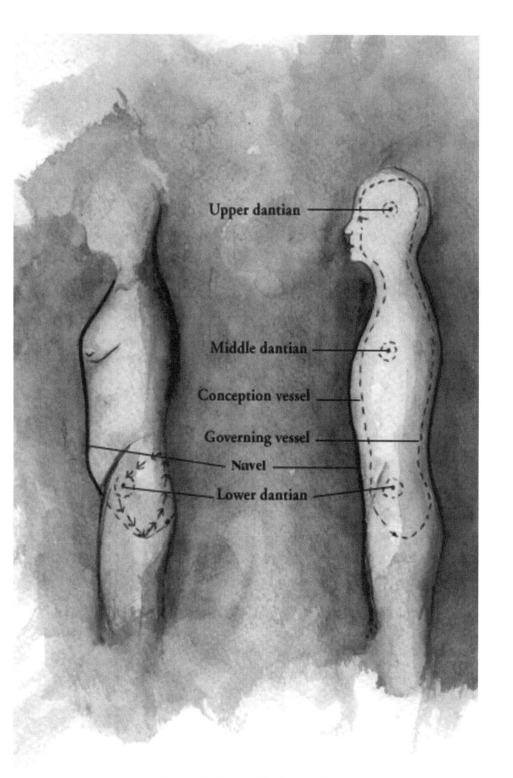

Figure 2: Great Circle breath

ing points of focus. Points of focus can include other people.

2. **Focus your attention on how your feet touch the floor and the relationship of the sole of the foot to the ankle, to the knee, to the hip joint, to the pelvis, to the spine, to the shoulder girdle, to the arms hanging from it, to the head.**

3. **Begin to slow your walk and incorporate an increased awareness of your breath.**

4. **Slow the walk to the point that you are standing in a comfortable position.**

5. **Place your breath in your belly.**

6. **Inhale and focus on the breath entering through this foot and moving up and through the pelvis. On the exhalation, take a step placing the other foot on the floor in front of you.** Be aware of the breath moving down your leg and out through the bottom of your foot. What is the color of the breath?

7. **Follow this by an inhalation into the sole of this foot as your prepare to lift your alternate foot.** What is the color of the breath?

8. **Repeat, investigating the relationship between breath and walking.** With practice, you should have the sensation of energy coming in and releasing out through the soles of your feet.

Journal: Describe the sensation in your feet and legs as your awareness of the internal respiration process increased. Describe the sensation in your spine and torso. In your neck and head, your shoulders, arms, and hands.

Exploration 7: Breath and Movement

Expansion and contraction are common to all living things. We experience them in the rhythmic pumping of the heart and in the ebb and flow of the nervous system. Our breathing is the rhythmic connection between ourselves and the general pulse of life. This exploration combines movement with the cycles of the breath through the contraction and expansion of the body. In the beginning, you may find you need to synchronize your breathing with your leg movements consciously, but in time your natural rhythm will develop, allowing you to enjoy the oceanic feeling of pulsation. Although performing the exercise should be pleasurable, for it increases the flow of energy in the body, it can make you feel a little anxious if you are not used to it. Take it one step at a time. You can begin either lying down on the floor or standing.

Lying on the Floor:

1. Bend your knees and put your feet flat on the floor, parallel, and the same width as your shoulders. Breathe in.
2. Breathe out, bring your knees up toward your torso, wrapping your hands around them to press them in to your chest.
3. Breathe in again, bring your arms out to the sides and lower your knees without necessarily touching the floor. As you continue the movement, focus the breath through all the pores of the skin. Over time, allow the body to begin to take on its own shape and direction. You may find that your legs want to go in opposing directions, while your arms reach in space in some way almost as if you were swimming in some giant vat of liquid.

Standing:

1. To perform the exercise standing, stand with feet in parallel position.
2. Repeat the same breath pattern as in lying, but this time include your pelvis in the movement.
3. Breathe in and feel the breath fill the entire pelvis and lower abdomen and, as you breathe out, send the breath from that area out through your arms and legs as they reach into space.
4. Repeat. Follow the direction your arms and legs want to move in response to the contraction and release in the pelvis. As you explore the potential of the breath to create movement, begin to play with the edge of each breath. See how far each extends before it pulls back in on itself to move in another direction. Do not force the edge of the movement. Rather, imagine it as if you were balancing on the edge of a cliff or building.

Journal: Note the changes to different parts of yourself that occur with different ways of breathing. What are the images that come to mind with different explorations? Are you reminded of people, places, situations, pieces of art, etc.?

Breath, Energy, Chakra

As stated previously, breath is related to *chi*, an essential life force. Associated with the Indian concept of *prana*, (breath), *chi* is invisible, silent and formless, yet it exists throughout your body. This energy system involves emotional centers that reside along the spine from your head to your pelvis. Some divide this system into physical (pelvis), spiritual (heart), and mental (head) centers. Each center is defined by the type of impulse related to that center, to a need for food and shelter (pelvis), for companionship (heart), and for power (head). Others contend that the seat of all emotions is in the pelvis, or central core, and that impulses are channeled through other emotional centers depending on the objective of the moment.

The system used in this text is derived from of the Hindu system of the seven chakra or emotional centers. According to Hindu philosophy, *chakras* are a set of spinning energy centers that run along the spinal cord beginning at the anus and ending at the top of the head. Each *chakra* has its particular function in the psychological and emotional life of the individual. For example, the survival *chakra* at the bottom of the spine is located in the area where the nerves from your spinal cord extend into your legs, which are used daily to carry out your wants and desires. The vocal *chakra* is located in the area of the spinal cord where the nerves reach into the shoulder, neck, and head. Although optimum health and balance is based on equality and balance among the *chakras*, individual *chakras* in different people vary in size. These differences, in combination with other perceptual capabilities, indicate specific talents and abilities.[30] For our purposes, the *chakra* system becomes a method for increasing awareness of the emotional centers associated with the brain, brain stem, and spinal cord.

Below is an outline of each *chakra* including: 1) the primary element associated with it, 2) its location within the torso, 3) the basic verb that identifies the desires of that *chakra*, and 4) a sound pattern that can stimulate an interaction between the *chakra* and the neuromuscular system.

---

[30]Shafica Karagulla and Dora van Gelder Kunz, *The Chakras and the Human Energy Fields* (Wheaton, Ill.: Theosophical Publishing House, 1989), 37.

The Seven Emotional Centers or Chakras (Figure 3)

Chakra One–Earth. The root (or first) chakra is located at the base of the spine in the area of the anus. Situated at the crossroads between the legs and the spine, this chakra is associated with the right to be alive and the fundamentals of being– shelter, food, clothing, healthy environment, friends. The primary element is Earth's energy and its pull, which grounds our physical and emotional life. The corresponding verb is "I have" or "I need". That is, I have the basics I need for survival (which is different for each character from a script). The sound is a long O, as in rope.

Chakra Two–Water. The water chakra is located in the area of the lower abdomen and the reproductive organs. With the mutability of water as its symbol, this chakra is related to the right to emotional expressiveness and desires associated with the attraction of opposites. The primary verbal phrase is "I feel", and the sound is a short OU as in due.

Chakra Three–Fire. The third (or power) chakra is located in the area above the navel and below the beginning of the rib cage. It is the emotional center that resides between the chakras concerned with some element of species survival in the lower part of the body and those focusing on the immaterial areas of existence. The element is fire and it functions as the emotional center for the right to act in the world. The corresponding verb is I can, and the sound is AH, as in father.

Chakra Four–Air. The fourth chakra is the eye of the hurricane and the location of the emotional center is in the area of the sternum. Often called the heart chakra, for the organ that with its repetitive beating keeps the body moving, it is the center from which the energy elements of love and compassion are shared with the rest of the world. Constantly in a state of flux, as is the air, this emotional center is always trying to promote emotional equilibrium. The corresponding verb is "I love", and the sound is AY, as in play.

Chakra Five–Sound. This is located in the area of the throat and the larynx. Hindus believe the entire universe was danced into being through sound: "It is through sound and communication that we continually create and breathe spirit into our world."[31] The con

---

[31]Anodea Judith and Selene Vega, *The Sevenfold Journey* (Berkeley, Calif.: The Crossing Press, 1993), 200.

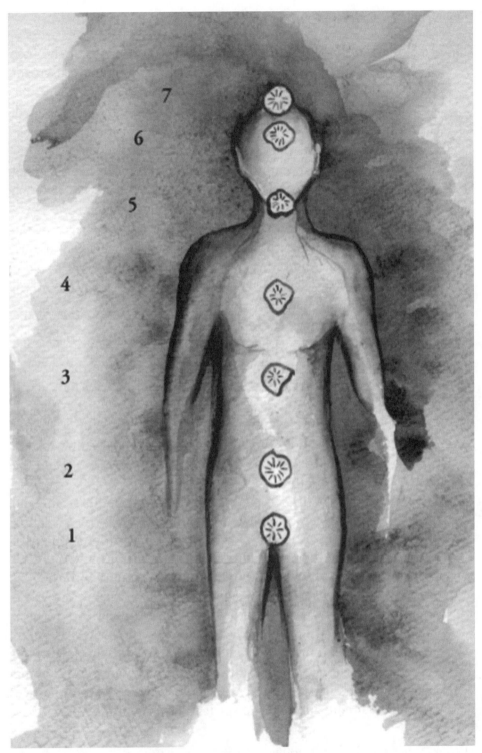

Figure 3: The Seven Chakras

cerns of this chakra are communication, creativity, and self-expression. The verb is "I say." The corresponding sound is a long E, as in seek.

Chakra Six–Light. Located at the center of the head at eye level or slightly above and sometimes called the third eye, the function of this emotional center is seeing and intuition, or what is sometimes called wisdom. With the corresponding sound which works up into the nasal passages, of M or N, and the verb phrase "I see", this area is the nerve center for the wisdom from the rest of the body that is being stored in the cerebrum.

Chakra Seven–Thought. The final chakra at the top of the head is the channel between the pull of the Earth and those forces of the universe that exist beyond it. The verb phrase "I know" indicates the root function of the chakra, which is understanding. It is assumed that knowledge evolves from a combination of introspection and experience. The unity of thought that develops from this combination influences how we respond to individual situations. The sound is NG, as in sing.

Exploration 8: Sounding

This "get acquainted" exploration of your *chakra* allows you to become aware of the energy and sound of each emotional center. It requires that you find a quiet place and spend a few minutes in a prone position.

1. **Complete an internal body scan, noting the area of each emotional center, beginning at the root chakra in the tail bone and moving through each center to the top of the head.** A method of discovering each center is to visualize that you have a ball in your pelvis that is spinning clockwise (as someone faces you). Watch the ball move slowly up the center of yourself, from the pelvis to the area behind the belly button, to the area just below the rib cage, to the area behind your sternum, to the area of your larynx, to the area between and just above your eyes, and finally, to the top of your head. As the ball continues to spin upward, note any color images that naturally occur. You can repeat this more than once and note physical (sometimes referred to as kinesthetic) images, memory images, or sound images that emanate from your unconscious.

Root and Water Chakra:

1. **Begin sounding in the first, or root** *chakra.* **The sound is O, as in rope.** You start this and all the other *chakra* sounds with a huh, or open h. This will gently lift the soft palate to allow breath followed by the sound to be expressed. As you begin sounding the O you should note a slight vibration in the area of your tail bone. Should you not feel this sensation, try pushing with your feet to create a slight rocking in your pelvis as the breath releases. Once you have established the O as a sound, feel the sound spread throughout the entire pelvic cavity.

2. **Repeat the process for the second chakra. Its sound is an O that sounds as a U as in due.** With a partner you can repeat this process from a hang-over position. Stand feet parallel, the same distance apart as the shoulders. Your head is released toward the floor, arms hanging in a relaxed position. The partner places one or both hands in the area of your tail bone, encouraging the person in the hang-over position to breathe into this area so that the lower back or lumbar region is raised upward. Once a breath rhythm is established in the hang-over position, repeat both first and second chakra sounds. The partner lets you know whether he/she can feel the vibration of the sound in and around the area.

Third Chakra:

1. **Breathe into the area of your solar plexus, within the V-shaped area of your rib cage.** This is the third chakra.

2. **Begin a slight pant as you watch this part of the abdomen rise and fall. Change the rhythm of the breath to several pants followed by an extended exhale.**

3. **Begin to vocalize the sound AH on each breath.** The pattern is a breath in, followed by several panted and vocalized AHs, followed by an extended AH. For example: Breathe in and release out on one breath an h followed by, ah, ah, ah, ah, ahhhh.

4. **Repeat until the sound fills the triangle between your ribs and your waist.**

Fourth through Seventh Chakra:

1. **Repeat the above process for the fourth through seventh**

chakra with the sounds AY, EE, MN, and NG. As you expand the sound of the chakra within each area, memories stored in that area of the neuromuscular system may bring themselves to conscious awareness. Do not try to hold onto any particular memory; literally allow memories to become caught up in the concentric wheel of the emotional center and spin out and through it, leaving the body with the breath.

2. **In subsequent sessions, you can play with different pitches associated with different resonating systems**. For instance, you can pitch the sound low for your chest resonators, in your mid-range for the mask and nasal area, and in the upper range for your head tones. As you work with different pitches, you will find that the sound will still root itself in your first chakra. You can also integrate these sounds with Yoga poses.

Journal: What is your sense of the size and dimension of each *chakra*? What colors do you associate with each? Do you feel connections between the centers as you intone the sounds for each center? Could you create a drawing that represents the relationship between each center?

Exploration 9: Subtle Energy and Shiatsu

Another method of becoming aware of your energy system is through awareness of concentrations of energy, or pressure points. These are points on your body that become a focus for massage in various forms of body therapy. Shiatsu is a Japanese form of pressure-point massage that helps to release stress in the muscle tissue through the application of pressure to points associated with your energy system. Comfortable, loose clothing is the best form of dress while you are giving yourself a massage. You should refrain from eating for an hour or two before you begin the work.

1. **Begin by lying on the floor, breathing slowly and deeply into your lower abdomen.**
2. **With relaxed hands and fingers, begin to apply gentle pressure to the area just under the rib cage, pressing gently toward the navel as you exhale.**

3.   **Inhale, and shift your hands to the right. Exhale, and press gently again.**

4.   **Continue in a clockwise direction until you have applied easy pressure all around the borders of your solar plexus.**

5.   **Now bring your hands to the center and top of the head. Place the fingers of both hands at the center seam and press.** Then move your fingers backward along the seam and repeat.

6.   **Continue all the way up the back until you have reached the crown of the head.** Pressure in this area is excellent for relieving headaches and some colds. Each time you place pressure in a new area, focus your breath on that point.

7.   **Hands still touching the head, place the palm of each hand on the temples (just to the side of the eyebrow ridges) and rotate slowly. Now apply a slight pressure to the depression between the inner corner of each side of the nose. Draw the fingers down to the depression at either side of the nostrils and press inward toward the center of the nose, one side at a time.** Feel the breath follow the pressure of your hands on your face.

8.   **Focus your eyes straight ahead and trace the line of your cheek.**

9.   **Now place a subtle pressure upward just under your cheek bones.**

10. **Apply pressure midway between the ends of the shoulders and the base of the neck to relieve tension in the shoulders.** The pressure points lie approximately one inch toward the back of the body in the sensitive depression above the shoulder blades. Again, be aware of the breath moving in and out of the pressure point.

11. **Find the point four fingers width below the kneecap to relieve tired legs.** At this point, slide off the bone toward the outside of the leg and apply pressure in the depression along the shin. Feel the breath fill the pressure point.

12. **Finally, there are two pressure points that activate the entire body. The first is the great eliminator that lies on the back of each hand, in the webbing between the thumb and the index finger, approximately one inch inward from the top of the webbing. The second, named gushing spring, is located in the center of the metatarsal arch, directly below the back**

of the foot. Note the breath/energy move from these points through your entire self.

13. **End your session on your back, focusing on the breath, and imagine you are inhaling positive thoughts and energy and exhaling any remaining physical tension as you breathe in and out through all points simultaneously.**

Journal: Which pressure points felt integrated to an experience of your breath and your entire energy system? Which pressure points felt isolated from the rest of the body? What was your experience of your body and breath when you completed the massage? Is there an body image that is a metaphor for this state?

Imagery: The Role of Your Nervous System

Your nervous system, with its connection to sensory images via the brain spinal column, provides for quick communication among your body parts, correlating and integrating various bodily processes. As can be noted in Figure 4, your nervous system can be divided into the central nervous system; those nerve cells associated with the brain and spinal cord, and the peripheral nervous system; the complex network of sensory and motor nerves that reach from the brain throughout your body. The nervous system can also be divided into the sensory (the senses) and autonomic systems (internal organs). Your sensory system interacts with the environment by receiving, interpreting, and responding to information.

The educational system assumes that our ears and eyes are the primary means by which we gather and process information. This view of our sensory system is replicated in the abstract nature of our language. For example, when we go from one place to another we say we will walk from here to there. We all have an experience of walking, but the language for the act does not incorporate the part of the body involved. In Sudanese English, going from one place to another is called footing–a use of the noun as verb that connects the body with the action. A similar (re)conceptualization of our individual body is necessary for the craft of acting. It requires that we relearn our experience of self. Part of this relearning or repatterning involves becoming aware of information related to touch and space provided by skin and proprioceptors.

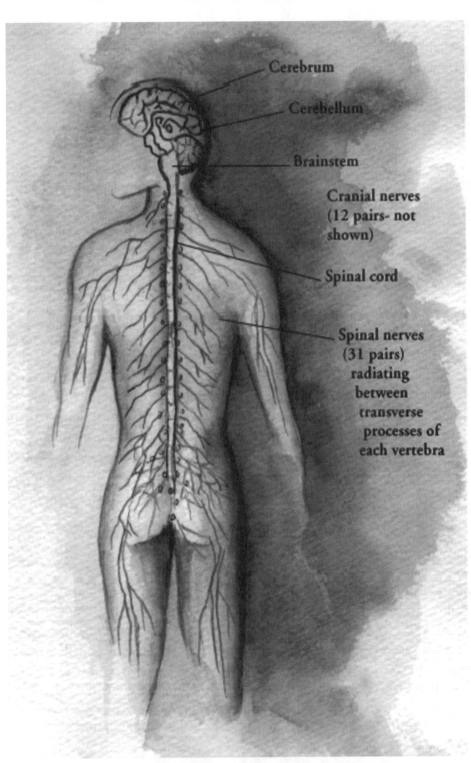

Figure 4: The Nervous System

Your skin is the largest single sensory organ of your body. Some have called it the surface for the brain. Housed within the skin are 640,000 sensory receptors, which are connected to other parts of the nervous system (including the spinal cord) by a system of over a half-million nerve fibers. The density of your skin varies from thin (over areas such as the eyelids, lower abdomen, and genitalia) to thick (over the palms of the hands and the soles of the feet). Your skin serves a variety of physiological functions including regulating temperature, protecting the body via covering and immune system, preserves food and water and is the site of vitamin D synthesis and exchange of gasses associated with breathing. The skin is, therefore, a significant organ ranging from its capacity to breathe, to sensations of touch in relationship to experiencing and responding.

Your skin also operates in combination with other sensory nerves to provide detailed information to your nervous system that influences your orientation to space. Called proprioceptors, these nerves provide information to the nervous system that is necessary for coordination. Proprioceptors are not only in the skin but can be found throughout your body. They include the expansion and contraction of muscle spindles, the joint receptors that monitor compression in our joints, and sections of the inner ear that apprize us of our equilibrium. These receptors transform a stimulus from the external environment into a nerve impulse that is conducted via the spinal cord to the brain in order to be translated into sensation.[32]

Physical action takes place when a signal or impulse comes through a combination of your proprioception and other elements of your sensory system–tactile, thermal, and pain receptors located in the skin, as well as visual, auditory, gustatory, and olfactory systems. In *The Natural History of the Senses*, Diane Ackerman describes these networks as caravans: "Most people think of the mind as being located in the head, but the latest findings in physiology suggest that the mind doesn't really dwell in the brain but travels the whole body on caravans of hormone and enzyme, busily making sense of the compound wonders we catalogue as touch, taste, smell, hearing, and vision."[33] An acting impulse is essentially an electrical stimulus traveling the pathways of these caravans. You literally sense or feel the information from your

---

[32]Andrea Olsen, *Body Stories* (Barrytown, New York: Station Hill Press, 1991), 15.

[33]Diane Ackerman, *Natural History of the Senses* (Random House: New York, 1991), xix.

surroundings by means of your entire sensory system, process or fuse with the information through your central nervous system, and make a decision for action that is revealed through the communicative centers in your face, arms, and legs. These choices are sometimes unconsciously controlled by your autonomic nervous system, as in the fight or flight response to danger. However, as demonstrated by the military, even automatic responses can be tempered by conditioning.

Exploration 10: Exploring Your Senses

Stanislavski remarks in *An Actor Prepares* that "An actor should be observant not only on the stage, but also in real life. He should concentrate all his being on whatever attracts his attention. He should look at an object, not as any absent-minded passer-by, but with penetration. Otherwise his whole creative method will prove lopsided and bear no relationship to life."[34] Each of us has a unique process of observation based on our ability to see, hear, touch, taste, smell, and feel that influences how we perceive and evaluate information from the environment. This exercise asks you initially to isolate these senses in order to discover the potential of each. Following the exploration of each sensory system, write a description of your experience in your journal. Note which senses you seem to write about in greater detail. With each sense, be aware of fusing with the sensory systems attributes and note what new levels of awareness you gain via this form of concentration and focus.

Seeing

1. **Take a walk through your community**. As you walk, experiment with the focus of your eyes, from looking straight forward to looking at the ground, to looking from right to left, to looking up at the trees or buildings. Now move your focus among all four areas.

2. **Now find a place to sit and place your eyes in sharp focus so**

---

[34]Constantin Stanislavski, *An Actor Prepares*, trans. Elizabeth Reynolds Hapgood (New York: Routledge/Theatre Arts, 1989), 91.

that you are collecting all the physical details of an object.

3. **Reverse this to soft focus as if the object were being observed through a soft lens.** Does changing the focus of your eyes affect your emotional life? If so, how? Write a description of your experience.

Hearing

1. **Pick three separate environments, one outdoors, one public, and one that involves nature. Make a twenty-minute visit to each environment.** During this visit you can walk or sit, moving as you feel necessary, depending upon the kind of environment.

2. **Give yourself an opportunity to experience each environment with eyes open and eyes closed.** What do you hear with eyes opened? Closed? Are there sounds in each environment that make it distinct? What kind of sounds are they–natural (wind, water), animal, human, mechanical?

3. **Write a description of each environment.**

Touching

Touching is primarily associated with sensors located in the skin. We know the temperature and texture of the objects that surround us by the information provided through the skin.

1. **Using your home environment as a place of exploration, begin to pick out various articles in your home to investigate through touch.** For instance, sit in a chair, close your eyes, and feel the texture and form of the chair through your skin. You can do the same on your bed or on the floor. Pick up various objects in your home and note their shape and texture. Do they feel cool, rough, smooth, warm, hot, dry, moist, wet, or other? With bare feet walk around your house and note the different reactions of the skin of your feet to different kinds of floors.

2. **Walk outside your home and note the same thing.**

3. **Describe the differences between touching with hands and with feet.**

Tasting

1. **Pick a favorite kind of food**. It can be a fruit such as an apple, a drink such as tea, or a main dish such as pizza or spaghetti.
2. **Over a period of a week or two, give yourself an opportunity to try different versions of the same food or drink**.
3. **Each time, make certain to describe the taste**. What is the difference between Earl Grey and Lipton tea? Between Roma and Macintosh apples? Between different kinds of cheese pizza? Can you taste the different flavors?
4. **Write a description of each**.

Smelling

Repeat the hearing exercise, this time note what it is you smell.

Feeling

Feeling refers to the proprioceptive information by means of which we continually negotiate our upright stance with respect to gravity. We use this feedback system daily as we manipulate busy streets, shift gears in a car, type at our computers, turn over a pancake on a griddle, and learn a new sport or dance technique. Most often we think of this system as the coordination that takes place between different combinations of large and small muscle groups. To identify this aspect of your life, keep a journal of a day and note the kinds of physical tasks associated with it, from such domestic chores as making the coffee, to methods of getting to work or appointments, to forms of recreation. How would you describe your use of self with each of these tasks? What is your relationship to gravity? What is the center of your awareness with each task? What muscles seem to be at work? At rest?

THE INTUITIVE BODY

Body awareness is a way of "attending to" yourself. All aspects of your life are contained in the inner worlds of your body. Continually enjoy the process of becoming more aware of your body. Learn to listen to your internal landscape and pay attention to your expressiveness in all of its manifestations. Each element–breath, postures, gestures, emotions, and tensions–are potential teachers. Developing the sensitivity required for responding to an impulse in rehearsal or on stage is a lifelong, day-to-day process. Similarly, expanded self-image involves not only a change in self-image but also a change in the nature of your motivations and the mobilization of your entire being.

The craft of performance requires a multifaceted approach to your work that assimilates information from all aspects of the self–mental, physical, emotional, and spiritual–and consolidates the knowledge in a single moment of impulse in rehearsal and on the stage. You can learn the craft first by increasing your level of awareness to reveal the unconscious and direct it toward conscious choices that in time will become intuitive choices. Second, you expand upon this base by providing new body experiences that increase the range of knowledge from which you can make intuitive choices. The rest of this text provides a series of explorations that you can individualize and incorporate into the process you have developed for approaching your work.

As part of the ongoing discovery, I encourage you to work initially with what I call an 'unknown text.' This can be a nursery rhyme, poem, song, monologue, or movement score for which you have not developed a specific approach and to which you are not emotionally attached. For example, you would not want to use a song that your mother used to sing when putting you to sleep as a child or a monologue that you had already used for an audition piece. Working with an unknown text becomes the opportunity to apply new states of awareness. A text used in this way is your guide to increasing your level of self-understanding and therefore your potential to cultivate your craft.

CHECKLIST OF POINTS TO REMEMBER

The chapter has provided an introduction to the basics of awareness. You have learned a method of working from a standpoint of exploration that incorporates discipline and attention to detail as part of the craft of acting. Below is a checklist organized by the three body processes–exploration, breath, and imagery–that act as your guides through this text. Review your journal entries for the chapter and note how you describe your experience of the use of the three body processes and how you discussed them with regards to your body's basic structures–bones, muscles and nervous system. Write a final journal entry that summarizes your experience.

Exploration

- Body listening is the beginning of exploring the internal landscape and expanding awareness.

- Exploring a specific body part is a way of understanding the whole.

Breath

- Breath is the key to the potential teachers that are within you.
- Focus on the breath increases your awareness of related energy states.
- Skin breathes.
- A key to stress reduction is breathing and focusing on the positive aspects of a challenging situation.
- Feel, fuse, and follow is the basis of physical action.

Imagery

- The body is the mind.
- Learning to perform is a process of bringing the unconscious to a conscious state of awareness so that it can expand your impulsive potential.
- The skin is the largest organ of the body.
- The nervous system connects your brain to your muscles.

The Rover Directed by Sarah Pia Anderson,
Kristina Goodnight as Hellena and Amber Fitzgerald as Florinda

CHAPTER TWO
DYNAMIC ALIGNMENT

Attention is built in many layers and they do not interfere with one another.
Talent without work is nothing more than raw unfinished material.

Constantin Stanislavski

WHAT IS DYNAMIC ALIGNMENT?

Dynamic alignment is the constant adjustment of your body's bony and muscular systems in relationship to each other. Thus, it is not a specific position such as one might find in a typical military or ballet stance, but a constant negotiation of the connections between bones, joints, muscles, ligaments and tendons. Note the actors in Figures 5a, b, c, d are demonstrating various poses–symmetrical, asymmetrical, standing, and sitting. They are in each pose aligning their individual experience of self, including their skeletal system, in relationship to others.

Dynamic alignment, therefore, extends our understanding of the functioning of the skeletal system. Many people conceive of the skeleton as a rigid framework on which all other body parts hang. This mechanistic analogy compares the body to non-organic structures such as buildings or machines. However, somatic specialists in structural and functional integration–Ida Rolf, Moshe Feldenkrais, Thomas Hanna, Joseph Heller, Frederick Matthias Alexander–consider bones not as structural units on which other elements depend but as *spacers* "whose function in terms of the body's structure is to determine the proper distance between its various parts, and to make certain that spacing is not compromised."[1] For example, the bone in your upper leg preserves a consistent distance between your hip joint and knee cap. This bone, aided by muscles, tendons, ligaments, and the other soft tissue, allows you to stand upright while providing a mobility in the joint that allows you to walk, run, hop, skip, etc. Each bone structure and joint has a specific placement and related space between, generated by

---

[1]Joseph Heller, *Bodywise* (New York: Jeremy Tarcher, 1986),48.

Dynamic Alignment

Figure 5a

Figure 5b

Figure 5c

thousands of years of evolution. The spaces between some bones are fluid with "ligaments that help to define the parameters of their movement, and the bones, by defining the placement and even the function of the flesh around them, that define the nature of the movement itself."[2]

Buckminster Fuller, architect and theorist, promoted the concept of the body as a tensile structure in which the bones act as spacers. He conceived of the body as interacting with gravity through two sets of forces, those that are compressing upon each other and those that are pulling away from each other. Generally, we conceive of compression and pulling as negative forces that cause tension within the body. When properly balanced, however, these forces interact to influence the body's energy. By becoming aware of gravity's pull on us and by discovering the balance and integration between the body's structures, we can consciously use compression and pulling as integrated aspects of the body's alignment. Through an understanding of the specific functions of the bones, muscle groups, and connective tissue, we develop a sense of the constantly changing nature of these forces and their relationship to dynamic alignment.[3] Dynamic alignment is therefore a constant interaction of the body's systems in response to the physical circumstances of an environment. It reflects your felt experience of internal connections in interaction with others around you.

Exploration 11: Your Bony Structure

Bones come in many shapes and sizes depending on their function (see Figures 6 and 7). A simple comparison of the bones of your legs with those of your arms reveals that the bones which function to bear greater loads of weight are larger and more dense than those that carry less. This is also true of your spine. At the lower end of your spine, in the lumbar region, the vertebrae are larger than those in the upper reaches of your spine, in the cervical area. Bones form a skeletal framework that protects your vital organs. They also support weight and act as levers.

---

[2]Joseph Heller, *Bodywise* (New York: Jeremy Tarcher, 1986), 48.
[3]Heller, 50.

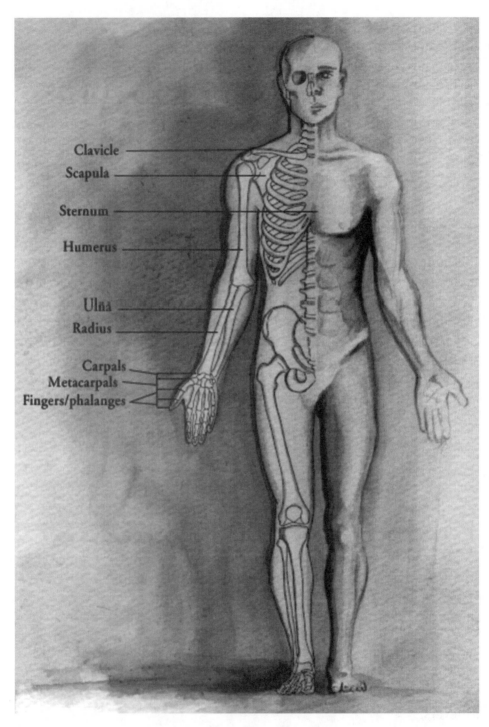

Clavicle
Scapula
Sternum
Humerus
Ulna
Radius
Carpals
Metacarpals
Fingers/phalanges

Figure 6: Bony Structure Front

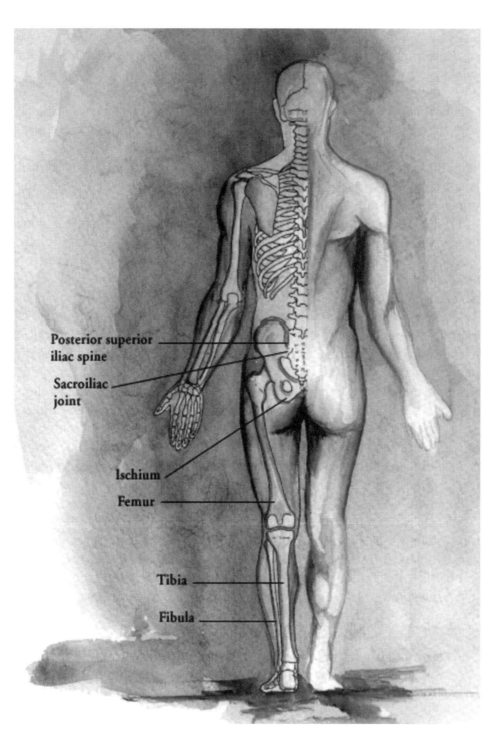

Posterior superior
iliac spine

Sacroiliac
joint

Ischium

Femur

Tibia

Fibula

Figure 7: Bony Structure Back

The bones in your skeletal system are generally divided into two separate but interlocking units, the axial and the appendicular. Your axial skeleton includes the bones we associate with the head and torso. They include your skull, vertebrae, ribs, and pelvis. The bones of your appendicular skeleton include your arms/hands and legs/feet.

Our typical image of bones as an inflexible foundation upon and within which the rest of our body exists is incorrect. Our bones are actually very flexible structures that modify themselves to reflect our current state. Athletes, for example, develop heavier bones, while the bones of someone who is in a cast for a long period of time become thinner. Your postural habits can also influence the shape of your bones and their relationship to each other. According to Dean Juhan, "A lot of sitting in squats, for instance, creates enlarged facets in the hip joints. A chronic slump can eventually alter the bony contours of the rib cage. Abnormal pressure on bone, such as that caused by tumors or by extreme postural aberrations, causes local erosion."[4] Efficient use of your bones takes place when bones follow their ideal path of action without any unnecessary contraction in the muscles. "The ideal path of action for the skeleton as it moves from one position to another, say, from sitting to standing or from lying to sitting, is the path through which it would move if it had no muscles at all, if the bones were linked only by ligaments."[5] The best care of the bones involves combining efficient muscle use with moderate exercise–dancing, walking, swimming, and bicycling–with periods of rest. A combination of efficient use and moderate exercise creates bones that are strong, resilient, and balanced.

The connection between bones is an interface of cartilage called a joint. The range of movement of which these connections are capable varies by location and function. Types of joints include immovable joints (like those of your skull); slightly movable or limited-range joints (as in the spine); and freely movable joints (as in the elbow, wrist, ankle, hip, and those in the hands and feet).

1. **Using the illustrations of the skeleton in figures 6 and 7 begin a slow massage of your body beginning with your head and working your way downward, focusing as you do so on the bony structure**. (This can also be done with a partner.) As you gently massage each area, become familiar with the names of the primary bony parts.

---

[4]Juhan, 103.
[5]Juhan, 90.

2. **Note the following, determining shape, size, and position in relationship to each other:**
    The attachment of the head to the spine.
    The entire shoulder girdle.
    The relationship between the ribs and between the ribs and the spine.
    The integration of the arm through elbow joint and fingers.
    The width of the iliac crest in the pelvis.
    The length of the leg from the top of the femur in the hip through the knee joint, ankle joint, and tips of the toes.

Journal: Immediately upon completing the exploration, draw a picture of your bony structure. Do not rely on what you have seen in illustrations; rely instead on your feeling sense of your bony structure. Are there any parts of the bony structure that you do not yet have a felt sense of? What is the exact circumference of your humerus, femur, tibia? How wide is your sternum? What are the differences in size of your vertebrae in different parts of your spine? What is the size of the tail bone at the end of the spine?

Muscles and Dynamic Alignment

Your muscles work in coordination with your bones to achieve various body alignments or postures. In their contracted state, your muscles work to produce, retard, or prevent movement in your bone system (see Figures 8 and 9). Muscles cooperate not only to produce movement but also to allow it, to control its speed and force, to guide its direction, to stabilize the more central structures against outward pulling force, and even to maintain internal awareness as you commit to a variety of physical actions from walking to shaking someone's hand or turning a somersault. The muscles of your body work together in groups to move your bony structures in the following motions (see Figure 10):

- flexion or bending
- extension or straightening rotation, either inward or outward
- circumduction, clockwise or counterclockwise (Circumduction is movement of the bone to describe a cone shape in space, the base being the distal end of the moving part, the apex being the center

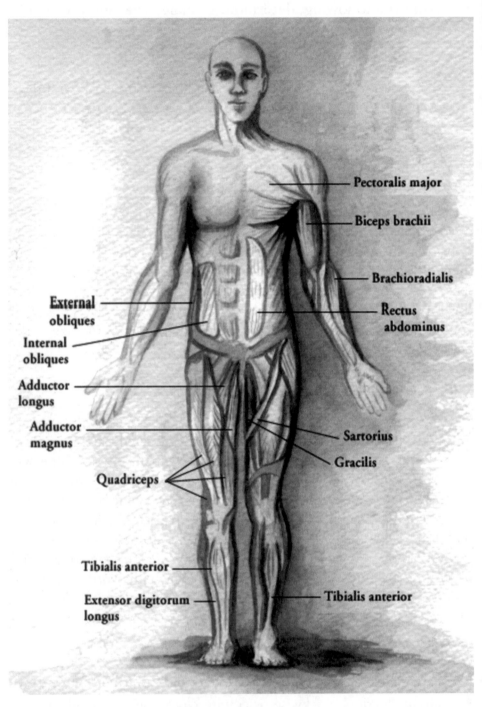

Pectoralis major

Biceps brachii

Brachioradialis

Rectus
abdominus

External
obliques

Internal
obliques

Adductor
longus

Adductor
magnus

Sartorius

Gracilis

Quadriceps

Tibialis anterior

Extensor digitorum
longus

Tibialis anterior

Figure 8: Muscles Front

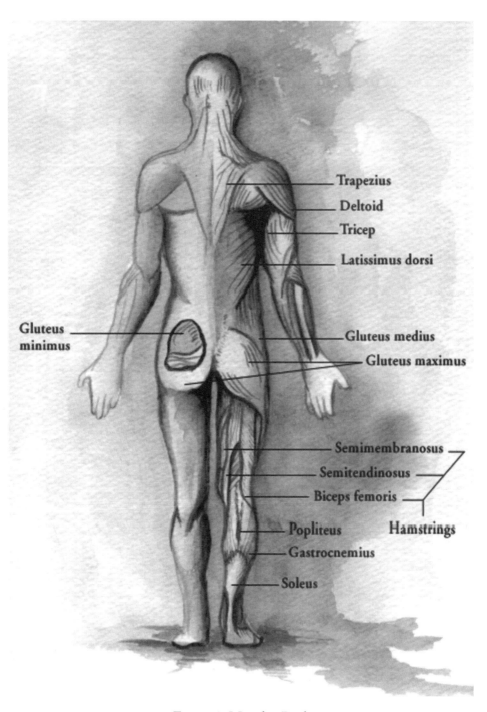

Trapezius

Deltoid

Tricep

Latissimus dorsi

Gluteus
minimus

Gluteus medius

Gluteus maximus

Semimembranosus

Semitendinosus

Biceps femoris

Hamstrings

Popliteus

Gastrocnemius

Soleus

Figure 9: Muscles Back

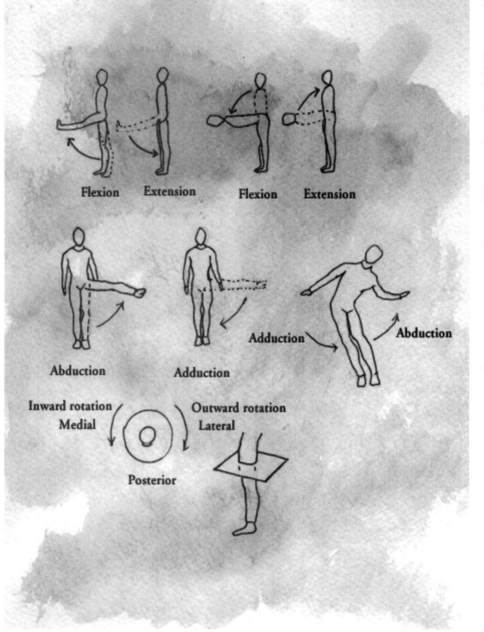

Figure 10: Muscle Actions

of the joint. One example is the movement of the outstretched arm while drawing a circle.)

- adduction toward the center of your body
- abduction away from the center of your body

Incorrect placement of the bones is the result of your muscles taking on the work of your bones. You can correct your placement as you discover ways to release unnecessary contraction in the muscle tissue. An increased understanding of the interaction between the muscular and bony system facilitates a release in your body's system. The primary method of increasing one's experiential awareness involves exploring the relationship between these systems. The increased awareness helps you move with ease and grace.

Your muscles do their work through a contraction or pulling inward on a set of muscle fibers. This complex process, initiated by the nervous system, creates a chemical reaction in your muscle that leads to a mechanical action in your muscle tissue. Unnecessary or constricted effort at the time of actual muscle contraction tends to shorten your body, as the overly contracted muscles have a shorter range of motion. This unnecessary, contracted state can be initiated by something as simple as incorrect or uneconomical use of a body part, usually the consequence of modeling others' movement patterns and incorporating them into your behavior. Or it can be the result of attempting to protect an injury. A third possibility is an imbalance in the system resulting from using some muscle groups more than others. This is often the case with people whose occupations require them to be in one physical position for long periods of time. Whatever the circumstances responsible for the unnecessary contracted state of a specific muscle group, it is important to integrate methods of releasing the tightened muscles within your daily practice.

There is a correspondence between awareness of muscle use and learning to release them. There are three levels of muscular discrimination associated with an active contraction in the belly of a muscle:

1) the initiation of an action brought on by intention
2) the static or contracted muscle state as you maintain a physical position
3) the final lengthening of the muscle as you release the body part

This process of contraction and extension is aided by the stretch reflex:

When a muscle is stretched, there is a reflexive contraction of that muscle following the stretch. The stretch reflex can be utilized to advantage in movement skills as in the windup or back swing of many motor skills. The back swing or windup creates a stretch of the muscles that produces the swing or throw. The plie is the dancer's windup for a jump. The first activation of these muscles is then reflexive and is provided by the stretch reflex.[6]

The stretch reflex protects the muscle group from being pulled away from the bones to which it is attached. To protect you from overusing this method of muscle development, you also have a response called the Golgi response, which helps to prevent over stretching. Golgi tendons are sensory organs integrated between the belly of the muscle and the tendon. Sensitive to extreme stretch of the muscle, they constrain the stretch reflex temporarily to prevent stress on the tendon. Moreover, as there is a contraction involved at some point in the stretch, you can use this reflex to strengthen muscle groups. Muscle groups strengthened in this way are generally longer than muscles built primarily through the effort of such activities as weight lifting, giving a longer look to the body silhouette.

You can experiment with all of the above by beginning with any muscle group of the body and exploring all of the various levels of contraction–active, static, and lengthening.

<hr>

Exploration 12: Muscular Awareness

The following is an exploration to help you become more aware of muscle groups and to encourage the release of unnecessary contraction. This exploration also introduces you to the relationship between contraction and breath. You begin to experience the sensation of breath on a cellular level and to become aware of degrees of muscular contraction.

1. **Begin lying on your back and complete the body scan**. Begin to notice the phrasing of your breath and allow it to slow down by

increasing the length of the exhalation. Begin to note the top of each inhalation and the bottom of each exhalation almost as if you were observing the top or bottom of an ocean wave.

2. **Slowly contract the muscles of your feet and ankles.** Permit the phrasing of the breath to dictate the speed of the contraction.

3. **Release the muscles of feet and ankles as you exhale.** Feel the contraction in the muscles as you breathe in and the relaxation of the muscles as you breathe out.

4. **Continue this throughout your body, moving up through the hamstrings and quadriceps of the thighs, the adductors in the inner thigh, the gluteal muscles of the buttocks, the abdominal and pectoral muscles of the torso, the latisimus dorsi and trapezius of the back, the biceps and triceps of the arm**. At first, you may not have any experience of the internal respiration process in relationship to the muscles but, with continued practice, your awareness will increase.

5. **Contract the entire body as a single unit, followed by a slow release of one muscle group after another.** Feel the energy from the muscles as each muscle is released sequentially from one group to the next.

6. **Contract your entire body by pulling your knees toward your chest, trying to make a small round ball.**

7. **Extend the ball into a full-body stretch, reaching your legs and arms in opposite directions, then shake out your entire body—arms, legs, torso, and head.**

8. **Release yourself into the floor and gravity**.

Journal: Imagine that you are a laboratory researcher who is trying to detect the relationships among various muscle groups. What are some conclusions you have come to following the exploration? Can you feel the work of the different muscle groups? The relationship between one group and another?

Dynamic Alignment and the Integrated Body

A integrated body is in constant evolution. Although most often considered as a physical experience, aspects of integration–alignment, grounding, balance–are useful concepts for both emotional and physical states. On an emotional level, grounding, or centering, refers to feeling at home with yourself, comfortable and aware. Physical centeredness is an attunement or alignment of the bony and muscle systems with each other and correspondingly with gravity. It is achieved through an understanding of the structural balance between different body parts. Phrases that help you to explore dynamic alignment are "ease up," "release into," "breathe into," "find the balance," "let go" and "link up and out."

You can conduct a mini-exploration of dynamic alignment and integration through the contrary body states of symmetry and asymmetry. A symmetrical state of the body exists when the head, spine, and limbs on the left and right sides of the body are creating the same shape (note two actors on right in Figure 5a). For example: The head rests on top of the spine. The spine is hanging long. The hips are parallel to the ground and the legs and feet are pointed in the same direction while the shoulders, arms, and hands are creating the same pose or shape. In a symmetrical pose, there is a vertical opposition to gravity in the alignment of the body's structure. Thus, gravity pulls down on the legs and the rest of the body, creating a compression of the body toward its central axis, the spine. An illustration of the opposite state, asymmetry, is provided by several of the actors in figures 5a, b and c. For example, actor far left in Figure 5a has head tilted slightly to right, pelvis reaching to the left, the right leg slightly pointed out, the right leg slightly behind the left, the right hand resting on the hip while the left hand presses forward. With the body in this position, gravity is not pulling directly down on the body, but differently through the weight distribution on each leg, the relationship of the spine to the legs, and the adjustment of the head and arms. Likewise, the body is not compressed inward toward the center line, but is a series of interrelated compressions between body parts. Take a moment and create a variety of symmetrical and asymmetrical poses. Move back and forth between symmetrical and asymmetrical poses. With each pose become aware of the subtle compression between body parts, the pull of gravity and the related internal kinesthetic connections.

Body Attitude, Dynamic Alignment and Neutral

Body attitude is learned and for the most part unconscious behavior. However, body attitudes can, unknowingly and inappropriately, become a part of a role. A concept that helps actors to minimize unconscious body attitudes is *neutral*. This idea evolved from the training theories of Jacques Lecoq, whose goal was to help performers become aware of their pre-socialized self in order to free their bodies for performance. A notion of neutral embodies concepts that include the self as a blank page. You are the "I" and the "not I". You are neither masculine nor feminine. You belong to no social group and hold no particular religious view of the world. You have not developed a specific sense of the past or the future, only of the ongoing present. You are in a state of what Zen Buddhists refer to as "beginner's mind." Finally, you incorporate psychological, emotional, and physical qualities that include detachment, nonjudgment, alignment, physical and emotional balance, groundedness, openness, acceptance, internal and external focus, and the ability to listen and breathe through your entire self. But, as Elderge and Houston point out, "Yet one cannot avoid being oneself. An actor can hope to perform a neutral action, but he cannot be neutral–neutral is a fulcrum point that doesn't exist."[7] Neutral is not a precise state but a conceptual image of an individualized mode of being. Dynamic alignment and neutral are complementary conceptual states. Each encourages you to become aligned, or what I would call rooted, to the core of your being. A concentration on embodying either state aides you in becoming a vehicle for exploration, an empty vessel, a container for possibilities and dynamic potential, a conduit for character. This potential comes from the core of your own uniqueness as you stand from. moment to moment. on the edge of the "cliff of possibilities" of your imagination.

IMAGERY AND KINETIC CONNECTIONS

The primary integrating technique of the nervous system is the process of *visualization* and its associated imagery. Visualization, imagery, and metaphor are three interrelated concepts. You extend your imagination through visualization and its associated imagery, expand your potential through the possibilities discovered in metaphors, and reformulate these discoveries in a single posture or gesture. Although each concept builds upon the former in logical

---

[7]Elderge and Houston, "The Neutral Mask," in *Acting (Re) Considered* ed. Phillip
  Zarilli (New York: Routledge, 1995), 123.

sequence, your experience is often a gestalt, with all elements coalescing in a single moment in time. In most acting classes, imagery and metaphor are used together. All the same, an image may or may not serve a metaphoric function. I may remember in detail images of an experience I had in the past, yet the memory may not function in the current situation as a metaphor. For an image to function as a metaphor, it needs to expand the imagination by answering the question, "as if it were?" Daily people refer to nature for simple similes that become metaphors for body attitudessuch as 'free as a bird' or 'deep as an ocean.' These references conjure an entire set of sensory images from watching birds fly across the sky to feeling the roll and pitch of the ocean as we look over the side of the ship and try to see the bottom of the sea. Each time we use a metaphor our imagination unites with our senses.

Visualization, or the ability to sustain, hold, focus, or concentrate on an image, has been at the center of much research on the self.[8] Visualization is an act of intention. Although it is often considered a process that is limited to the cerebrum, the act of visualizing is connected to the entire body via the nervous system. You can, for instance, make a gesture of your hand, then close your eyes and mentally repeat this gesture by relying on the physical memory of the act as stored in somatic memory (which includes muscle tissue), or you can intentionally visualize it by placing breath or colored energy in different parts of your body. Thus, the visualization process can simply involve using the imagination to create an image that you then explore or it can involve past experience.

Like body sensing, visualization is a three-part process comprising *focus*, *suggestion*, and *unification*. This three-part process is an extension of the feel, fuse, and follow method described in chapter 1.

The first step, *focus*, brings you to a level of concentration on the task of using an image that is analogous to feeling and connecting with your breath as it enters your body.

The second step, *suggestion*, involves fusing the image with your breath and acknowledging the power of the image to transform your structural system.

---

8 Two sources are: Jeanne Achterberg, *Imagery in Healing: Shamanism and Modernism Medicine* (New York: Random House, 1985); Mike Samuels and Nancy Samuels. *Seeing with the Mind's Eye*, (New York: Random House, 1975).

The final step, *unification*, engages the combination of breath and image in the reorganization of your energy system. (As you remember from chapter 1, energy is the combination of breath and image.)

This three-part process can be used in the exploration of dynamic alignment, which includes placing breath, discovering the basic structure, centering the pelvis, extending and lengthening the spine, connecting with appendages, grounding the energy, and finding the balance. This approach to discovering dynamic alignment is also a method of warming up the body for performance, and creating a physical character. Appendix A provides a method for warming up the body.

Placing the Breath

The phrase "placing the breath" includes the process developed in the explorations from chapter 1. However, the phrase also suggests placing the breath for a specific purpose. Functionally, the breath can be used to increase relaxation, awareness, and focus. The breath can also be combined with images to investigate alignment, create the physical life of a character, discover and channel emotions, and find the phrasing of a text. The first step in each of these performance tasks is becoming aware of the placement of the breath. The initial question becomes, "Where within my body do I experience the breath?" or, "Where is the breath placed within my body? Is it placed where I need it to be for the current task?" Once these questions are answered, you can guide the breath to fulfill the needs of the activity. Placing the breath thus becomes the first task of the actor in the movement studio, rehearsal, or performance.

In the investigation of dynamic alignment, breath plays the role of releasing the muscles, particularly, those in and around the joint structures. This is accomplished by focusing on the internal respiration process and fusing with the breath as it moves through the body on a cellular level and by integrating this breath with images. A cellular response to breath was provided by Explorations 3, 4, and 7. In this chapter, we will concentrate on using breath in combination with imagery. It is a method of using the breath we will return to in future chapters.

Exploration 13: Breath and Imagery

The majority of us expand our experience of breath by placing it within the torso and extending it from this area to the rest of the body. The goal of this exploration is to provide you with a sequence of images to center and expand your experience of breathing. The images used in this exploration are based on previous work with actors and dancers. You may discover other images that are more effective for you. You should begin with the suggested images and allow them to transform if other images, via your associative memory, reveal themselves. An important element in this exploration is the sequencing of images, from those that involve only one part of the body to those that engage the body as a whole. In working with a sequence of images, you are learning to integrate a series of tasks.

1. **Complete a body scan and ask, Where do I feel the placement of the breath in my body?**
2. **Note the phrasing of the breath.** Allow the exhalation to be slightly longer than the inhalation.
3. **Connect the experience of the breath and fuse the breath to the image of your diaphragm as an elevator that moves down toward your pelvic floor as you inhale and up toward your lungs as you exhale.** Working with this image, become aware of the sensation of breath reaching down through your pelvic floor as you inhale and up through your torso as you exhale.
4. **Change the image. Now focus on your rib cage as an umbrella that opens as you inhale and closes as you exhale.** Working with this image, become aware of the sensation of breath that fills the spaces between your ribs and between the shoulder blades and collar bone.
5. **Unite the images of elevator and umbrella.** This is accomplished by beginning to focus on one image and adding on the second image. For instance, focus on the image of the diaphragm as elevator and add the image of the rib cage as umbrella. Integrate the two images and note the experience of your breath. Continue to use the suggested images or adapt them as necessary to place the breath down into your pelvic floor and into the spaces of your upper torso.

6.   Begin to imagine the pelvic floor as a smoldering fire that is brought to life by the breath.

7.   The heat from this fire extends down through the soles of the feet, up through the spine and head, and out to the tips of your fingers and through all the cells of your body.

Journal: Describe your experience of the breath from your initial body scan through the final stage of feeling the breath reach through your feet, head, and finger tips. Is there an element, such as water, fire, or air, that the breath feels like? Does it have a particular color? Does this color change as it moves through different parts of your body? Did the images, such as the elevator for diaphragm or umbrella for rib cage, remain or did they transform to other images? If so, what were those images?

Centering the Pelvis

Your pelvis is the structural and emotional center of support for your alignment, center, and balance (see Figure 11). Constructed like a bowl, the pelvis is a complex set of bony structures, muscle tissue, and nerves that unites your spine and upper body with your locomotive appendages, the feet and legs. Thus, your pelvis is the point around which the entire weight of your body balances. It is impossible for the rest of you to remain in one position if the pelvis is in motion. As a unit, the pelvis functions primarily to support and protect the internal organs; to provide a place of origin for the muscles of the trunk, lower limbs, and proximal portion of each arm; and to "transmit the weight of the trunk and upper extremities to the lower limbs."[9]

The primary bony structures of your pelvis are the sacrum at the back of the pelvis, the ilium forming the sides, the ischium forming the bottom, and the pubis forming the front. Three points of connection with the rest of your body allow the pelvis to move as an individual unit. These are the two hip joints and the articulation of the sacrum with the fifth lumbar vertebra. Your pelvis thus connects the spine with your lower and upper body.

For many people, a problem of the pelvic area develops from an inappropriate use of the muscles through over contraction in either the

---

[9]Lulu Sweigard, *Human Movement Potential* (New York: Harper and Row, 1974), 31.

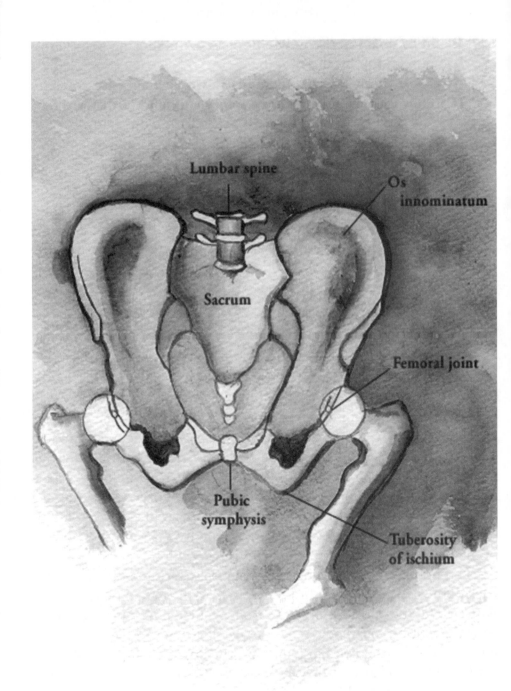

Figure 11: Pelvis

lumbar region of the lower spine, in the gluteus, or both. This over contraction causes lumbar lordosis, or swayback, and is often associated with hyper-extension of the knees. Another common problem is an over contraction of the lower abdominal area, the pelvic floor, and the gluteus maximus. This results from an image of physical beauty borrowed from magazine adds. Poses of men and women in tightly controlled poses encourages imitators to overly contract the muscles of the lower abdomen, which inhibits breath and emotional flow. This problem is solved by a redistribution of the muscle system and a reevaluation of the individual's self-image, influenced by the cultural creation of unhealthy standards of beauty. By releasing old habits, you will release the muscles of the back and engage the muscles of the front of the torso to create balance in the pelvic area.

The purpose of the following explorations is to help you discover the intricate relationship between the muscles of the pelvic area and the rest of the body. Before and between each exploration, allow yourself to fully rest on the floor on your back and complete a body scan.

**Exploration 14:
Getting Acquainted with the Pelvis**

---

1. **Start by lying on your back and slowly drawing up your knees toward the ceiling until your feet are parallel to each other, the same width apart as your shoulders and flat on the floor.**[10]
2. **Slowly tilt your pelvis back and forth in a gentle rocking motion.**
3. **Continue this motion, being aware of allowing the breath to participate in the action through a fully released abdominal breath.** The more relaxed the breath, the more released the action of the pelvis at the hip joints.
4. **Now imagine a clock dial painted on the back of your pelvis:**

---

[10]This exploration is an adaptation of Moshe Feldenkrais' pelvic clock exercise as described in *Awareness Through Movement* (New York: Harper and Row, 1977). I have expanded on the original version to include an increased awareness of the spine and the integration of the feet and legs.

Six o'clock is drawn on the coccyx and twelve o'clock is at the top of the pelvis where it joins the spine at the fifth lumbar vertebra.

5. **With these two points in mind, raise the hips so that the back of the pelvis, except for the position of twelve o'clock, is off the floor.**

6. **Lower the pelvis so that it reverses its direction and the area of twelve o'clock is lifted while the weight of the pelvis rests at six o'clock.** Continue to move back and forth between these two points. Be certain you are continuing the relaxed abdominal breathing with which you started. Also begin to notice the relationship between the pelvis and other parts of the legs and torso. Try to answer the following questions: Where is the pressure of my body against the floor as I move my pelvis to twelve o'clock? To six o'clock? What is the role of my feet and legs while completing this movement? Is there a way I could incorporate the muscles of the front and back of the pelvis that would make this movement economical? More relaxed? More fluid? Is there a way I could incorporate the feet and legs that would make the movement economical? More relaxed? More fluid?

7. **Once you discovered six and twelve o'clock, begin to fill the rest of the circular pelvic area with other portions of the clock.** You can place three o'clock in the area of the right hip joint, nine o'clock at the left hip joint. The other hours will take their appropriate places between.

8. **Begin to explore the entire circle of the clock, moving from twelve o'clock, to three o'clock, to six o'clock, to nine o'clock, and back to twelve o'clock.**

9. **Complete this circle and reverse the direction, moving first toward nine o'clock.** Notice areas of the circle that seem more difficult to move through than others. If, for example, you find the circle fluid over the entire perimeter of the clock except from three to six o'clock, return to this area, trying new methods of incorporating the muscles and the muscles in relationship to the breath until the movement becomes fluid and easy.

10. **Follow the initial clock exploration with journeys across the face of the clock, from twelve o'clock to five o'clock or three o'clock to nine o'clock.** Again, as in the earlier movements, continue to notice both the use of the muscles in the pelvic area and

their relationship to the organization of muscle use in the rest of the body.

11. **When you have finished exploring the entire pelvic area using the image of the clock, straighten out your legs and complete another body scan, noticing how you are giving your weight to the floor.** Is it the same or different from what it was before the exploration?

12. **Expand your experience of this exploration by using the same image but placing your feet and legs in different positions.** For instance, bring both knees upward and over the chest, place both feet toward the ceiling with ankles entwined around each other, one knee bent and the other leg straight, one knee over the chest and the other leg straight, knees flopped in opposite directions toward the floor. Each of these positions will cause you to engage the pelvis and hip joints in new ways. Becoming aware of personal tendencies on your back without the vertical pull of gravity will help you begin to notice how you integrate different areas when you are standing.

13. **Expand your experience by changing size of clock.** Pressing gently with your feet to initiate the movement, begin moving around the edges of the circle of the clock. Each circumnavigation allows the clock to get bigger and bigger until the very edges of your pelvis are touching the floor. Be aware of the related release in the spine, neck, and shoulders as they respond to the circling of the pelvis. Continue the circle, but allow the circumference of the clock to become smaller and smaller until it reaches the center of your pelvis. Breathe into and out of that center. Be aware, as you breathe in of the breath touching the edges of the pelvis and, as you breathe out the breath traveling up the spine and head and into the feet and fingers.

14. **Expand your experience by adding imagery.** Imagine a giant brush at the center of the clock that is brushing the edges of the pelvis with paint as you circle first one way and then the other. Or imagine that the pelvis is filled with colored water that sloshes around the center and touches the outer edges of the pelvis.

Journal: After you finish each exploration, describe your experience. Pay particular attention to areas of the body that did not feel as if they were moving with ease. Also pay attention to your discoveries about your own method of organizing yourself, based on the exploration, and note your reaction to the use of the breath and images. Are these techniques easy or difficult for you? And if so, in what sense? In the method of focus and concentration they require? In incorporation of the breath? The kind of images?

Exploration 15: Images to Release the Pelvis

One aspect of economical use is the appropriate *tonus* or muscle contraction of the flexor muscles, located primarily on the front of the torso, and the extensor muscles, located primarily on the back of the torso. The relationship between these two complementary muscle groups can be visualized as sympathetic to each other. For instance, appropriate pelvic placement is achieved when the muscles in the front of the pelvis contract or narrow across the front while the muscles along the back of the hips widen. One method of adjusting this placement is *constructive* (see Figure 12). This is the position of the body in which the different muscle groups need to use the least amount of contractual effort to maintain an ongoing relationship with each other. It is also a position in which you can be actively engaged in an imagistic task without being likely to go to sleep. Constructive rest, like some meditation postures of the body, is a position of repose in which you are actively engaged in a task. Unlike most meditation postures, however, you generally keep your eyes closed.

1. **Lie on the floor and bring your knees toward the ceiling. Instead of your knees being the same distance apart as your hips, allow them to be slightly farther apart than your hips but with your feet on the floor.** Now allow your knees to drop toward each other so they are resting somewhere in the center line of your body. If you find that your knees tend to fall away from each other, take a piece of rope or other material and tie the knees together. The upper part of your torso and head should be resting comfortably on the floor.

2. **Reach your arms toward the ceiling and allow them to fall across the front of the body so that they are crossing each other.** (You may find that your chin reaches toward the ceiling in

this position. If this is the case, try putting a folded towel under your head to see if it releases your chin toward your chest and places your head in a more comfortable relationship with your spine.)

3. **Once you have achieved the constructive rest position, begin to focus on your breathing, allowing the breath to move into and out of your lower abdomen.**

4. **Fusing with the breath, you can begin to focus on your pelvis using one of the following images.** Experience the buttocks as two separate loaves of unbaked bread dough being squashed into the floor by their weight and flowing sideways away from each other to widen the space between them while portions of the bread dough come over the hips to meet in the center of the pelvis. OR Feel a pair of tight levis that you must zip up the front; at the same time, watch the hip pockets on the back of the pants move away from each other and toward the pelvic bones in the front of the body.

5. **Keep in mind that some images will work for you and others will not.** Do not get stuck on one image; rather, try one for ten minutes and move on to another. If while trying one image another comes to your consciousness, allow it to replace the initial image as long as it stays within the goal of the original image. It could be that this is your subconscious giving you cues about how to work with these images.

6. **Try to incorporate as much specific sensory information as possible into the initial image.** For instance, you could imagine the pelvis as a toy accordion (with handles on either side and vertical pleats on the front and back) that is opening in the back and closing in the front. However, you will deepen your experience of the image if you add sensory input to the accordion. For example, feel the accordion being opened wide as the hips become an accordion and the soft white pleats of the accordion open wide in the back as the firm handles (hip blades) of the side of the accordion pull to the side and the white pleats slowly come together in front. Incorporate the breath into the image so the exhalation brings the soft white pleats of the accordion closer and closer together in the front of the pelvis. What color is the accordion? As the pleats move apart, what sound do they make? What is the texture of the bread dough? What does it smell like? Sensory details help you

to engage the images in greater depth.[11]

7. **Finally, when you feel the urge to move, do so gently in small rocking or jiggling movements**. These will help the body to release old patterns. If you lose concentration, do not criticize yourself; instead, just return to the task of focusing on the image.

Figure 12: Constructive Rest

---

[11]The images in this text are adapted from Lulu Sweigard's work. I have added sensory awareness and breath to the original images.

Exploration 16:
Connecting the Pelvis with Breath

---

1. **Lie on your back and lift your knees to approximately a ninety-degree angle with your feet flat on the floor.**
2. **Begin to breathe in and out of your lower abdomen.**
3. **On exhaling, contract the muscles in the lower pelvic region of the abdomen while keeping the muscles in the buttocks released and lift the pelvis slightly off the floor.** Allow the work of the exhalation to send your navel to your spine and lift the pelvis off the floor.
4. **Now inhale and feel the breath moving toward the outer part of the buttocks as you release the back into the floor and the spine lengthens.**
5. **Repeat several times to discover the rhythm that unifies the exhalation and inhalation.** With each repetition, notice the reaction of the muscles in the lumbar region of the lower back and in the gluteus.
6. **Rest with your knees pulled toward the abdomen and note any changes in the lower back.**
7. **Reverse the process of breathing.** Instead of exhaling as you lift the pelvis off the floor, inhale, keeping the focus on the use of the muscles in the lower abdomen.
8. **Rest with your legs long.**

Journal: Describe your experience of the relationship between your pelvis and your breath. Did you notice a change in the manner in which the muscles contract? Which combination of inhalation and exhalation with the pelvis tends to release which muscle groups in the pelvic area? If your focus is to strengthen the lower abdomen, which breath combination would you use? If you want to tighten the gluteus, what would you use?

Extending and Lengthening the Spine

Your spine works with the pelvis to integrate your upper and lower body. Because of this task, it has more trouble adjusting to the upright

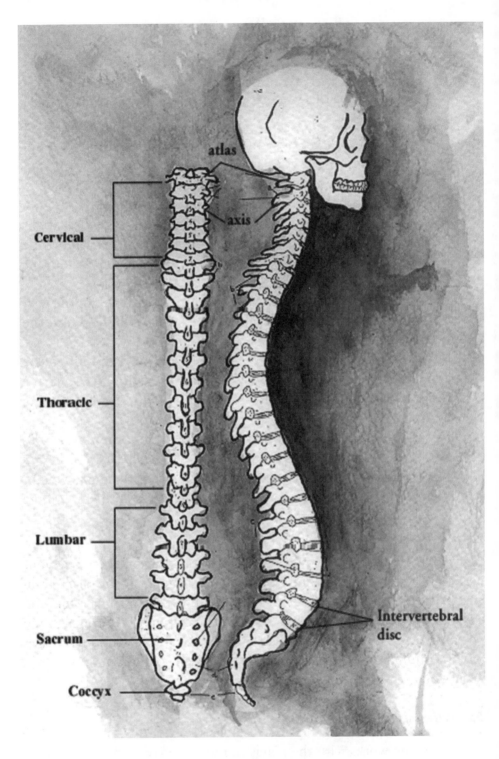

Figure 13: Spine

position than any other portion of your body. The spine is composed of 24 separate vertebrae that can be divided into three separate groups–the seven cervical vertebrae in the area of the neck, the twelve thoracic vertebrae in the area of the rib cage, and the five lumbar vertebrae in the area of the waist and hips. All three vertebral groups share a similar structure but differ in size depending upon where they are in the spinal column (see Figure 13).

Your spinal column has several functions. The first and most important is supporting and transferring weight from the lower levels of your body (feet and legs) to the upper levels of your body (head and arms). The differentiation between the vertebrae ensures movement in a variety of directions. Your spine also provides a protective passageway for the spinal cord and related nerves.

The shape of your spine can be compared to a pyramid, with larger lumbar vertebrae at the base, gradually narrowing to cervical vertebrae at the top. It is, however, unlike a pyramid in its flexibility. Like other flexible columns, it relies on balancing curves that develop after birth. The cumulative adaptation of your various vertebrae to each other from the base upward gives the distal/upper spine a relatively large range of motion compared with its sacral base. The intervertebral discs that connect the vertebral bodies act as buffers or cushions and consequently are shock absorbers which allow your spine to curve forward in the cervical and lumbar regions and backward in the thoracic and sacral regions. Thus, the shape of your spine resembles an elongated, inverted S.

Since your spinal column must support great weight, resist shock, and protect the spinal cord, movement between any two vertebrae must be slight, although movement of the entire column is considerable. Motion is easiest where the vertebral bodies are smallest and where the discs are thickest–the former in the cervical, the latter in the lumbar spine. Movements of your spinal column include *flexion* (forward bending), *extension* (backward bending), *lateral flexion* (bending to the side), *rotation* (twisting), and *circumduction* (end point rotation). These differ in degree in the three regions as well as within each region. The direction of motion in any region is controlled by the shape of the associated vertebrae.

You can explore the movement of the total spine by working with a partner (preferably someone of the same height or taller) who gently holds your head while you allow the rest of your spine to follow. Your partner moves your head forward to *flex* the spine, backward to *extend* the spine, sideways to experience *lateral flexion*, or in a circle to experience both *rotation* and *circumduction*. If a partner is not available, you can approximate the experience by imagining your head being manipulated in a variety of directions by an invisible force.

**Exploration 17:
Getting Acquainted with the Spine**

The following set of suggestions will help you get acquainted with the cervical, thoracic, and lumbar regions of your spine and understand how they are functionally integrated with your appendages. Do not feel limited to these movements; during these explorations, you may discover more efficient ways of integrating the appendage with the torso. Complete each movement, being aware of the beginning or initiating element of the action and the ending of it. Also allow a complete disengagement or a relaxation of the muscles between each movement. Doing so will help you to become aware of the level of muscle contraction needed for action and the level of muscle contraction associated with nonaction for that particular position of the body.

1. **Lying on your back, complete a brief body scan.**
2. **Using the pressure against the floor generated in your heels, begin a gentle rocking motion that moves you up and down from your head to your feet.** Observe which areas of your body have a sense of gentle vibration or rocking in them. Using your knowledge of the spinal vertebrae, form a kinesthetic picture of each vertebra, from the tail bone through the lumbar region to the thoracic and cervical vertebrae. What does the relationship between the spine and the pelvic bowl feel like? Can you find an approach that incorporates your breath into this movement? A use of the breath that increases your awareness of the different areas of the spinal column? Let the rocking motion slowly drift away.
3. **Take your right arm and place it above your head, palm up. Reach it toward the area above your head, which remains on the floor, and return it.** What parts of your spine become

engaged as you lift your arm? Try this several times.

4. **Keeping your arm in the same place, reach your arm upward as you turn your head to the left**. What parts of the spine did you get acquainted with this time? Investigate innocently with the attitude of a child, moving back and forth between arm and head and discovering more about both as you become aware of the integration between the two. Can you coordinate this movement with your breathing?

5. **Repeat on the other side.**

6. **With your arms at your side, reach your right arm toward your feet**. What parts of the spine did you engage this time?

7. **Begin a small-oval stroking motion on the floor toward your feet and up toward your waist and back**. How does this change the engagement with the spine?

8. **Repeat. Try it with the other arm and hand.**

9. **Placing your arm horizontal to the body, move the arm in a slow arc from the waist to above the head**. How does the changing position of the arm influence the relationship with the spine? What about lifting the arm above the body and reaching for the arm on the opposite side?

10. **Try it with the other arm**.

11. **Bring your attention to your legs. Begin to move either leg away from the body and return it to a normal position**. Repeat several times.

12. **Try it with the other leg.**

13. **Using opposite arms and legs, reach down with your leg as you reach up with the arm.**

14. **Repeat using arms and legs on the same side of the body.**

15. **Roll over on your stomach and repeat.**

16. **Lying on your back, bring your knees up. Place your feet flat on the floor. Now drape one leg over the other. Release the legs in the direction of the leg that is on top. Contracting the abdomen, bring the leg back to center. Repeat**. What area of the spine is part of this action? Can you increase the area involved in the space between the vertebrae by incorporating the breath and the use of the abdominal muscles?

17. **Repeat with the other leg.**

18. **Lie with your back on the floor and, listening, notice how much of your spine you are now aware of.**

Journal: What parts of the spine and related integration with the torso were you aware of at the beginning of the exploration? At the end of the exploration? Draw a picture of your experience of your spine. Do not try to replicate one you have seen in an anatomy book, but the actual experience of your spine.

Exploration 18: Seesaw

This partner exercise on a mat helps you to discover the integration of the separate parts of the spine in lying and standing positions. It also helps you to gain an awareness of the muscle balance in the pelvis necessary to support the spine.

1. **Partner one lies on the floor with knees flexed and feet together in full contact with the floor. Partner two, standing, faces Partner one. The feet of the person on the floor (Partner one) enclose the feet of partner two.**

2. **Partner two bends toward Partner one and grasps Partner one firmly by the wrists. Partner one also grasps Partner two by the wrists. Partner two begins to gently pull backward and move into a squat position.**

3. **As Partner two moves back, Partner one contracts in the abdomen and raises his/her head at the same moment and starts to move forward and up, using the combination of the contraction in the abdomen and the pushing into the mat with the feet.**

4. **As Partner one comes to standing position, Partner two releases onto his/her back, keeping the knees flexed while slowly breathing in and rolling down one vertebra at a time.** Partner two needs to be certain to gently place Partner one on the mat (and the reverse), taking time for the partner to be able to lengthen the spine while releasing the back to the floor.

5. **Repeat several times.** As you repeat the exercise, you should find that your awareness of the separate vertebrae of the spine increases. You also become more aware of the necessity of using your lower abdominal muscles to come to sitting and standing positions, and of the integration of breath into the movement. At

some point you should discover a place of balance as one partner is coming up and the other is going down. You are, in this position, equally dependent upon each other. With continued repetitions, the relationship between the two partners will begin to feel like a seesaw. This exploration can also be used as a rehearsal technique for discovering the push and pull of characters in a scene.

Journal: Where did you feel the lengthening of the spine while doing the seesaw? In the lift of the body up? In the release of the body down?

The Head

Your head sits at the top of the spinal column and is held in place by a series of muscle attachments in the shoulder girdle, spine, and ribs. Through different muscle organizations, your head has a wide range of motion, including rotation to either side, flexion and extension, gliding, and circular movements.

The head plays a significant role as the container of the primary sensory channels used to survive in today's world; the eyes and the ears. Unlike hunters and gatherers, who needed to be able to detect the motion of animals through their feet or figure out the weather by the feel of the wind against the skin, our technology demands we interact with one another and communicate with machines through touch or voice. The result is an emphasis on the head as the location of perception and the initiator of action, an emphasis that often creates a level of unnecessary contraction in the neck area as we spend long periods in front of a computer screen or perform other tasks requiring hand-eye coordination.

Although all body therapies consider the release of the head as a significant component of alignment, the Alexander technique was initially developed to correct a problem experienced by its originator, F. Matthias Alexander, with the integration of his head and the rest of his body. Although originating from his problem, the principles Alexander espoused do not focus entirely on the head but on the total body. Two of Alexander's basic principles involve freeing the neck and lengthening the spine.[12]

---

[12] These two phrases were adapted from Wilfred Barlow, M.D., *The Alexander Technique* (Rochester, Vermont: Healing Arts Press, 1990).

Neck free: The neck is free when the muscles of your neck and upper back are released while participating in movements of other body parts. Do not try to keep your head in a fixed position. Instead, focus on the dynamic, as in dynamic alignment, to allow your head its delicate balance on top of the spine. The head floats up as your tail bone releases into the pull of gravity and your pelvis balances atop your legs.

The torso lengthening and widening and filling out in depth: To lengthen your spine does not mean to hold it straight, but to allow the natural curves of your spine to be filled with breath. Consider your torso as a hollow tube filled with breath. Your shoulders are allowed to open and widen. Feel the energy of your body flowing outward from the center of your torso through the finger tips. Your hips are relaxed within your joints and your spine lengthens upward as your legs and knees move easily away from your torso. Your legs are not pulled inward toward your pelvis, but are grounded into the floor through the soles of your feet.

Exploration 19:
Releasing the Muscles of the Neck

The goal of this partner exploration is to provide a means of experiencing Alexander principles by having someone else guide your body to new levels of awareness by using a gentle massage technique. Thus, you begin to associate the principles with an attitude of relaxation.

Working with a partner, do this exercise with one person as the guide. Take a brief rest, and then have the other person guide. Remember, as you are working you need to sustain an integrated focus that simultaneously operates on two levels–a focus both on the other person and your own experience. A student describes her experience of self-discovery during the exploration with her partner:

> *Oddly and ironically, the words I chose to coach her loosened me up. Also, I knew that if I touched her bearing tension in my own body, I would transfer my tension to her. As I tried to let go within my own body I found myself saying things to her like, "Let your vertebrae relax against my fingers, step by step." She even commented*

to me that she felt particularly open, let go, and elongated.[13]

Begin with one person lying on the floor, while you assume a comfortable sitting position at that person's head. Applying a light touch with your hands, change the balance of your partner's head so that the muscles in the nape of the neck lengthen and the head rotates more comfortably on the shoulders. Do not overstretch muscles by applying too much pressure. Correctly done, the massage will help to create a new balance in the body.

1. **Take a minute to place your hands gently on the forehead of the person in front of you, discover that person's breath rhythm, and try to integrate it with yours.**

2. **Lift the head, cupping it gently in your hands.** Do nothing else at this point until you can feel that your partner is allowing you to hold the complete weight of the head.

3. **Gently roll the head side to side while easily pulling directly upward along the axis of the spine; do not pull the head so the chin lifts.** You will probably notice a release in the muscles of the neck and shoulders.

4. **Stroke and massage the neck. Carefully placing one hand palm up below the base of the neck, massage gently from neck to the ears.** You will see the shoulder visibly widen and flatten. Repeat on the other side. Repeat several times in a manner similar to that used in milking a cow or stroking a cat.

5. **Gently replace the head on the mat.**

6. **Going to one side of your partner's body, lift an arm so that it is well supported.**

7. **Gently jiggle the arm, from the hand into the shoulder socket, until your partner gives up control of the arm to you.**

8. **Begin to massage the whole arm, beginning in the center of the back between the scapula, drawing the arm steadily downward and away from the torso, continuing through the hand and into the fingers.**

9. **Repeat with the other arm.**

10. **Move to the leg, lift it, supporting it underneath the thigh area. Repeat the gentle jiggling motion used with the arm, waiting for the person to give you the weight of the leg.**

---

[13] Bobbie Saltzman, Personal communication, 1994.

11. **Once the leg is released, begin to pull gently downward as you make little circles of the leg at the hip joint.** Do not force anything. If there is a constricted place, allow it to be there and work within the person's range of movement.

12. **Slowly lower the leg and gently brush from the hip down the outer side of the leg to the feet.**

13. **Return to the head to ensure that it remains free of tension.** Placing your hands on either side of your partner's shoulders, do a little jiggle back and forth and then stop to see if it reverberates through the rest of the torso.

14. **Massaged person rolls to either side and comes to a sitting position with the torso released to the front, knees relaxed, head dropped.**

15. **Use your fingers to walk up the spine from the tail bone through the cervical vertebrae. Slowly bring your partner to a sitting position.** There should be a lengthening in the spine.

16. **Help the person to stand and walk behind. Place your hands on the upper neck to release the spine upward.** You might find it helpful to locate the top of the spine at the center base of the head. It can be found by placing a finger of each hand in a horizontal position under the opening of the ear and pointing inward. If the fingers were extended toward the center from each side, they would meet at the center base of the head at the top of the spine.

Part 2:

Your major sensory systems–vision and hearing–reside within your head but are connected through neural pathways to the rest of your body. A kinesthetic association of these systems with the rest of your body helps you to create internal links between body parts. This portion of the exploration expands your awareness of these links.

1. **Stand or sit in a comfortable position.**

2. **Concentrate your attention on your eyes. Very slowly without moving your head, move your eyes left and right.** Note any movement of internal muscles at the back of the head or along the edge of the spine as you move your eyes.

3. **Begin a movement of the eyes to the left or right, but followed by a slight movement of the head.** Note the movement of the muscles as you did in step 2.

4. **Enlarge this gesture of the head in slight increments until you are turning your head completely to the left or right.** As you enlarge the movement be aware of the increasing engagement of the spine from the cervical vertebrae through the thoracic and lumbar vertebrae and finally the sacrum. Also note the inclusion of the joints of the shoulders and hips that extends to the fingers and toes.

5. **Return to just moving the eyes, but include the awareness of the total body in the gestures of the eyes.** You can increase your awareness of the rest of the body by inhaling prior to the gesture and exhaling as you move your eyes to the left or right.

6. **Pick a favorite piece of music. Lie with your back on the floor, release into your breathing, bring your attention to your ears, and listen to the music.**

7. **Using your ability to visualize the interior of your body, see the music moving through your ears and into the inner recesses of your body.** Do not attempt to force it along a particular path but allow the music to trace its own path.

8. **Repeat using a different piece of music.** You will discover that different pieces of music engage different parts of your body.

Journal: Describe in your journal your expanded awareness of your head and its connection with the rest of your body.

Connecting with the Appendages

The joints of the appendages in your upper and lower torso are complementary (see Figures 14 and 15). Your shoulder and hip joints allow for rotational movement, while the joints in your elbows, knees, wrists, and ankles focus on gestures that move primarily on the *sagittal* (forward and backward) plane. These contrasting movement abilities are related to the function of each area. Your arms and associated shoulder girdle provide a means to bring objects within the realm of your head and communication centers. By contrast, your legs and feet have evolved to provide locomotion and a means of flight if necessary.

Each joint of an appendage is a *synovial* joint, which means that it contains a fluid that protects the bones and cartilage from rubbing against each other. This fluid shifts as your body moves and is a source of proprioceptive information. The concept of stillness in performance is related to the stillness at the center of the pelvis that radiates out to

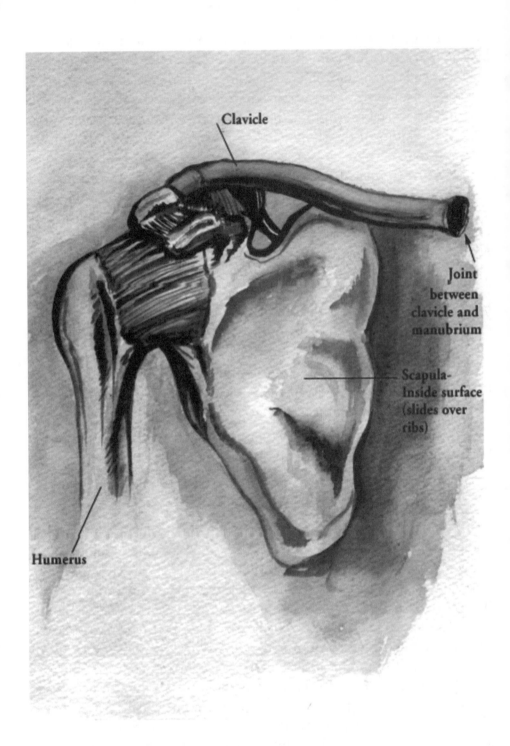

Figure 14: Shoulder Girdle

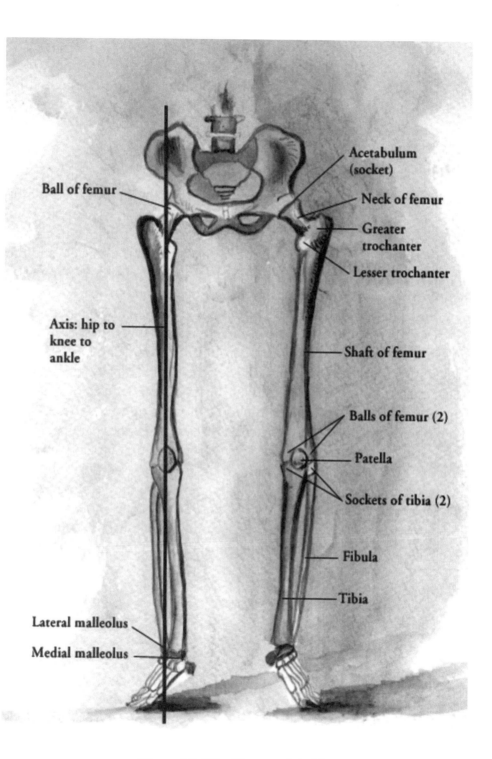

Figure 15: Hip, Knee and Ankle

the center of each joint to create stillness there as well. The image of stillness at the center of the synovial joint can help you to achieve total body stillness. This state of stillness is similar to that of a meditating monk or an animal in a state of readiness.

Your shoulder girdle

The shoulder girdle is a network of bones attached to your rib case, or cage, by a network of soft tissue. Except for the support that it provides to your arms, there are no weight-bearing components in your shoulder girdle. Instead, it is a set of bony structures that wrap around the rib cage. The only connecting joint is between the clavicle and the upper part of the sternum. The ideal military, ballet, or gymnastic stance, customarily depicted as chest out, shoulders back, actually demonstrates an inefficient use of the upper torso. This posture causes a restriction in the upper torso, shoulders, and spine that creates tension in the pectoral muscles on the front of the torso and in the muscle group attaching the shoulder blades to the torso. Ideally, the muscles that attach your shoulder girdle and arms to the trunk are balanced between flexor and extensor muscles to prevent tightness in this area. The shoulder girdle is released so that breath and energy are perceived as releasing into the force of gravity. The joints that attach your sternum to the clavicle are not stretched but in a released position. The muscles attaching your shoulder blades are released to lie close to your ribs, with the internal and external borders of your shoulder blades flowing with the curve of your ribs. Some people use the muscles of the upper shoulder to hold the body upright. This creates an unnecessary tightness which influences the muscles of the entire torso, including those between the shoulder blades and spine and between the humerus and shoulder girdle.

Your lower extremities

The entire alignment of your body can be changed by an efficient use of the supporting elements, from your pelvic bowl through your hip joints, limbs, knees, ankles, and feet. When your lower extremities are in an ideal position, your weight is centered through your pelvis at your hip joints. Your thigh, calf, and foot are centered in a position that can be bisected by a line drawn through the centers of the hip, knee, and ankle joint. A hyperextensive thrust of your leg backward often pushes your pelvis forward with a corresponding movement of your head backward to compensate. This position also causes stress to the joint structure of your knee.

In aligning the pelvis with the lower limbs, most people exhibit a variety of possibilities, which result from modeling that took place as they were learning to walk. These include a slight outward rotation of the leg, hyperextension in the knees, a tendency to walk on either the inside or outside of their feet, or some combination of the above. It is not possible to immediately repattern this form of muscle use. However, it is possible, through focused awareness, to slowly teach the muscles to think in new ways that incorporate minimal stress in joints and ligaments by centering the weight in the pelvis and through the hip joint and by realigning the relationship between the hip, knee, and ankle joints.

**Exploration 20:
Investigating the Joints: Upper Body**

Generally, we view the joints of the body as separate units that are not necessarily integrated with each other. Nevertheless, when we watch someone move with what we term grace, we are observing a complex process; no matter how small the movement, each segment of the body responds to and unites with every other segment. The lack of this level of functional integration is the result of unnecessary contraction in sets of muscles that restrict motion. Called follow-through in some sports, good joint action exists when there is an equal distribution of force at each joint as the physical action is carried throughout the body. For example, proficient use of a gesture of the arm includes a clear distribution of force (energy) from the hand through the arm, elbow, and shoulder, to the back of the scapula and to the front, through the center of the body in the vertebrae and into the earth. The initiation of this movement begins in our axial skeleton, thus concentrating our energy in the center of our torso. Conversely, it can begin in our appendicular skeleton and cause us to move directly into the space.

Part 1

1.   With a partner, have one person sit on a bench while the other person begins to slowly trace the edges of the shoulder girdle from the internal and external edges of the scapula in the back of the torso to the clavicle in front. The active partner should try to identify the top edge of the humerus of the sitting person and its relationship to the clavicle. It may be necessary to lift the upper arm and gently jiggle it as you explore the joint.

2.   Use your turn as recipient as an opportunity to practice listening to the information about yourself that is being provided by the other person's hands. As your partner traces the outline of your shoulder girdle, you can create a kinesthetic picture of the scapula and where it sits in relation to the ribs, the spine, and the pelvis and in relation to the clavicle. Can you feel the difference between bony and muscular structures? Once you have traced the shoulder area, go down the arm tracing the area of the elbow, lower arms (radius and ulna), wrist, and hand. Try using the idea of providing a physical image through touch for the other person by carefully tracing each section.

3.   Trade places and repeat.

Part 2

This exploration is done with a partner or group of partners. There are watchers and doers. The doers complete a set of acts and the watchers act as auditors for the doers, repeating to the doers only what they observed, without judgment. For example: After watching someone lift an elbow toward the ceiling, a watcher would say, "What I saw was that you initiated the movement in the elbow, then began to engage the upper arm, the shoulder area, and then the muscles of the back of the neck." A watcher would not say, "When you lifted your arm the movement was very easy as you lifted the elbow, but once the elbow got to your head you started to tense up the muscles of the back." Tense is a word often used pejoratively to mean "do not be so tense." Its use, when trying to help someone understand how they are incorporating muscle groups, is only likely to cause an increased level of muscular contraction.

1. **Find a comfortable space in which to work. One person watches. The other person stands parallel and begins to lift his/her hands up and then down, using the obvious hinge structure in your wrist joint.**

2. **Continue this motion, concentrating first on one hand, then the other, and then both.**

3. **Increase the size of the movement until it begins to incorporate your elbow, upper arm, shoulder area, entire body.** Note the adjustments you need to make along the way for the movement to get larger.

4. **Follow this by slowly circling your hands in both directions in a series of small circles that gradually become larger.**

5. **Reverse this series of movements.** Again note the adjustments that take place as the movements get smaller and larger.

6. **Now initiate a small gesture of any sort with your hand, elbow, shoulder.**

7. **Repeat with a variety of sizes of gesture.**

8. **Repeat, but initiate the gesture from the upper torso** (from your upper rib cage, clavicle, sternum, allowing the gesture to be a very small). Now increase the size of the gesture, letting it express itself through the arm and hands.

9. **Partner provides information from observation. Reverse places. Repeat.**

Journal: Describe and draw your current experience of your shoulders as an extension of your upper body.

Exploration 21:
Investigating the Joints: Lower Body

Part 1

This is a solo exercise that begins by lying on the floor on your back.

1. Bring feet up so that they are parallel and the same distance apart as your shoulders.

2. Place one hand on each side of a hip joint and begin a slight rock-

ing motion of the entire body by pushing your feet into the floor. As your pelvis rocks back and forth, begin to explore the hip joint with your hands, trying to find the different muscle groups that are integral to standing, sitting, and walking.

3. Replace the rocking with a lift of one foot and the other, but continue investigating the same area with your hands.

4. Placing your hands on the inside of your thigh, allow one knee to fall to the side and then return and pull it toward center. Repeat several times. Can you feel the adductor muscles on the inner thigh that you engage as you bring the knee toward center?

5. Leaving your hands in the same area, reach with your right knee away from the body until your foot is dragged away from the body by the action of the knee.

6. **Turn the knee toward the body and move toward it, dragging the foot in the opposite direction. Repeat.** What do you observe in the joint with this movement?

7. **Place your hand on the outside of the hip and feel the work of the muscles as the knee moves away from the body. Repeat with your left knee.**

8. **Place your feet on the floor and bring the right knee into your chest and hug it with your arms. Repeat small circles of your knee toward and away from the torso. Release, put the leg down, and bring up the other leg. Repeat. Release, put the leg down, and bring up both legs. Create circles using both legs.**

9. **Straighten the legs toward the ceiling and continue the circles in either direction. Return to bent knees.** What is the difference in the movement with your legs bent or straight?

10. **Put your legs down and rest a moment.**

Part 2: Partner or Group

1. **Divide into watchers and doers.** Watchers sit at the edge of the working space, doers find a comfortable standing position.

2. **Doers begin by making small circles on the floor with the ball of one foot.** The circles the foot makes get larger to include the entire foot, the knee, and finally the hip.

3. **Reverse the direction of the circle and decrease the number of body parts included until you are again using only the ball of the foot.**

4.   Repeat with other leg.

5.   **Balancing on one leg, swing the other leg backward and forward, in a movement initiated in the hip but supported by the pelvis.**

6.   **Repeat, but this time initiate the movement from the knee. Repeat starting from the foot.** Try this set of movements on the other leg. Try swinging the leg back and forth in front of the body. How is this similar or different from the previous exploration on the floor?

7.   **Start walking around the room; let the walk be initiated from the hip. Repeat, initiating from the knee, the foot.**

8.   **Relax. Discuss and describe the movement of the doer and trade places.**

Part 3: Partner or Group

1.   **Divide into groups of four.** Two people are watchers, the other two are doers.

2.   **Using balls of various sizes, throw the ball back and forth across a space of approximately 10 feet. When you receive the ball, concentrate on receiving it with your entire body. As you throw the ball, throw it with your entire body. Try different ways of sending or receiving the ball.**

3.   **Discuss the different integrations of the body and trade places.**

Journal: What differences did you notice in your use of the joint structures of your arm and hip? Describe or draw your current experience of your pelvis, hip, knees, ankles, and feet.

Exploration 22:
Moving from Lying to Sitting to Standing

The goal of this exploration is to begin to watch for the most economical movement of the body in moving in and out of three positions. In watching the movement of others, note:

1) which muscles they use to accomplish a task

2) whether they are supporting from the center

3) lengthening up the spine, releasing through the tail bone

4) narrowing in the chest and front of the pelvis

5) widening across the shoulders and back of the pelvis

6) finding the balance between flexor and extensor muscles

7) grounding through their feet, using the joint structures of the hips, knees, and ankles in balanced relationship to each other.

The group is again divided into watchers and doers. In discussing the movement continue to use positive and neutral language. An example of negative language use would be, "Your knees are not balanced over the toes." An example of a positive and neutral use of language would be, "I noticed that your knees appear to move inward toward the center line of your body." By stating exactly what you see, you become a better observer, and your observations are more helpful to the person you are addressing.

1. **Begin by lying on the floor on your back. Complete a quick body scan.**

2. **Get up from the floor.**

3. **Observe how you incorporate yourself to do so and then lie back down, also observing how you do it.** From where do you initiate the movement? How do you use your head, arms, and legs to complete the movement?

4. **Get up again, but before doing so, focus on taking a breath into your entire pelvic area and get up on the exhalation.** How did this change the movement? Reverse the breath. What do you discover?

5. **Get up again, but this time initiate the movement from your head.**

6. **Repeat, but initiate the movement from your hands, your torso, your pelvis, your legs.** Is one way easier than another? Why?

7. **Get up again, but this time concentrate on getting up in a forward direction.**

8. **Now try it again, this time trying to get up toward either side.** Does any of this remind you of a previous life experience?

9. **Lie back on the floor and rest a moment.**

10. **Get up as easily as possible, as if someone had just called to you from another room on a quiet Sunday afternoon.** How

did you do it?

11. **Lie down and get up again, but this time as if you had just heard a set of gunshots right outside the door.** How did you do it?

12. **Find a chair and sit in it.** Observe how you did it.

13. **Get up.** How did you do this?

14. **Repeat, using all the material from previous lessons on exploring breath, initiating from different body parts, moving into different directions.** What is the most efficient way to use yourself in moving from sitting to standing?

15. **Get up from the floor and stroll over to a chair and sit.**

16. **Get up and stroll to another place in the room and lie down.**

17. **Do the latter with different tempos–fast, slow, medium.** Now find a comfortable stance. Feet should be the same width apart as shoulders. Allow your head to move toward the floor. Hang over in this position a moment and then reverse the process, rolling up one vertebrae at a time.

18. **Discuss. Trade places.**

Journal: Draw picture of your self moving from lying, to standing, to sitting. What is the visual image of your experience of the integration of your spine, head, arms, and legs in each position and moving between them. The drawing does not need to be literal.

Exploration 23: Contact

Two people face each other, right foot forward and left foot back as in Figures 16a,b,c. Relax your knees and release toward the floor. Leave your left hand at your side and extend your right hand palm outward to touch the palm of the person in front of you, fingers reaching toward the ceiling. Allow enough pressure between the hands to establish that you are both responsible for your mutual balance. Once the position has been established, use the feel, fuse, and follow technique from Chapter 1 to focus on and place your breath. During the exhalation of the breath phrase, feel and fuse yourself with the breath with the energy system of your partner. This exploration and its variations is a good way to start work on a scene.

Contact

Figure 16a

Figure 16b

Figure 16c

1. **Using your hands, gently push toward the heart area of the other person as you breath out.** As one person begins to take charge, the other person yields, breathing in. The goal for each is to feel the other person, fuse with that person, and follow that person's energy. Extend the experience by being aware, that as you yield to your partner, you are compressing energy via to the energy that exists in your pelvis that is related to your relationship with gravity. Send this energy to your partner as he/she releases.

2. **Repeat, creating a circle of energy between the two of you.** You will feel this through the connection between your palms and from your palms through the arms to the central torso, up through your head, and down through your spine, pelvis, legs, and feet. As you continue to work, focus on the breath moving through you, over and around each of the joint structures, from the attachment at the head to the shoulders, arms, hands, spine, pelvis, hip socket, knee, ankles, feet.

3. **Repeat on the opposite side.**

4. **Variations:**

   A. **Connected with index fingers instead of palms, one person guides the other around the space while the other person follows. Reverse roles. This can also be done in groups of three or more.**

   B. **Maintaining visual contact, one person guides the other person through placement of their eyes.**

   C. **Maintaining aural contact, one person guides the other person via non-verbal sounds.**

   D. **Combining kinesthetic, visual, and aural awareness, one person guides the adjustment of the other's body through the adjustment of their own body.**

Journal: What was the energy dynamic between yourself and your partner? Were you pushing and pulling each other? Releasing into each other? Helping to balance each other? Supporting each other? Connecting with each other? Some combination of all the above? If you had more than one partner, compare and contrast your experience.

Exploration 24: Imagery for the Torso

There is a relationship between the position of the pelvis and the muscles of the lumbar region of the spine. A sway back is often the result of tightness in the muscles of the lumbar region–a lack of widening and lengthening the back muscles. There is also generally a corresponding narrowness in the muscles of the upper back region of the shoulder blades. As with the pelvis, constructive rest position can be combined with images to release muscles in the lumbar region while increasing tonus in the abdominal muscles. As in previous explorations, you will want to add more sensory detail than is provided by the basic image. The more detail you add, the more the images will help you to re-pattern your muscles. The desired goal of the image is listed first, followed by the potential images. Spend time with one or two images in any one session. In time, you will find that it is easy to visualize one image and then another without any loss of focus or concentration. Remember, you can create your own image.

To lengthen the spine downward:

1. **Begin in the constructive rest position.**
2. **Feel your back resting on a warm, flat surface with your buttocks sliding away from you as the warmth spreads from the center of your back toward your tail bone.**
3. **Feel the bony structure on each side of the pelvis as a rotating disk that is slowly moving back and down as it takes the energy from behind the navel and sends it out the tail bone.**

To widen the back and release the upper torso:

This image helps to release tightness in the muscles of the shoulder girdle and the spinal column. Ultimately, it should help to create a more-flexible shoulder girdle and ribs.

1. **Begin in the constructive rest position.**
2. **Experience the rib cage as a toy accordion with handles on each side, just under the arms, and vertical pleats on the front and back.** Feel the gentle pressure of the accordion closing inward toward the center until it is no wider than your neck. Pay particular attention to the opening of the pleats in the back, especially the center of the back.

> ## Exploration 25:
> ## Breath Imagery for Head and Torso

1. **Begin in constructive rest.**
2. **Focus on the inhalation of breath as it reaches down into your pelvic bowl.**
3. **On the exhalation, watch the breath move up your spine as it simultaneously moves out the tail bone and through the center of your hip joint, thigh, calf, ankle, and feet.** Indulge in the experience of the breath moving freely from pelvis through the upper and lower body. Is the breath a specific color? Mixture of colors? Are there images associated with it?
4. **Repeat this breath until a circular pattern is established.**
5. **Stand with feet comfortably apart in parallel and repeat the process.** Use the breath as a point of focus to recover concentration. Slowly walk around the room, aware of the breath and its integration into every step.

Journal: Record the changes you experience of dynamic alignment as well as the type and style of images. What colors or images have power for you? Do you notice a similarity between images used for different lines of movement? As you go about your daily life, walking across campus or shopping for groceries, cultivate an awareness of your release into dynamic alignment. Are there situations in which you feel more released? Less released?

Grounding the Energy: Gravity

Gravity acts on us from the moment of birth until death. Our relationship to gravity, displayed by our upright posture, raises our eyes off the earth and focuses our attention on the horizon, which influences our interactions with the environment. Our primary perception of the earth, particularly for people who live in urban environments, is as a solid, hard surface. Yet, we know the earth is actually a mutable set of interactive forces, one of which is gravity. One way to increase your experience of this force is to imagine the surfaces on which you walk as soft and responsive to your step instead of hard and resistant. You can imagine that when you step there are energy waves emanating from your feet as they interact with the fluid pull of gravity. Practice this method of conceiving walking in different contexts, with different shoes, and with no shoes at all. Note the difference in your experience of being grounded in each context and foot ware. Other methods for increasing your awareness with regard to gravity and grounding follow.

Exploration 26:
Grounding from an Upright Stance

Martial artist, James Kapp, maintains that "People don't get grounded. They are grounded as a natural extension of their relationship to gravity."[14] The exercises that follow have been devised to help you increase your experience of being grounded. They work specifically on releasing muscle tension from the hips through the ankles.

Loosening the ankles

This exercise helps to unblock energy held in the ankles by stretching the Achilles tendons.

1. **Kneel down, then raise your left knee and place the foot down flat a few inches behind your right knee.**
2. **Shift your weight onto the ball of your left foot, stretch your arms forward, and rock back and forth, pressing your foot into the floor as you rock forward.** Try to keep your breathing rhythmical and the rest of your body relaxed.
3. **Repeat, reversing the position of your legs.**
4. **Kneeling down and sitting back on your heels, spine straight, will also help to loosen your ankles.**

Shaking the legs

1. **Standing with feet hip-width apart, bend your knees and distribute your weight evenly over the balls and heels of your feet.**

---

[14]James Kapp, Personal Communication, June 2000.

2. Lift one foot and shake it from the ankle so that it becomes floppy and relaxed.
3. Shake the same leg vigorously from the knee.
4. Shake the whole leg from the hip joint.
5. Note difference in your two legs.
6. Repeat other leg.

Awareness

1. Stand with your legs apart, weight evenly balanced.
2. Bring your awareness to your sacrum at the base of the spine.
3. Keep your left foot on the ground but move your awareness slowly down your right leg until, when it reaches your right sole, all your weight is on your right foot.
4. With your weight still on your right foot, move your awareness slowly across to your left foot. As your awareness travels up your right leg, gradually transfer your weight via your pelvis to your left foot. You can use the image of water being emptied out of one leg and filling the other. Repeat two or three times.
5. Return to an even weight distribution.
6. Repeat the exercise, but instead of focusing your awareness on the transfer of weight, focus the breath/energy from the pelvic bowl to either leg/foot, back to the pelvic bowl, and to the other leg/foot. Imagine the incoming breath as one color that is transformed internally and is exhaled as a different color.

Journal: Describe how your experience of being grounded changed as you did the exercises.

**Exploration 27:
Dynamic Alignment, Gravity, and Movement**

Your body can move in one of several planes. They are the *saggital* (forward and back); *lateral* (to the sides); *diagonal* (to the corners either in the front or back); and, finally, in the *vertical*, (upright or up and down plane). Due to the rotation possible in your head, arms, and legs, you can initiate a gesture from any one of these appendages into any of the planes. For example, starting from an open, released position, lift your right arm up to the side until it is horizontal to the floor in the *lateral* plane. Now move it forward, noting as you do so that it is moving into the *diagonal* plane. Continue to move your arm forward and it will be in the *sagittal* plane. Lift your arm straight up to a *vertical* position above your head and turn your palm so that it faces behind you (another section of sagittal). Finally, allow your arm to move horizontally to the side of the body, observing that it moves through the backward right *diagonal* as it returns. The movement through these planes takes you from the *symmetrical*, in which there is an equal balance of body parts, to *asymmetrical*, in which the body parts are not mirroring each other.

1. **Stand with your feet in parallel.**
2. **Experience yourself as a long pencil with your feet as the eraser and the top of your head as the tip.**
3. **Begin to draw a line from the ceiling to the wall in front of you with the tip of your pencil.** There will probably be a place where you will begin to fall forward. Note the relationship of the muscles to the joints at this point. Do the same thing to the back wall as well as to both side walls. You will discover that your balance is centered in the pelvis. This is the core from which you will explore the different planes of movement.

Puppets

1. **One person becomes the puppet the other becomes the puppet master.**
2. **If you are the puppet master, you want to help the person discover the body's kinetic oppositions by placing them in opposite planes.** One example would be a position of the body that places one leg in a forward right diagonal and the right leg in a left back diagonal. The puppet uses his/her internal focus to note the point of origination of the action within the pelvis, the gesture of the appendages, and the final target of the movement in space.
3. **Trade places and repeat.**

Mirrors
1. **One person lead the other follows. The leader completes a gesture and the follower completes the mirror or opposite of it.** For example, a gesture that incorporates the forward left diagonal, the other person creates a movement that uses the backward right diagonal. What active verbs associated with different planes of movement? For example, active verbs related to forward and back or the sagittal plane that may describe your interaction with the other person include: advance, assist, promote, deliver, foster, send, succor, sponsor, support, confirm. What images do I associate with a symmetrical body? An asymmetrical body? What emotional states do I associate with a symmetrical body? An asymmetrical one? Some words associated with symmetry are: balance, order, poise, equalize, stabilize, steady, constant, evaluate. Synonyms for asymmetrical include: irregular, erratic, random, variable.

Space

1. **Fill a room with chairs or blocks at different angles.** (They do not have to be the same kind of chair.)
2. **Take different positions on the chairs or blocks, being aware of the planes of movement as you do so.**
3. **Continue to move from chair to chair using symmetrical and asymmetrical movements to get in and out of the chair.** Can you describe the poses with reference to the planes of movement?
4. **Continue the exploration, allowing the breath to become part of the investigation.** Can you use the breath to accent or change the way you sit in the chair?
5. **Keep working and allow sound to become an additional part of your investigation.** You can initiate the impulse for sound from a chakra area or use any combination of consonants and vowels that occurs to you. You might even discover a word or a phrase that rises out of your associative memory.
6. **Label the chairs, ie. throne, senate seat, beach chair, electric chair, etc.** What active verbs would you use to describe the way you put yourself in a chair or chairs? What adjectives would you use to describe your walk between chairs? What emotional states are associated with different ways of sitting in the chair?

Journal: What were the active verbs and or images that you noted during the exploration? Were certain planes of movement associated with particular kinds of verbs or images?

Exploration 28: Falling Actions

When performed quickly and with control, a falling action can be spectacularly breathtaking as well as reveal a character's psychological and emotional state. When working with falls, note the difference between the static joint within the pelvis and the dynamic and moveable joints of the spine, shoulders, hips, elbows, knees, wrists, and ankles. Work with these joints to allow yourself to fall in any direction–forward, backward, diagonally, or laterally–in a set of sequential actions that protect the body from being pulled too quickly by the force of gravity. The awareness and incorporation of joint alignment in working with these falls will protect you from hurting yourself in a combat class or rehearsal. *Be certain to work on a mat throughout this exercise.*

Formal Falls

Formal falls are one way of learning the sequencing of movement in which each body part follows another in logical succession. As you experiment with the following falls, take time to systematically understand the relationship of the body parts to each other, to gravity, and to the floor. This will promote safety.

Front falls:

1. Stepping forward on one foot, lifting the other leg back, reach your arms forward, palms toward the floor.
2. Fall forward to catch your weight on your hands, back leg still extended in the air.
3. Lower yourself to the floor by flexing your elbows and then sliding your hands forward as the supporting leg extends.
4. Practice several times and then move from a front fall to a forward role.

Side falls:

1. From a side position, arms and legs pointed in the same direction, reach your body to the left, dropping your left arm and placing your hand on the floor while releasing the left hip.
2. Slide your left hand sideways as your legs extend in the opposite direction.
3. Take weight first onto your left hip and then, as your body extends, on the entire left side.
4. At the end of the fall, your left arm extends, your head rests on your shoulder, and your right arm is parallel with your extended legs.
5. To recover, reverse the order, leading with the upper side rib cage.

Back falls: There are two ways of performing a fall to the back, one used by dancers and the second by fight choreographers.

1. A Dancer's fall begins from a standing position, by crossing the right foot in back and lowering to the right knee. This will bring you to a sitting position on the floor with your left leg extended forward.
2. Reach to each side with your hands as you curl down the spine while extending your right leg and using your hands to help support and control your torso.
3. A fight choreographer's fall begins in the same position. Instead of placing the knee behind you, release your weight straight to the floor with the lifted leg stretched forward.

Spiral falls:

1. From an erect, standing position, legs turned out, twist your torso to the left. As you do so, your right leg will tuck itself behind as you contract into your left hip.
2. Deepen this spiral action to the left by lowering yourself to the floor, balanced on your left hip.
3. Descent should be controlled.
4. Adjust your feet under your center of gravity in response to changes in the position of your torso.

Informal or Moving Falls

1. Begin moving around the floor of a room covered with mats and, without conscious planning, fall in any direction, letting the fall take you into a movement on the floor. For example, start to spiral downward and let the spiral become a body roll on the floor.
2. As you explore the possibilities associated with falling, observe how the knowledge you gained investigating the planes of movement helps you to safely execute falling and rising actions.
3. Run across the floor as if you are trying to get away from someone, fall to the floor, turn and scoot on your rear, take it into a backward roll, and return to standing. Keep experimenting with moving and falling.
4. Allow yourself to be influenced by the following verbs: collapse, crumble, drop, plunge, cascade, droop, surrender.
5. What situational images are associated with different combinations of fall and recovery? What stories start to evolve?
6. Pick one story and create a movement score which nonverbally tells that story.

Journal: Describe the different internal sensations of each balance and fall. In which did you feel you could complete the action and remain grounded, balanced, and centered? Which were difficult? What adjustments do you need to make? What was the difference between formal and informal falls?

Finding the Balance

Balance is, as suggested in the different forms of falling, a negotiation of gravity and consequently a component of dynamic alignment. The question implied in the phrase "finding the balance" is, "Are all body parts in equilibrium?" The following exploration uses the image of an empty suit (see Figure 17) as a method of placing yourself into a position of balance. As an exercise, the empty suit offers you an opportunity to use the visualization process to release the muscle system. An advantage of the empty suit is that, once learned, it is a quick and easy way to become physically and emotionally grounded and aligned in a public place. You can engage the images anywhere, from waiting outside an office for an audition to standing on a crowded commuter train going to a rehearsal.

> ## Exploration 29: The Empty Suit

The empty suit is made out of a fabric you would like to have close to your skin. The suit is in one piece, with bell-shaped trousers and tassels at the end of the legs. The coat portion has a soft, circular collar and a zipper that extends from the pubic area all the way to the top of the collar. Complete a body scan lying down, then move into a constructive rest position and place and fuse with the breath. In constructive rest, see the trousers supported at the knees by the cross of an imagined hanger suspended from the ceiling; the arms of the coat rest across the front of the coat. The suit has many wrinkles in it. To straighten out this wrinkled suit, imagine the following images.

The Trousers

1. Feel the upper part of the thigh of the trouser falling together as your knees are supported over the bar of the hanger.
2. Feel the crease of the suit's fabric at the thigh joint sink into the empty seat of the trousers.
3. Feel the trouser leg twist inward across the front until the long crease is in the mid-front, centering with the knee and thigh joint.
4. Concentrating on one trouser leg at a time, feel the length of the crease from the ankle to the thigh.
5. Feel the looseness of the bell-shaped lower trouser leg as it sags together in folds.
6. Experience the foot as a tassel, made up of different lengths of thread or yarn (long toward the toes, shorter at the heel).
7. Watch the tassels release on the floor around the edge of the foot.

The Coat

1. As you start to zip the zipper, feel the crosswise wrinkles on the back of the coat being smoothed downward from the lower part of the back and slowly moving upward.
2. Feel the vertical wrinkles on the back of the coat at the inner borders of the shoulder blades being smoothed outward until the coat

becomes very broad shouldered.

3. Feel how good it feels to have the fabric of the coat smoothed down the back and beyond the tail bone.

4. Now feel the zipper in the front of the coat being closed to the top of the soft circular collar.

5. Feel the crosswise wrinkles in the collar being smoothed upward until the top of the collar reaches the base of the head.

Figure 17: Empty Suit

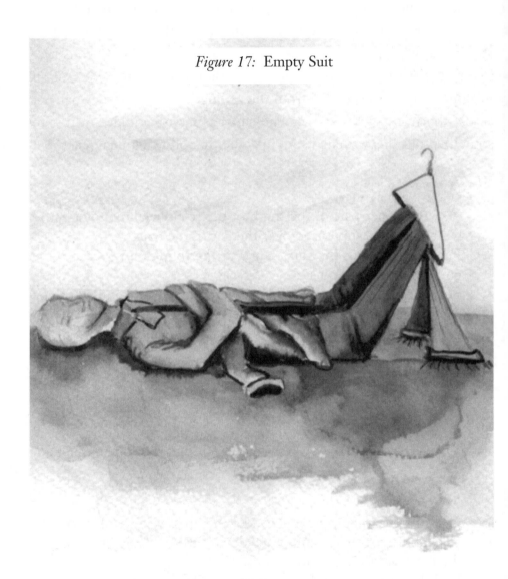

The Empty Head

1. Feel your head as a large, empty ball filled with breath.
2. Can you feel the distance between your ears and between the front of your head and the back?

The Entire Body

1. Once you have completed visualizing the entire empty suit, remain in constructive rest a few moments longer, finishing the session with a second body scan.
2. Note any changes. Then get up and slowly walk around. With your internal eye, review the empty suit images.

Journal: Develop an image that is your version of the empty suit. As you evolve the image, do not forget the narrowing across the front, the widening across the back, the lift of the head away from the torso, the crease in the hip joint, the plumb line down the center of the leg through the knee and ankle, and, finally, the reach of the feet into the earth.

Exploration 30: Partner Balancing

Partner balancing is a way of exploring your balance and its relationship to the functions of the joint structure. Each balance requires that you discover the relationship between your joints from your feet, through your ankle, knee, hip; through your hip's connection to spinal vertebrae, head, and shoulders. Finding the center of balance is also a way of discovering the role the eyes play in balance.

Partners should make clear choices about their visual focus during each balance. You can make clear choices about when to look at each other, focus on some object in space, or close your eyes. It is particularly important to keep aware of your relationship to gravity during each balance. Try to work with as many different body types as possible.

Balance Poses

Figure 18 a

Figure 18 b

V Position:

Two people stand side by side to each other, sides of feet touching, and holding onto each other at the wrists. Maintaining your center, lean slightly away from your partner as in Figure 18a. The feet should stay on the floor with the ankle acting as a fulcrum for the lean. Be certain that the body stays relaxed. The space between the partner's feet and head finally assumes a fully extended V shape. Once a comfortable relationship is established between the two people, both can gently roll their heads to either side or bend and straighten one knee or the other.

C Position:

Moving from this basic V position both partners can create a C by turning to face each other and taking right wrists in the same pattern as if they were shaking hands. They bend the knees and focus on pulling away at the hips. curving the lumbar region of the spine as in Figure 18b.

Figure 18 c

Back Position:

With backs to each other, interlock at the elbows, and then begin to sit, finding the place of balance from which, if you go farther, you will be on the floor as in Figure 18c.

Journal: Each of these balance positions can be a potential starting point for rehearsing a scene. Considering this, describe your experience of each balance. Which balances presented the greatest physical risk for you? The least risk? Which required more physical cooperation between you and your partner?

LOCOMOTION

The Shona of Zimbabwe have a saying, "To walk is to dance, to talk is to sing." Among the Shona, walking is a metaphor for movement and dance or the constant interplay of dynamic alignment expressed in the daily lives of the Shona people. We have four primary means of "walking." We can: *walk*, changing weight from one foot to another without going into the air. We can *jump*, trying to leave the realm of gravity with both feet. We can *hop*, trying to leave the realm of gravity with one foot. We can *leap*, trying to leave gravity with one foot and land on the other. Or we can combine any of the above. For instance, a skip is a combination of a hop and a step, or walk. Unless we are dancers, most of us use one method of locomotion, walking, which we do at different speeds, from slow pacing or ambling to jogging or sprinting. On a rare occasion, such as moving from a boat to a dock or across a ditch, we might leap. We also might jump to get off a chair or in response to something frightening in the environment. But we probably have not hopped anywhere since we played games as children.

```
┌─────────────────────────────────────────────────┐
│                 Exploration 31:                  │
│     To Walk Is to Dance, To Talk Is to Sing      │
└─────────────────────────────────────────────────┘
```

1.   **Begin this exploration by walking around the room. focusing in different directions with your head.** For instance, keep

walking forward but look to the side, or look up, or look at the diagonal. Stop periodically and begin again, with the head focused in a specific direction, allowing your entire self to follow. Observe the realignment that takes place in the rest of you.

2. **Try out different forms of walking around the space, such as ambling, strolling, sauntering, or striding.** What kind of personal momentum does it take to move from one form of walk to another? How is your breath incorporated into striding or other modes of walking?

3. **Pick a walk and hum in time with the movement, allowing it to evolve into a consistent melody.**

Leap:

1. **Return to walking, head comfortably focused forward.**

2. **Slowly pick up speed until you are moving from a walk to a jog to a run and lengthen your stride with each forward motion.** Let the propulsion of the back leg, combined with a slight contraction in the lower abdomen, send you into the air in a small leap.

3. **Continue leaping but increase the swing in the arms to support the extension of the leap.** How is the breath incorporated into the movement? Enjoy the exhilaration that comes from leaving and returning to gravity. As you work with the leap, use the following verbs to modify your leap: soar, surge, vault, hurdle, and bound.

4. **Complete a series of leaps that move from soar to vault to bound or any combination of the above.** How is the breath incorporated into the movement? Allow the sound of the movement to be expressed with the breath.

5. **Gradually return to a run, jog, and finally a walk.**

Jump:

1. **Be aware of the plumb line that extends through the center of your body from the top of your head to the center of your pelvis, bend your knees, dropping your tail bone down, noting the crease in the hip joint, and releasing your knees over the center of each foot.** Be aware of rooting the breath and

energy through your feet into the floor.

2. **Slowly straighten your legs by initiating the movement in the muscles of the lower abdomen.** Repeat several times.

3. **Balance your weight on the balls of both feet.** You are now at a high level; your balance has shifted above your normal level.

4. **Slowly move through normal level by bending your knees again to move to a low level or below your typical pelvis level.**

5. **Move up and down on the vertical plane between low level and high level pelvis.** Continue this for several repetitions and, as you repeat it, become aware of the shift taking place in your relationship to gravity, of the articulations of each bone and muscle of the feet when you move from a low to a high level.

6. **Bend your knees and, using the initiation of the contraction in your lower abdomen and the exhalation of the breath, jump up away from gravity and, on the inhalation release back into gravity by bending your knees.** Continue to use both contraction and breath as you repeat the jump several times. Try moving forward in space with it. Also try backwards, sideways. Which directions are easy? Which difficult? Begin a jump that pounces on an imaginary object, cringes as it jumps away from another object.

Hop:

1. **Return to an easy jump until you decide to try it on one foot, at which time it becomes a hop.**

2. **Hop on one foot four or five times and then return to the other foot.** In how many different directions can you comfortably move through the room? Forward? Backward? In a circle? Diagonally? What are some images that come to mind with this physical activity?

Breath and Locomotion:

1. **Return to walking around the space and note your breath and its relationship to your heartbeat.** Allow the phrasing of your walk to match the phrasing of your breath. Be aware of feeling and fusing with the breath under the entire surface of you skin as if you were a giant balloon.

2. **Continue to walk, but begin to change the phrasing of the breath.** The breath can be taken in quickly and released slowly or taken in as a series of slow inhalations followed by one quick exhalation. You can consider the breath as creating the rhythmic underpinning for the movement of your body.

3. **Continue to make choices that allow your walk to be transformed by the rhythmic changes of your breath.** You may find that at some point the walk naturally evolves into a run, leap, jump, etc.

4. **Allow sound to be expressed with the exhalation.** As you play with the combination of breath and movement, try not to plan the next movement; let the natural impulses of your intuitive self guide you.

5. **Pick several pieces of dissimilar music that have a steady underlying beat and begin to move around a space, whether a movement studio or your apartment.**

6. **Experiment with all forms of locomotion to several musical selections.** Does some music seem as if it needs a hop? A jump? Play with changing your body orientation in space (forward, backward, sideways, diagonally, circularly) or your facial focus (up, down, sideways, etc.). Does spatial orientation or focus change the movement and the interpretation of the music?

7. **Develop words you associate with each form of locomotion.** For example: jump–hurdle, lunge, pounce, cringe, flinch, wince; leap–soar, surge, vault, bound; walk–amble, saunter, stroll, stride; hop–spring, bounce, recoil.

8. **Create a scenario and movement score that incorporates one or more of these words.** An example would be someone waiting at a bus stop where a car careens out of control and hits a small child. You might have hurdled yourself away from the car, sprung up to help the child, but recoiled at the sight of his injuries.

9. **Perform this scenario for others.**

Journal: Were some methods of locomotion easier than others? Were there combinations of locomotor movements that you returned to again and again? Describe your experience with the music. Describe your scenario.

CHECKLIST OF POINTS TO REMEMBER

The primary theme of this chapter has been the exploration of dynamic alignment through the integration of breath and imagery. Remember that alignment, like the concept of neutral, is a dynamic, not a static state. It is a jumping-off point that is discovered anew in each rehearsal, in each moment. Also, review your journal and note how you have described your experience of the explorations. How has your image of your body changed?

Exploration

- Learning is making unconscious behaviors conscious.

- Neutral is a form of dynamic alignment and a beginning place from which to explore.

- Dynamic alignment is a continuous state of discovery.

Breath

- Visualization is a technique to expand your awareness.

- Be certain to integrate breath and imagery with movement.

Imagery

- Dynamic alignment is a constant process of discovering a state of being grounded, balanced, open, and centered.

- Your pelvis is the center of your emotional and physical support.

- Placement of the pelvis can be achieved through using images that focus on widening across the back of the pelvis while narrowing across the front.

- Constructive rest is a position from which to investigate images.

- Your shoulder girdle is attached to your bony system only by a single joint at your sternum.

- Focusing on the line from the center of your hip through the center of your thigh, calf, and into your ankle helps to balance the body.

- Release your head upward like a helium balloon.
- "Empty suit" is a way of exploring alignment and balance.

Ti Jean and His Brothers Directed by Yvonne Brewster,
Lisa Maxine as Bird and Alicia Teter as Cricket

CHAPTER THREE

ENERGY, METAPHOR, ACTION

When an actor responds to an imaginary stimulus, he himself chooses and shapes that stimulus. He has the potential for a deep contact with that stimulus, since it is privately chosen. This contact brings up energy for the actor's use. On one level or another he is given energy by his inner prompting, associations, that part of his life which is already lived.

Joseph Chaikin

Somatic psychologist Stanley Keleman describes a life as "rhythmical waves of pulsation, waves that we can slow down, hold still, or speed up. Through inhibition we regulate the amplitude, volume, and rate of the waves of expansion and contraction."[1] Constantin Stanislavski describes energy as flowing "down the network of your muscular system, arousing your inner motor centers"[2] and stirring you to external activity. The quality of this energy is revealed in physical actions:

> Energy, heated by emotion, charged with will, directed by the intellect, moves with confidence and pride, like an ambassador on an important mission. It manifests itself in conscious action, full of feeling, content and purpose, which cannot be carried out in any slipshod, mechanical way, but must be fulfilled in accordance with its spiritual impulses.[3]

The regulation, control, adjustment, and manipulation of these energy waves to achieve personal desires is an expression of your history. As suggested in previous chapters, we learn in our formative years the appropriate physical displays for a variety of social situations, from the visit of a favorite relative to such ritual events as weddings and funerals. We bring to the craft of acting tendencies to move based on

---

[1] Stanley Keleman, *Embodying Experience* (Berkeley, Calif.: Center Press, 1989), 10.

[2] Constantin Stanislavski, *Building a Character*, trans. Elizabeth Reynolds Hapgood (New York: Theatre Arts/Routledge, 1989), 50.

[3] Stanislavski, *Building a Character*, 50.

these sensory memories. Your performance is influenced by this movement style, which Warren Lamb calls the merging of posture and gesture (PGM).[4] Your body posture sets the tone of the interaction while the gesture expresses your desires. The merging of posture and gesture is, therefore, your internal life made visible.

Your physical actions can be described, as they are identified in the Personal Inventory in Chapter 1, by body part used, as in arms, legs, and head; the direction in space the body takes (forward, back, diagonal); and the general movement shape (symmetrical, asymmetrical). However, movement can also be described in terms of its primary dynamic. This approach is based on the movement research of twentieth-century theorist Rudolf von Laban, who was born in 1879 in the Austro-Hungarian empire. His father, an army officer, was stationed in various parts of Europe and the Near East. Laban's education therefore included the opportunity to observe people in diverse environments. His need to express this experience prompted him to study art and dance in Paris from 1900 to 1907. In 1910, he started a dance farm, or dance community, that initiated a series of art festivals. His work with this dance community was curtailed by the outbreak of World War I, at which time he moved to Zurich, where he developed a method for analyzing movement. Between World Wars I and II, he established dance schools in many European countries, including Germany, Italy, and Hungary, created a choreographic institute, directed pageants, and became director of the Allied State Theaters in Germany. In 1935 his work was banned by the Nazi party as not sufficiently nationalist. Subsequently, he moved from Paris to Manchester, England, where he published a series of books outlining his methods of movement analysis, education, and notation.

Through observing and analyzing individual movement, Laban discovered most people have *energetic qualities* that are a result of an internal dynamic. This individual dynamic is the result of the interaction of the different aspects of self (essential and social). These largely unconscious aspects of self interact through the neuromuscular system to generate physical choices that fall into the range of what Laban termed *effort*:

---

[4]Warren Lamb and Elizabeth Watson., *Body Code* (London: Routledge, 1979).

"Effort" is the term used to refer to the inner urge or drive towards movement. The resulting movement will be either an action (a gesture, step, body shift, working action) if fully developed, or, in one initiated which then dies away, a "shadow movement" (a small body movement, seemingly, with no external aim; a raised eyebrow or frown, a tapping finger, a shoulder twitch, a fleeting look of recognition).[5]

When people interact, they commit to a set of actions that usually take a particular attitude or tendency toward one or more of these efforts. Laban divided the efforts into four categories: *flow, weight, time,* and *space.* Each category is subdivided into two opposites that represent a continuum.

1) flow continuum from bound to free.
2) weight continuum from strong to light.
3) time continuum from sudden to sustained
4) space continuum from direct to indirect.

Individual movement styles create a *movement signature* that is a combination of different efforts as sustained (time) and bound (flow), for example, or sudden (time) and direct (space). Learning to distinguish visually and kinesthetically the various efforts increases your potential choices by expanding your range of movement. Furthermore, an understanding and awareness of effort qualities provides a method for analyzing the movement of others.

The explorations based on this approach to the effort qualities are initiated by discovering the general state of the body for each quality and its related continuum. Individual explorations have a strong kinesthetic component, which provide an opportunity to investigate with an effort quality via related images. This method of discovery is followed by explorations to help you deepen your understanding of the qualities by applying information gained from earlier explorations to specific physical tasks, the use of metaphor, and physical characterization. A distinction is made between physical states that release into the pull and compression forces of gravity, referred to as indulgent, and

---

[5]Rudolf von Laban, *Modern Educational Dance* (Boston: Plays Inc., 1963), 155-6.

physical states that resist gravity's forces, called resistant. Indulgent qualities are free, sustained, light, and indirect. Resisting qualities are strong, bound, sudden, and direct. This chapter also provides a method for creating a character based on Laban's effort qualities and an approach to analysis that can be used in observations of people inside and outside of the movement studio.

LABAN'S ENERGY SYSTEM

We can do every imaginable movement and then select those that are the most suitable and desirable for our own nature. These can be found only by each individual. For this reason, practice of the free use of kinetic and dynamic possibilities is of the greatest advantage. We should be acquainted both with the general movement capacities of a healthy body and mind and with the specific restrictions and capacities resulting from the individual structure of our own bodies and minds.

Rudolph von Laban

Flow Qualities

Flow refers to the manner in which we manage our movement, or as some would say 'how' we manage our movement. It can be either *successive* or *simultaneous*. Successive, or sequential, flow is experienced as a series of muscular contractions from one body part to another. Simultaneous flow involves the muscles moving at the same time to accomplish a physical task. For example, when walking across the floor, your body moves in a sequence of gestures that can be initiated in the hips, knees, or feet. A walk is a successive movement. If it were an obviously simultaneous movement, the entire leg from hip to toe would move as a unit. A sequential movement that moves through you, either from your head to your feet or the reverse, is analogous to a body wave. There can also be waves of individual limbs and from limb to torso.

Free flow is a movement difficult to stop suddenly. The flow of energy projects itself through you with no specific target. Words used to describe it include:

fluid
uncontrolled
abandoned
wholehearted

Figure 19: Flow

Bound flow refers to stopping or inhibiting the flow of movement. On the continuum of free to bound, there is movement that is beyond stopping– like someone tumbling over a cliff–and there is movement that is absolutely held–like someone holding her breath. Between these two extremes are a variety of states in which the muscles are in various states of contraction. Words used to describe these states are:

> careful
> controlled
> restrained
> cautious
> limited

Whether you move the entire body at once—simultaneous movement—or as a sequence of parts—successive/sequential movement—you are managing your flow of energy. Thus, you are literally "feeling" the situation and deciding how to act as a consequence of your interpretation of the moment. Note the photograph of the toddler in Figure 19. Her spine and appendages are freely and fluidly integrated with each other. Her head is bounded by the back of the chair and thus is held in its relationship to the rest of the body. Most people's movement vocabulary contains a similar combination of free and bound flow.

Exploration 32:
Flow Qualities–Bound to Free

Before beginning any exploration, warm up using a combination of body listening, breathing, stretching, and visualization techniques. This approach will allow you to explore the material in greater depth and with greater ease.

Free and Bound:

1. **Begin walking around the room. Imagine that you are walking on the beach, an entire week of sun and relaxation in front of you; you are absolutely free of responsibility.** The very idea of having no immediate tasks makes you begin to play on the beach like a three-year-old, running toward the waves, throwing sand against the wind, and chasing sand flies.

2. **Suddenly, all your muscles contract at the same time.** You find it difficult to move. It is as if you have become a dense mass.
3. **You concentrate on releasing the muscles of your upper torso, arms, and right leg, but the left leg still feels like a mass of clay.**
4. **Now, as if your body were playing tricks on you, your right leg seems to have become clay, but your left leg moves freely.**
5. **You keep moving around, trying to change the feeling of your leg by walking around, sitting, lying down, and standing again.** You notice that the "clay" feeling has finally left your legs, but now your hips feel like clay.
6. **Finally, you begin running up and down the beach in desperation, jiggling each part of your body until you are able to recapture that sense of physical freedom you had when you first started playing on the beach.**
7. **Stop in neutral and return to walking around the room.**

Flow:

8. **Create any task–for example, putting on or taking off articles of clothing (coat, hat, shoes).**
9. **Perform the task in a state of successive flow. (Simultaneous flow.) Find moments in the task when the flow is free.** When the flow is bound. Experiment with various combinations of bound to free or free to bound. What happens to your breath in each state?
10. **Return to a neutral state.**

Journal: Each exploration develops new levels of energy awareness through the different qualities on the effort continuum. When working with the qualities, you will want to expand your ability to work from physical metaphor by using your journal to record your reactions to your experience of each quality. The entries should include: (1) the words and phrases that come to mind when you begin moving in the quality, and (2) a completion of the following sentences. I move like _____; I feel like_____; I respond to the world by interacting like _____; I sound like_____.

     Possible answers for light would be: (1) gentle, float, drifting, subtle, teasing, playful, indirect. (2) Answers for the blanks in the sentences could be: I move like a cloud; I feel easy, gentle; I deal quietly with people. This journal entry is a means of beginning to define your movement signature. It is also a source of information for creating the physical life of a character.

Weight Qualities

Our relationship to gravity can be either *strong* or *light*. Our relationship to gravity tells us 'who' we are with regards to the pull of the earth. Are we resisting gravity, releasing into it, or negotiating with it? Our experience of gravity is extended into our communication style and thus our interactions.

A *strong* movement results from a level of contraction in the muscles that causes a forceful exertion in a particular direction. This exertion can be in response to an individual physical choice, such as a strong gesture with any body part exerting itself against gravity. It can also be a response to an outside kinetic force when a body or body parts are moved forcefully. Strong static force results from internal counter tensions, producing a firm, braced condition. In each case, the muscle system is working at a level of contraction that can vary in intensity depending on the personality and the situation. Strong interaction with resistance from outside is met with resistance from the inside. There is a narrowing of the body's energy system. Verbs often associated with strong are:

resist
force
defy
oppose
prevent

These movements require participation from the center of gravity in the pelvis, used either as a base or for elevating the body away from the floor.

A *light* movement requires minimal force or tension and counter tension. A light exertion of the muscles away from gravity keeps the body off the floor sufficiently and thus prevents the skeletal system from slumping. A light use of the body does not require extreme tension to keep the body off the floor. There is a widening of the body's energy system as experienced with the breath.

Light interaction with outside force means there is limited resistance such as: a light touch, a gentle push, a fine touch, a delicate touch, with slight and sensitive tension. Light actions convey the feeling of being carried by the air (in actions and positions). Activation in the center of the torso (chest, sternum, ribs, and upper back) along with support from the lower trunk provide optimal conditions for producing lightness. Verbs often associated with light are:

tame
subdue
calm
pacify
placate

In defining the form of a gesture and its relationship to gravity, the weight continuum defines the style of the action or the who, the personality of the character, as they sense their position in relationship to the emotional and physical balance of a particular social situation. Student Shawn Dorazio responded to the work with strong and light as follows:

> *Both strong and light are tiring but after I exhausted my energy I started to play the continuum more. I realized that strong doesn't need to be fast and forceful but can be quiet and rooted. Light doesn't have to be lack of weight as much as thinking effortlessness.*[6]

In contrast, note the woman on a stormy day in Figure 20. She is using the strength of her body in relationship to gravity to prevent the umbrella from being blown away from her. To achieve this, she has firmly and forcefully planted her feet a relative distance that helps her to center her pelvis in relationship to her spine. The total stance is reminiscent of a rooted tree.

---

[6]Shawn Dorazio, Personal communication, 1995.

Figure 20: Weight

Exploration 33: Weight–Strong to Light

Strong:

1. Following a general warm-up, begin by lying on the floor.
2. Imagine you are being held to the earth by some invisible force that prevents you from standing.
3. **Commit all your strength to the physical action of trying to get up from the ground.** Each time you start to get free you are pulled back to the ground by a force stronger than yourself. Initiate your attempts with different parts of your body–your hands, legs, torso, head. Note what is happening to your breath.
4. **Finally, you manage to pull yourself to upright and walk around the room, aware that the force that was holding you still has a grip on your feet.**
5. **Walking you are aware of moving to defy, combat, oppose, and resist the force that would pull you down.**
6. **Release your walk of resistance and return to your normal walk.** Note how the walk that was resisting, opposing, defying, and combating the force is different from your normal walk.
7. **Continue walking but stop suddenly, where the force that is in the ground emerges in front of you.**
8. **Find a stance to oppose this force, which has now moved closer to your side, although you continue to resist its pressure.**
9. **The force keeps changing position and is trying to pull you to itself. Defy the force by committing your entire self to resisting and escaping it.** This may mean that you need to pull, push, or thrust the force away from you. This may put you into a mode of running away from the force. Run, feeling the force behind you trying to pull you to itself, first from one direction and then from another.
10. **Return to neutral.**
11. **Lie back down on the floor.**
12. **Get up and note how much effort it took to get up.**
13. **Lie down again.**

Light:

14. **Imagine yourself as a giant, deflated person-balloon similar to those in parades.**

15. **Feel yourself being inflated as the balloon fills from the feet upwards.** First your feet fill with air, followed by your calves, thighs, hips, pelvis, rib cage, shoulders, head, arms, and hands. As you become more and more filled with air, note that you have a desire to rise and move around the room. The only thing holding you to the floor is a set of strings tied at your ankles, knees, hips, wrists, elbows, and top of the head.

16. **See someone come and snip the strings that are attaching you at your head, wrists, and elbows to the ground.** As they cut the strings, your upper body begins to float upward.

17. **See someone come and snip the strings that are keeping your hips, knees, and ankles connected to the floor.** As they snip these strings, you slowly come to an upright position.

18. **Begin to float around the room.** As you float, become aware of the gentle breezes that calmly push you one way and then another, maybe even delicately lifting you off the floor.

19. **Finally, a slow leak develops in your balloon and you glide gently back to the floor.**

20. **Come to standing.**

21. **Using your kinesthetic memory and the physical organization for both strong and light, move around the room going from walking to running, jumping, leaping, hopping, turning.** How do you organize yourself differently for a strong run and a light run? A strong hop and a light hop? A strong leap and a light leap? A strong jump and a light jump? A strong turn and a light turn? If you had to describe a strong run, what adjectives would you use? Light run? Strong hop? Light hop? Strong leap? Light leap? Strong jump? Light jump? What breath phrasing are you using with each? How can you use the breath to more specifically embody strength? Lightness?

22. **What possible situations would create an experience of resistance to and/or release into gravity? Create an improvisation using one of these situations.**

Journal: Repeat initial journal questions.

Figure 21: Time

Time Qualities

Time qualities refer to the *duration* of a movement. *Sudden* quality is a fast movement of *short duration* and corresponding *acceleration*. *Sudden* has a moment of stillness and then a burst of energy. A sudden quality can be felt as an immediate discharge of energy or as a decisive arrival at a new place. With regards to its energy focus, sudden is experienced as a narrowing of energy or breath. Sudden gestures can continue after you have arrived and are experienced as feelings of urgency, which often include shivering, fluttering, or vibrations. Words used to describe it might be:

urgent
sharp
staccato
excited
instantaneous

Sustained is a slow movement of a longer duration and longer deceleration, during which the energy widens into space. Sustained is a constant loop of transformation. Words or phrases used to describe it:

prolonged
legato
lingering
indulging in time

It can be felt as a gradual change from one situation to another or as an unhurried departure.

Time as a quality dictates the 'when' of any action. Thus, it is an indication of the style of reaction of an individual to people and events. Are they slow or quick to respond? As a consequence, do they seem aggressive or passive in their stance toward others? Note man in Figure 21. His upper body is indulging in the moment of opening the chest. Thus, his gesture can be read as a combination of ecstatic and embracing of the joy of being outdoors in the sun.

Exploration 34:
Time Qualities–Sustained to Sudden

Sustained:

1. **Place feet parallel, knees comfortably bent.** You should be supported in the lower abdomen with the tail bone dropped toward the floor.
2. **Breathe in and out from the lower abdomen, sending the breath out through your head, the palms of your hands, and the soles of your feet.**
3. **Repeat.**
4. **Inhale, allowing yourself to rise until you are balanced on your toes.**
5. **Exhale, sinking until your knees are slightly bent, heels flat on the floor.**
6. **Once this pattern is established, start moving around the room, keeping the sense of rising and lowering in extended, continuous time.** Allow your arms to replicate the phrasing of the legs and torso, reaching out into space as you exhale and releasing in toward the body as you inhale.

7. **Maintaining the relationship with the breath, reach into space with head, hands, shoulders, feet, knees, hips, back, elbows.** It may feel as though you are under water. Keep the continuous nature of the movement that seemingly has no distinct beginning or end.

8. **Move at different speeds and still maintain the same quality.** Ask yourself, How do I initiate the movement? Once I begin to explore the quality, what is its relationship to the breath? Do I work within any specific breathing pattern?

9. **Finally, reduce the movement to a walk.**

10. **Observe how you organize your body around this sense of time.** What do you note about the relationship between your pelvis, spine, legs, arms, head?

11. **Return to a normal walk.**

Sudden:

12. **Imagine that you are walking down a busy street and a small boy runs out into the street.**

13. **Quickly chase after him, dodging several moving cars to prevent getting hit yourself. Get to the boy, snatch him up, and then return to the sidewalk, again dodging all the cars.**

14. **Return to your normal walk.**

15. **Imagine you are walking along a trail in a dense forest at twilight. You are enjoying the beauty of the trees when an arrow hits a tree next to you.**

16. **Startled, you start running.**

17. **While running, you discover several people chasing you and you must propel yourself around a series of trees and boulders up ahead.**

18. **You manage to negotiate the obstacles and get to a clearing, but now your pursuers have almost caught up to you.**

19. **They begin shooting arrows at your feet and other parts of your body. The only way you can prevent yourself from getting hurt is to move quickly out of the way, first one body part and then another, sometimes even your entire body.**

20. **Return to your normal walk.**

21. **Remembering the kinesthetic qualities of sustainment, try walking, running, leaping, jumping, falling, skipping with**

sustainment. What adjectives would you use to describe each? Walking? Running? Leaping? Jumping? Falling? Skipping?

22. **Return to your normal walk.** Remember the physical state of suddenness. Investigate the other possibilities of this time quality through the locomotor movements mentioned above. What words would you use to describe each?

23. **Return to your normal walk.**

24. **Allow this walk to be transformed into a stride as you walk around the room. Change this to stalking, creeping, crawling.** What flow, weight and time qualities are contained in each of the above? What possible situations might cause you to move in such a manner?

25. **Return to your normal walk.**

26. **Allow this walk to be transformed into a dart, a dash, a sprint, a bolt. Repeat, moving back and forth between each.** What qualities are contained in each of the above? How are you engaging your breath with each? What situations might call for you to move in such a manner?

27. **Return to your normal walk.**

28. **Allow the walk to be transformed into a run and begin to flee, to avoid, to elude, to evade some person, mechanical being, animal.** What qualities are contained in each? What situations might call for you to move in such a manner?

29. **Return to your normal walk.**

30. **Allow the walk to be transformed into drifting through the room.** Allow this walk to evolve into an object or animal that glides, floats. What qualities of movement are contained in each experience? What situations might call for you to move in such a manner?

Journal: Repeat the observations from the journal section of Exploration 32. Begin to add information based on your observations of your own movement. How would you categorize your movement in Laban's terms?

Space Qualities

When we physically negotiate our way through many different environments and social situations, we are spatially thinking about our next action. In the process, we continually incorporate various degrees of *direct* or *indirect* spatial qualities. For an external observer, we are answering the question "where"—where we will move next and whether our pursuit of that goal will be direct or indirect. Direct can be defined as keeping strictly to the path or to the point; as such, it represents a narrowing of your energy. Words or phrases used to describe it are:

> pinpointed
> channeled
> zeroing in
> single focus
> restricted use of space

Attention must be kept directly on the place of arrival or points passed through during a curve; the space on either side of the pathway of the action has no importance.

Indirect/flexible is a movement that wanders through space, several

Figure 22: Space

parts of the body going in different directions simultaneously as the energy widens into space. Indirect always leaves an opportunity for something else to happen. As it reflects a personality characteristic, it appears as a slight hesitancy. Words used to describe it include:

roundabout
wavy
undulating
deviating
flexible
overlapping

There are always many shifts in the body among different foci. Additionally, walking in a dark room, unable to see, might require indirect focus. Dramatically, a direct action displays itself as self assurance while indirect action engages the potential of comedy in the set up followed by the unexpected punch line. Spacial qualities are also indication of our relationships to each other. Note the relationship between women and man in Figure 22. The women maintain a spacial distance between themselves and the man on the sidewalk by indirectly looking at him and adjusting their position on the sidewalk. Thus, they combine an indirect focus of the eyes with a direct intention of the body that makes a definite social statement.

Exploration 35:
Space Qualities–Direct to Indirect/Flexible

Direct and Indirect:
1. **Begin walking around the room using your normal walk.**
2. **Take a direct path that uses right angles.** You can move sideways, forward, and backward, but keep your focus forward. How do you integrate your breath into the decision to change directions? Stop. Now just walk around the room taking any path you want, but do not bump into any person or object.
3. **Extend the action of walking to an imaginary game of basketball.** See yourself surrounded by other players who want to take the ball away from you. To keep the ball, you have to con-

stantly and unexpectedly change your path in relationship to the other players. This causes you to constantly change focus and direction.

4. **Come to neutral.**
5. **Imagine you are encased in a giant, invisible bubble of some unknown material.**
6. **Reach out and touch the edges of the bubble with various body parts.** With the sides of your arms. Investigate the bubble with your feet. With the sides of your torso. Continue the investigation of the dimensions of the bubble with your head, the sides of your legs. Note the ways you are organizing your body to explore the dimensions and texture of the bubble.
7. **Return to neutral.** Where is your breath in relationship to your point of stillness? What is your kinesthetic image related to this point?
8. **An imaginary mosquito lands on your nose and then flies away. It returns to land on another part of your body and moves away. You decide to get it. Try to follow the movement of the mosquito with your eyes. Try to catch the mosquito with one hand. Try both hands.**
9. **Return to neutral.**
10. **An imaginary snake begins to crawl in front of you. You decide to stamp on it with your foot but it keeps moving. You keep trying to step on it but it moves one way and another. You keep trying to follow its movements by guessing which way it will go next. You cannot seem to judge enough in advance, and the snake finally slithers off. What happened to your breath during this scenario?**
11. **Return to a normal walk, move from direct to indirect.** Allow any part of yourself to initiate the change in direction. If you were going to describe moving indirectly, what words would you use? What would they be for direct?

Journal: Repeat the observations from the journal section of Exploration 32. In what situations do you think you might be likely to move in a direct manner? An indirect manner? You have completed an introduction to the four effort qualities of Laban. How would you use the categories of flow, weight, time, and space to describe your movement signature? Can your movement vocabulary be described into terms of the resistant to indulgent categories? Does your movement signature change depending upon public or private environments? The social situation?

Exploration 36: Imitations

Imitating others increases your movement vocabulary as well as providing an opportunity to analyze the movement of another person. The following imitation exercises can be used with any of the effort qualities. Below is a list of the effort qualities, with the resistant and indulgent qualities indicated. You can work with these qualities as discrete energy states or you can combine them as images/metaphors.

	Resistant	Indulgent
Flow	Bound	Free
Weight	Strong/Firm	Light/Fine
Time Qualities	Sudden	Sustained
Space Qualities	Direct	Indirect/Flexible

Follow the Leader

1. Divide into groups of three. One person in each group becomes leader; the others will follow.
2. Leader explores a full a range of locomotor movements such as walking or running, acrobatic movements such as somersaults, cartwheels, jumps, abstract movement with a variety of dynamic qualities. The followers imitate the leader as closely as possible, aiming to reproduce the dynamic quality.
3. Following a period of exploration, the performers should stop and discuss the movement range used by the leader, noticing whether any movements dominated or were left out.
4. Repeat, rotating leadership. Once everyone has had a turn as leader, the groups make assignments for each of their members. Each member individually practices the suggested qualities and brings them back to the group for comment.

Contrast Mirroring A goal in this exercise is not to imitate the other person but to contrast the quality of the movement both as posture and gesture. Thus, if the partner is doing a strong gesture, the mirror of it is a light gesture.

Impulse Circle The goal of this exercise is to explore the effort qualities as a continuum.

1. The group forms a circle.

2. **One person completes a movement/sound from one of the effort qualities such as light.**

3. **The next person in the circle repeats the same movement/sound, but slightly increases its intensity.** The following person makes it even stronger, etc. The final person in the circle repeats the same movement/sound, but this time it is very strong. This exercise can be completed with all of the four effort qualities—weight, time, space, and flow. You can also vary the continuum around the circle, going from light to strong to light again, etc.

Exploration 37: Gestures

Gestures can be divided into several categories, each representing a different function. These culturally specific categories represent a broad range of nonverbal language, the functions of which can be identified as *social, functional, emotional,* and *motivational.*[7]

Social gestures are culture-specific communications that replace a gesture with a word. These gestures are called *illustrators* and *regulators.* Two examples from American culture would be the up-and-down gesture of the head to mean "yes" and the two-finger "V for victory" sign. Illustrators are a form of social gesture used by the communicating party to accent a particular idea: the way to the market is very close, a long way off, etc. Being context specific, illustrators are likely to be understood by two parties in a conversation, despite differences in cultural background. Regulators are social gestures that control the

---

[7]This reference to different forms of gesture is taken from the video documentary *Reading People: The Unwritten Language of the Body,* Lake Zurich, Illinois: The Learning Seed.

means by which members of a group decide whose turn it is to speak. Participants rely on a variety of responses, including facial gestures, eye movements, and postural shifts. Regulators are always specific to community. Additionally, they indicate an individual's emotional state.

Functional gestures refer to actions of daily life; the physical actions we use for common tasks such as washing our hair, brushing our teeth, fixing food, and taking care of other household tasks. There are, however, many household tasks that are specific to each of us, depending on individual cultural background, occupation, and lifestyle. For example, someone who lives on a farm will incorporate a very different set of gestures into daily experience compared with someone who lives in a metropolitan area; a person raised as a Buddhist will engage herself very differently in a set of physical actions associated with her religious faith than a Protestant.

Emotional gestures, or affect displays, are indicators of the emotional mood of the communicator. They include many movements that are often habits, ranging from twisting the hair to tapping the fingers to rearranging elements of clothing. Cultural norms often dictate the degree and form of emotional display appropriate for given situations.

Motivational gestures have the specific goal of influencing the behavior of others. We often think of them in terms of either their momentary or long-term function in any situation. Emotional and motivational gestures can overlap in the moment with social and functional gestures. For example, politicians shake people's hands at political rallies as a form of social gesture (greeting), but attempt to convey an attitude that motivates the individual to vote for him/her.

1. **Using the contrast mirror exercise, imitate the leader's actual physical gesture, but change the quality of the movement.** You can use any category of gestures–social (greetings, farewells, illustrating a story, regulating the flow of a conversation), functional (from everyday life or an occupation), emotional (anger, joy, fear, tenderness, sensuality, joy) and motivational (inspiring a team to succeed, leading an army to battle).

2. **Gestures can also be combined, for example, expressing a postural and gestural attitude of joy through a social or functional gesture.**

Journal: Following the exercise note, which gestures you used when you were the leader that are part of your daily movement vocabulary. What new gestures did you discover? Using one of the new gestures as a starting point for your imagination, write a character description using the effort qualities. You can refer to previous journal entries for flow, weight, time, and space.

Exploration 38:
Daily Life and Arbitrary Actions

---

1. **Create an action score based on your daily life (brushing your teeth in the morning, doing a morning exercise routine, making coffee, riding the bus or train to work, feeding a pet, etc.) or create a list of arbitrary actions such as sit, stand, fall down, walk around the space, lean against a wall, sit on the floor. Be very detailed with the list of actions.** For example, an action of brushing your teeth can be divided into a series of movements that include walking to the bathroom, turning on the water, getting the toothbrush, getting the toothpaste, putting toothpaste on brush, etc. This expanded score will allow you to explore the dynamic potential of individual movements.
2. **Complete each movement in one of the effort qualities.**
3. **Experiment with combinations of qualities for the set actions.** For example, you could brush your teeth lightly but strongly throw the toothbrush back in the drawer.
4. **Experiment with combinations for individual actions.** Using the toothbrush example, you could start to brush your teeth lightly and, in the process of brushing, increase the strength.

Exploration 39: Properties Improvisation

Bring a variety of props that might be used in association with the physical life of a particular character–chairs, balls, paper bags, articles of clothing, fans, canes, hats, cigarettes. Try different movement qualities with different props. Create a short movement sketch that nonverbally reveals the effort affinities of the character.

Exploration 40: Metaphor

External plasticity is based on our inner sense of the movement of energy.
Constantin Stanislavski

We are most familiar with the use of metaphor in relationship to language, but, as we have learned from other chapters, metaphor in its relationship to imagery and our imagination is an important aspect of energy. As choreographer Daniel Nagrin writes, "Every action, in or out of art, can be seen as a metaphor for something else. Metaphors are what we do for a living."[8] Metaphors surround us each day as we make comparisons between our daily life and what our imagination considers possible. For example: You are watching a bird fly across the sky. You try to imagine what it feels like to cover space without being bound by gravity. The next time you jump off a stool or run in the wind, you remark to yourself, "I feel as free as a bird." Metaphors are our method of integrating our body with our imagination, or the body and the mind.

Since metaphors incorporate the dynamic potential to create from lived experience, they are a performer's primary tool. This desire to create metaphors is part of the joy of living in your imagination. The following exploration is in two parts. The first focuses on playing with effort qualities and evolving a set of images/metaphors. The second uses the images/metaphors to create a character.

Part 1

1.   **Using a variety of movements, from locomotor movements to everyday gestures to abstract movement, explore the individual qualities (light, strong, etc.)**
2.   **Write down the images that occur to you as you are exploring.**
3.   **Locate the images in different referential sets of metaphors.**
     For example: Images/movements in relation to the following:

---

[8]Daniel Nagrin, *Dance and the Specific Image* (Pittsburgh: University of Pittsburgh Press, 1994), 97.

1) senses–for hearing these might be blaring, groaning, gurgling
2) mood, characterization, or attitude–arrogant, confused
3) emotional states–ardent, calloused, caustic, eager, joyous, sad
4) age–callow, codger, coltish, decrepit
5) nonhuman images/movements–bellow, grunt, hiss, screech, snarl, squeal, whine, atomic blast, boiling water.

4. **Identify the effort qualities that describe these images.** For example: a groan could be strong, sustained, and bound. A groan could also be sudden, free, and indirect. A confused emotional state could be light, indirect and sudden. Ask yourself, What metaphor describes a strong, sustained, bound groan? One answer might be a lamenting cry. A light, indirect, and sudden confused emotional state might be described as a panicked wind.

5. **Go back and explore the metaphor from the standpoint of other qualities.** If in the exploration of the quality "strong" the image of a lamenting cry emerged, for example, see if you can add onto the description of the cry by exploring its opposite light. What kind of cry do you discover?

Part 2

1. **Pick one of the images and answer the questions you have asked for the initial effort explorations.** I move like a_____, I feel like_____, I respond to the world by interacting like a _____, I sound like_____. Also ask: Where is the center of physical support for myself as this image? What is the emotional center for myself as this image?

2. **Use the process of visualization to fuse with image on a cellular level.** One method to experience the image on a cellular level is to place the image within an emotional/chakra area. Fuse the breath to the image. Breath into the image, expanding its size. Note the adjustment the image makes in your pelvis. Allow your spine to align with the image and your ribs to release into the image, your head extending from the spine. Finally, see your appendages connecting from the image.

3. **Create an improvised context, or place, that allows you to interact with others as this metaphoric character.** Potential examples include meetings between people for whom there is some sexual attraction or a situation in which some power relationship exists, such as ruler and ruled, parent and child, boss and employee.

4. **Create an action score related to that context.** A potential score for any of the previously listed contexts is: Person A: sitting in a room, crosses legs, shifts in chair, looks at clock. Person B: opens door, looks at person A, starts to walk toward A, halts. Person A: turns away from B, etc.

5. **Once you have established a repeatable score, begin to explore the primary metaphor by transforming the image through changing the dynamics of flow, weight, time, or space as you play the actions.** For example, a character who is metaphorically a striking red rose (free, strong, sustained, and direct) may start to wilt (free, light, sustained, and indirect), change color by getting dark, blotched edges (free, light, sudden, and indirect), and finally begin to loose petals (increased intensity of free, light, sudden, and indirect). The same rose could receive the proper amount of water, the color would deepen, and the petals slowly begin to open to reveal a fully developed rose (increased intensity of free, strong, sustained, and direct). Be aware of it and use your breath to stay continuously engaged with the image and the emotional connection it creates.

The ability to use imagery was an exciting discovery for Kristina, an undergraduate acting student:

> *But what I discovered that was so wonderful was that when I completely concentrate on an image, everything else more or less falls into place. There are so many times when I am rehearsing when, even if I am in the moment, there is still a little part of me conscious of my external movements and gestures. I guess I should not expect myself to alleviate that problem right away, but last night was one of the first times when I felt completely focused on the image. And it was an amazing feeling when I allowed it to completely take over. My mind did not feel like it needed to judge anymore. Yet it was also a little bit scary because it was such an unknown experience and I did not yet fully trust it. I guess that will now be my goal, trusting the fact that a powerful image can guide my body.[9]*

Journal: Continue as in previous observations to record the images that arise from your unconscious. What metaphors are more prevalent than others? Do you find that they reflect some movement qualities more than others?

---

[9]Kristina Goodnight, Personal communication, 1994.

ACTION

The first two sections of this chapter have helped you to expand your understanding of different effort qualities, their relationship to your movement preferences, and the possibility of using them to extend your imagination via metaphor. Nevertheless, as previously discussed, our movement language does not consist of a single effort quality, but of two or more effort qualities in combination. Laban organized possible effort combinations into what he referred to as the *eight basic actions*. According to Laban, these actions are an indication of individual psychology and personality. As Laban describes it:

> Weight, Space, Time, and Flow are the motion factors toward which the moving person adopts a definite attitude. These attitudes can be described as: a relaxed or forceful attitude toward weight, a pliant or lineal attitude toward space, a prolonging or shortening attitude toward time, a liberating or withholding attitude toward flow.[10]

A quick response, for example, is guided by an internal or external need to have the situation resolved immediately. As described by Laban, actions associated with quickness include:

a direct and strong punch
an indirect/flexible and strong slash
a direct and light dab
an indirect/flexible and light flick

A slower response is guided by an inner hesitation or an external observation of the situation which suggests that a decision to act can be delayed. This response is associated with some action states and resistance qualities, such as a direct and strong press and a flexible and strong wring. Actions associated with less resistance include:

a direct and light glide
an indirect/flexible and light float
a direct and sustained press
an indirect and sustained wring

---

[10]Rudolph von Laban, *Modern Educational Dance*, 160.

The following explorations help you to research these actions in order to explore related personality states. Each exploration ends with a written description of a character based on the images associated with the action. These character sketches/biographies can be used as reference points for future explorations. If working with a group, divide into watchers and doers for Explorations 41 through 44. Watchers choose one person to observe. They act as coaches for the doers. They encourage doers to explore the effort actions with all parts of their body. The basic sequence used for thrusting and slashing can be used for the other efforts.

Exploration 41:
Eight Basic Actions: Thrusting/ Slashing

Thrusting is sudden, strong, and direct. The action is one that moves in a straight line away from you, in toward the body, or to a specific destination. The actions encourage stamping and punching gestures.

Slashing is sudden, strong, and indirect. It moves flexibly through space, causing you to leap and twist.

1. **Begin to move in the space in a sustained, continuous fashion with no accents to your movements.** You can speed up and slow down, but you must continue moving in a sustained manner. As you feel the impetus, you can add either thrusting or slashing movements and then return to sustainment. Groups of people may form and develop a pattern and move together in a similar tempo/rhythm.

2. **Remain conscious of your breath and emotional state and how it changes as you explore each action.**

3. **Write down images that evolve from exploring the states. From these images, write two short first-person character sketches/biographies.** These sketches include the basics of who, such as place of birth, age, occupation, family background. In your sketches, also describe the movement qualities of self as character and as part of the gestural language that regulates communication, illustrates a story, indicates emotional state, or serves as part of a social communication.

Exploration 42:
Eight Basic Actions: Gliding/Floating

Gliding is sustained, light, and direct. Gliding movements are flat, without undulations or curves; they also include direct movements that resemble moving through space with a clearly determined goal (glide like a skater, glide like an airplane, glide like a skateboard).

Floating is also sustained and light, but it is indirect instead of direct. It often moves from the wrist, fingers, and elbows to take you indirectly about the space. The legs lift lightly off the floor in careful rising and falling steps (float like a boat, float like a balloon, float like a cloud.)

Exploration 43:
Eight Basic Actions: Wringing/Pressing

Wringing is sustained, strong, and indirect. This form of gesture creates wringing movements that knot in and open out. Initiate a wringing movement by twisting one limb first in one direction and then another. Complete the same gesture with each limb, followed by all body parts in combination.

Pressing is sustained, strong, and direct. It implies resistance from one body part to another, or from one body part to an external or internal force, and includes pressing away from the body into space. Pressing is a resistance to gravity, either against another portion of yourself, against space in general, or against an object in the room. Create a series of postures, either pressing against yourself, a chair, another person, the wall, table, etc.

Exploration 44:
Eight Basic Actions: Dabbing/Flicking

Dabbing is sudden, light, and direct. It occurs when you dart here and there with pointed gestures of feet and hands.

Flicking is sudden, light, and indirect. It occurs when the hands and feet lead the rest of you, sparking you to action. The fingers become alive, scattering and gathering, and the knees and feet make round-about gestures in the air, lightly stepping and springing.

Actions associated with flicking and dabbing are small gestures most often associated with the hands. However, you can expand your approach to the use of this action by flicking different substances off different parts of your body or dabbing different parts of your body with different substances. For instance, flick a fly off your face, flick water on a piece of paper, dab your fingers in pudding, dab your feet in mud, dab paint on your arm. Try to come up with a variety of substances to flick off or dab with. This can lead into a scenario that becomes an improvisation in which flicking and dabbing become the prime motivation for the relationship.

OBSERVATION AND ANALYSIS

As performers, we are always observing the world in which we live for images to file away in our memory to retrieve when necessary to create a character. The majority of these observations are informal responses to people we see walking on the street, sitting in a restaurant, or visiting a museum. Periodically, we are cast in a role that requires a formal method of observation. The approach provided in this chapter combines your understanding of Laban with your ability to observe the effort qualities in the movement choices of another.

Observing the movement of others, as Moore and Yamamoto point out in *Beyond Words*, is a process that incorporates many of the skills you have already learned, including relaxation, concentration, specific and general focus, other awareness, or, as Moore and Yamamoto phrase it, attunement.[11] Many have discovered that some of their best observations of the behavior of others takes place in shopping malls or outdoor cafes that allow them to find a comfortable place to sit and watch the life around them. Moreover, the media age provides the opportunity to gain a vast array of information from "surfing" the programs offered on television, from evangelical church services, cooking shows,

---

[11]Carol-Lynne Moore and Kaoru Yamamoto, *Beyond Words* (New York, N.Y.: Gordon and Breach, 1988).

home videos, MTV, Country-Western music stations to art exhibitions and exhibits.

Whether your observation will take place at home in front of your television or at the local mall, bowling alley or browsing through a museum or art book, the following set of guidelines will help you observe effectively. First, make certain that you have a comfortable place from which to observe. If you are physically uncomfortable, it will be difficult to concentrate on the movement of others. It is also important that you place yourself in a position that is relatively inconspicuous in relation to the person or people you are observing. People generally begin to change their behavior once they realize they are being watched.

Once you have found a comfortable place from which to observe, allow yourself to focus in a relaxed manner on the subject of observation. The initial observation should answer general questions concerning the general posture and changes in posture of the individual. As you begin to observe, jot down simple notes on the time and place of observation, who was observed (young woman, old man, etc.), and the movement, expressed as diagrams or words that will bring back the memory of the movement. After a period of general observations, use the observational time to pay attention to the details of movement.

Some suggestions about specific movements to look at are the following: (1) the shape of the hand so that it shows clearly how an object is held; (2) the rhythm that evolves from repeating an action; (3) the weight and time and space qualities of an action; (4) the quality of transition between actions; (5) how much of the body is involved in an action; (6) rhythm of an action; (7) mood associated with an action; (8) vocal patterns associated with the gestural pattern. These are not written in a specific order. Your observations will, however, encompass all of them over time .

After a period of observing, it is important that you take yourself out of the observing mode and into a period of recuperation, which will vary depending on the subject of observation and your personal state. This recuperative moment can be as short as looking away for a brief moment, or as thoughtful as getting up and relocating yourself in another position from which to observe. The more you can apply the technique of relaxed focus, the easier it will be to maintain your concentration.

An accurate analysis of the movement of another does not take place in one period of observation; it is the accumulation of several periods. As you complete each period, ask yourself, using the chart provided below, "What do I not yet know?" You want to create a "thick description" of the person. These observations serve as the beginning of a character notebook that you can expand upon and use whenever you need information to create a new character.

This method of observation can also be used to develop a character from visual sources. For example, you can apply the same process of analysis to drawings and paintings of people from a particular historical period, or to photographs of people taken from written and filmed ethnographies, magazines, or collections of photographs. If you build this form of research into your working life as an actor, you will develop during your career an entire notebook of resource material.

Outline for Analysis

The following outline includes information you will want to record for anyone you are observing. With each observation session, you will be adding more detailed information. Ultimately, you will develop a detailed account of the movement, or movement signature, of the person you are observing. Some people discover they like to draw sketches to accompany their written observations. Others supplement the written document with photos or videotaped material. The goal of the observation is to organize a set of data that you can refer to as needed in the development of characters. These same questions can also be used for a self-analysis that expands upon the personal inventory outlined in Chapter 1.

Where Observed: Did the observation take place in a shopping mall, restaurant, street corner, theater, dance club, museum, home, video store, etc.?

Who Observed: Who did you observe–an individual, a group? If possible include a short biographical statement, including information on age, gender, ethnic identity, place of birth, education, etc.

Context of Observation: Describe the location of your observation and any interactions that took place as part of it. For instance, if you were observing children in a park, did you talk to them? What was the nature of the conversation? Or was your observation based on secondary source material, such as a video, historical account, televison, film?

Most Active Body Parts: What are the most active body parts of the person observed–legs, arms, torso, head, hands, feet? What are they doing–sitting, standing, moving?

Use of Space: When the person moves through space, what direction does he/she take with their body? Is the path direct or indirect? The specific direction of movement? Or moving in general? Do they carry themselves away from gravity or are they released into gravity? When moving, how much space do they cover? What is the size and shape of the bubble that surrounds them? What about when they are sitting?

Organization of Body Parts Within Phrased Movement (Gestures): Does the gesture language tend to be simultaneous, sequential, or in some combination of the two?

Forms of Gesture, or Kinesthetic Display: What forms of gesture is the person most likely to engage–social, illustrators, regulators, functional, emotional, motivational? What parts of the body are engaged in individual gesture vocabularies?

Use of Effort: What is the person's general affinity toward flow, weight, time, and space? Can their movement be summed up as falling into either the resistant or indulgent categories? What body parts initiate changes in posture or gesture?

Combinations and Transitions: What effort qualities tend to be combined (strong-sustained, free-sudden)? What action qualities? Is there a way the person under observation organizes the muscle system to make transitions between gestures with differing qualities?

Interactions: How do they use their eyes or other body parts in interactions with others? Direct? Indirect? Combination? Do their movements, including touching others, have a tendency to be sustained, sudden, combination? An individual? A group? A person from the opposite or same sex? Are they fluid, bound or a combination of both in their interactions with others?

Metaphors: What metaphors would you use to describe this person?

CHECKLIST OF POINTS TO REMEMBER

Laban's efforts provide a guide to recognizing individual tendencies and understanding your movement signature. It is also a means of increasing your expressiveness. Using this work, you have moved from the specifics of individual efforts to their unification in the eight actions. You also have continued to increase your ability to combine breath and imagery to create specific energy states. Finally, you have learned a process for creating a character and a method of analysis that you can use to create a series of movement profiles for future character investigations.

Exploration

- Be certain to warm up prior to working.

- Change takes time, and if you want to expand your creativity you need to practice in everyday life as well as in times set aside for class or rehearsal.

- Approach all your work as an open question.

- Images and metaphors are gateways to the imagination.

Breath

- Allow the images to flow through your body as the breath does.

Imagery

- Gestures can be categorized as social, functional, emotional, and motivational.

- Explore effort qualities in their pure state before combining them.

- Note your internal landscape and external focus during periods of transition between qualities or combinations of qualities, as this is the key to transformation.

- Learn to play with images you have discovered from states associated with effort qualities of flow, weight, time and space as well as the eight basic actions of punching, slashing, floating, gliding, pressing, wringing dabbing and flicking.

PART TWO

APPLICATION

Essential to the collaborative nature of theatre is an awareness of your interaction with different communities, from family and friends to artistic associates—actors, directors, designers, playwrights and, finally, the audience. The rehearsal, or the act of exploring a text, is the center of this interaction. This section applies the skills and process of breath awareness, exploration, and imagery to work with masks and texts. The mask chapter serves as a transition between the early chapters that focused primarily on increasing awareness, and the final chapter, which is concerned with product and performance. The final chapter provides a method of applying awareness to the creation of a character, embodiment of a text, and interaction with actors, directors, and audience.

Ti Jean and His Brothers Directed by Yvonne Brewster, Juan Manzo as Bolom

CHAPTER FOUR
MASK, MYTH, AND ARCHETYPE

Most anthropologists and psychologists agree that the mask liberates man. Behind it he is free both to express joy, pain, or anger without social or religious restraints and to mimic and mock those who sanction and impose the restraints. Man's irrational, imaginative, and fanciful observations and feelings are given temporary form and, consequently, a temporary reality. In effect, the mask turns the world into a temporary stage.

Susan Valeria Harris Smith

The term *mask*, or face-covering, can refer not only to the Halloween or Mardi Gras mask we wear for a ritual occasion but also to the social mask, carefully constructed of clothing and physical habits, which is part of our daily lives. This social mask conveys our position in society. We use it to find the appropriate partner, employment, and friends. As students, lawyers, doctors, salespeople, daughters, fathers, wives, partners, lovers and others, we define and are defined by this mask. Our social masks are an intricate interweaving of our essential natures (present at birth) and the habits of a lifetime derived from and developed in relation to our environment. This generalized social mask modifies our behavior as we switch environments from public to private or peer group to natal family, according to the role of the moment.

Currently and historically, facial and body masks have been used by the world's theatre to symbolize social masks. Ancient Greek actors wore masks that were conventionalized manifestations of facial expressions. The mouth of each mask contained a megaphone to help project the actor's voice. The miracle and mystery plays in Medieval Europe used masks to portray dragons, monsters, and allegorical figures such as the devil or the seven deadly sins. Half-masks; a mask covering only the upper part of the face, were used by the commedia dell' arte companies of Italy. In Asia and Africa, the majority of theatrical forms still use masks–body, face, or painted face–as a means by which the spiritual forces of the universe enter the bodies of the performers. Wearing the mask, performers enact the myths of creation and explain the nature of existence. In contemporary theatre, masks have been used in plays such as *The Great God Brown* by Eugene O'Neill and in modern versions of Greek plays.

The use of masks in actor training originated with the work of Jacques Copeau (1878-1949). Influenced by the work of Dalcroze, Appia, Craig, and Stanislavski, Copeau opened the Ecole du Vieux-Colombier in 1920 to create a poetics of stagecraft. The program he originated ranged from courses in theatrical theory and criticism to traditional conservatory classes in acting, voice, and movement. In his view, mask training helped actors by giving them an opportunity to return to a childlike method of exploration and discovery, free from the social constructions of personality.[1] The mask, according to Copeau, helps the actor to understand the relationship between the social constructions of a character's behavior and their acting tendencies and thereby broadens their imagination. As he explains it:

> [The mask] symbolizes perfectly the position of the interpreter in relation to the character, and demonstrates how the two are fused one to the other. The actor who plays under the mask receives from this object of cardboard the reality of the character. He is commanded by it and obeys it irresistibly. Barely has he been shown the mask, when he feels pouring out of himself a being of which he was unaware, that he did not even suspect existed. It is not only his face which is altered, but his being, the character of his reflexes where feelings are being formed which he would have been incapable of imagining with his face uncovered. . . . Even the accent of his voice will be dictated by the mask–by a persona–that is to say by a personage without life as long as it is unwedded to the actor, which came from without, yet seizes him and substitutes for self.[2]

Thus, the theatrical mask interacts intuitively with your imagination in much the same way that the social masks you wear interact with your essential nature. The mask frees you to be an aspect of your

[1]Jacques Copeau qtd in Mira Felner, *Apostles of Silence* (London: Associated University Presses, 1985), 40. In *Souvenirs du Vieux Colombier* (Paris: Nouvelles Editions Latines, 1931), 51.

[2]Jacques Copeau, in Felner, 43. In "Reflections d'un comedian sur le 'Paradoxe de Diderot," *Ecrits sur le Theatre* (Paris: Michel Brient Editeur, 1955), 25-26.

intuitive/metaphoric self. From the stillness inside the mask, you live in a double state of existence–you are yourself and you are the mask, the *I and the not I.*

Throughout this chapter we will be exploring three types of mask: *the self, the neutral,* and *the archetypal.* Designed to help you deepen and develop your imagination, each mask will increase your ability to work intuitively. Two of them–the self and neutral masks–are actual masks. Limited to the face, these masks encourage you to delve into the core of your being (self mask) and use your imagination to transform your body and the mask (neutral). In section three, you work with archetypal masks. These are not actual masks but metaphorical masks, or what I call body masks. The sequence from self to archetype deepens your kinesthetic experience. This self-other process of learning also helps to refine your relationship between self as person, person as actor, and actor as character. Finally, mask explorations help to prepare you to work with different styles of production.

Ideas included in this chapter are:

- Motion and stillness are not separate phenomena. There is always motion in stillness and the reverse. In each moment there is a visceral stillness related to an inner source of motivation that, when expressed externally, is dramatically powerful.
- The art of acting is related to simplicity. More is often said through less. You will develop an inner concentration that will help you to become aware of subtle degrees of change in time, space, and energy.
- The basic building block of good acting is essence. You find the essence of a moment by asking the question, What is the most basic need of the moment and how is this expressed through action?

SELF MASK

In the process of creating our social mask, we have, for a variety of reasons, learned to suppress parts of our essential disposition. The essential part of the personality is often hidden under a social mask that projects the opposite energy qualities. For example, a strong, determined personality is hidden behind a postural/gestural language that primarily uses the indulgent qualities of light, sustained, and free. While we need to appreciate and acknowledge our personal histories, it is not necessary for our purposes to know the specific details of why we have evolved our social mask. What is important for performing artists is the ability to access all parts of themselves. Acknowledging and appreciating the essential aspects of self makes available a greater range of options. The exploration of self also helps us to realize, by extension, the importance of a scripted character's commitment to their social mask. The following mask exercises will help you to explore your essential self and the uniqueness of your expressive gifts.

Making the Mask

The self mask is a mask of your face as it exists. It is made with the help of a partner, plaster bandage (which can be found at most pharmacies), Vaseline, and water.

Step 1. Cut the plaster bandage into strips of many different shapes and sizes.

Step 2. Cover your face with Vaseline, especially the areas that have hair on them such as eyebrows, eye lids, edges of hairline, and beard if you have one.

Step 3. Lie on the floor in a comfortable position, with towels under your head to catch any excess moisture. You may want to play quiet music in the background to help you to relax.

Step 4. Take a few minutes to breathe and allow your face to assume its most comfortable position. When you are ready, signal to your partner that he/she can begin to make the mask.

Step 5. Dip a segment of the plaster bandage into the water, shaking off the excess and then placing the bandage on the face. It is good to begin with larger strips on the external part of the face and slowly move to the inside area. As you move into the central area of the face, use the smaller strips of bandage. As you put each strip on the face, make certain that you smooth it into place, creating as smooth a surface as possible. Completely cover the entire face except the mouth. Also, do not cover the entire nostril area; cover only enough to retain the shape of the nose, leaving enough room for the person to breathe.

Step 6. Once you have covered the entire face with bandages, use a small amount of water on your finger tips to smooth out any rough spots.

Figure 23: Self-Mask

Step 7. Wait for the mask to dry; it will take approximately 30 minutes. The masked person can remove the mask.

Step 8. Once the mask is dry, you can reinforce the edges with more plaster bandage strips. Use a pair of scissors to cut out the eyes, and reinforce the edges of the eye holes. Attach a string from the edge to the eye hole so that you can tie the mask to your head.

Working with the Mask

Begin each working session with the mask by taking time to warm up, following the outline provided in Appendix A. Follow the warmup with a period of time of observing self in the mask via a mirror as illustrated in Figure 23. This self observation has two parts. First, look at yourself in the mirror, noting the relationship of your face to the mask. Second, put on the mask and look at yourself in the mirror in mask.

Exploration 45: The Lyric Self

---

1. **Take time to browse through a bookstore, through jacket covers in a music shop, or in a library to uncover a piece of poetry that intuitively seems as if it represents some core part of you.** It need not come from a traditional source of poetry; any piece of lyric writing is appropriate.
2. Memorize the poetry as you would a script and make several audio recordings of it, each with a different interpretation.
3. With the mask on, begin to play with the language of the piece (this can be done either with the taped script or by repeating the piece to yourself), permitting yourself to respond impulsively to the imagery in the poetry and allowing your entire self to be a literal expression of the text. Try not to define the movement imagery immediately; instead, give yourself time to play with the possibilities.
4. Continuing to explore, note those movements that begin to repeat themselves over and over.
5. **Create a movement score with this vocabulary and perform it for others.** You can read your poem either prior or after performing the movement score.

As one student discovered:

> *Starting from neutral stillness and letting the body text emerge. I think you could work on a simple piece like this for a very long time and always be learning something. Distilling and concentrating movements further and further down to extract their meaning and purity.*[3]

---

[3]Mark Philpot, Personal communication, 1995.

This exercise can also be completed with one person moving and another person or persons reading the poetry. The goal of the moving person is to listen to the phrasing and intonation of the person speaking. The goal of the speaking person is to try to respond to the movement of the moving person. When used in this way, the exercise often expands the choices of both the speaker and the mover.

Journal: What did you note about how you approached this exploration? Did you attend more to the imagery in the poem, the vocal qualities of your partner's voice, the physical movement of your body? Some combination of all three?

Exploration 46: Musical Alter-Ego

1. **Pick a contemporary singer who represents your musical alter-ego.** Whatever the genre, the performer should represent someone with whom you identify. Using your knowledge of movement analysis, write a description or draw the basic set of postures and gestures the performer uses.

2. **Explore a recording singer's music using the postures and gestures from your movement observation.** Answer the following questions: What do you note about your reaction to the experience psychologically, emotionally, physically? How does this reaction influence your image of yourself? Does it change it? Does it expand it?

3. **Perform the piece in the self mask as a lip synch for others.**

One student described his process:

The process starts out very deliberately and with simple imitation. You start trying on movements like pieces of clothing and at first they don't quite fit and are definitely in a style you would not be caught dead in but slowly the outfit starts making sense and within the process the new suit begins to have its own logic.[4]

Journal: Which perceptual modes did you use to analyze the movement of your alter-ego? Your eyes? Your ears? Your kinesthetic sense?

---

[4]Mark Philpot, Personal communication, 1995.

What movements of the alter-ego's postural/gestural vocabulary were the most significant in the creation of your version of the alter-ego? How is your movement vocabulary similar or different to that of your alter-ego?

Exploration 47: Day in the Life

1. **Choose an event from some part of your day.** This does not need to be something complex; it can be as simple as getting up in the morning and making coffee. It should, however, incorporate more than one action. For instance, do not limit it to just getting out of bed, but include getting the paper and letting out the cat.
2. **In mask, repeat this phrase until you feel you have evolved a consistent movement score for which you are aware of your objective/intention for each physical action.**
3. **Repeat it again, still in the mask, but with an awareness of potential obstacles that exist to your accomplishing each task.** These should be naturally occurring obstacles—material, physical, emotional—that exist for you in your home.
4. **Perform in mask the scenario for others.**

Journal: What was the immediate situation that came to you as you were given the assignment? Describe your performance using Laban's effort categories. Describe what you believe to be the essential part of yourself or your unique means of perceiving the world.

Exploration 48: Discovering the Comic Self

Clowns function in rituals and drama around the world to satirize the potential excess inherent in social masks. The author of *Mythic Imagination*, Stephen Larsen, suggests:

> Psychologically, we could say that clowning has always addressed itself to the Jungian concept of the shadow. The

grotesque, hidden, and unacceptable aspects of personal life are unveiled and shown to be universal. We recognize the outrageous braggart as a pure type and, if we are psychologically attuned, as classic element in our own makeup. They are members of our "inner cast of characters." [5]

Each of us has stories we share with our closest friends detailing how a failed attempt to maintain social decorum created a humorous moment. These include breaking the social code through momentarily dropping our social mask. Creating comic moments comes from learning to enjoy the potential ambiguity that exists in such situations. It embraces the possibility that the inner desires and drives of each of us can be discovered in a moment of revelation. In this exploration you will combine the "day in the life" exploration with your analysis of your physical habits (chapter 1-Personal Inventory).

1. **Take any physical habit you have previously discovered. This can be a stance, a gesture, facial expression, or any combination.**

2. **Heighten your awareness of this stance/gesture/facial expression by concentrating on feeling and fusing with the gesture inhalation and following the inherent energy of it on the exhalation.** For example, if a consistent postural/gestural pattern for you is to scratch your head and at the same time turn it to the left, you should breathe in, allowing yourself to feel and fuse with the gesture and breathe out and observe how the gesture changes in size and intensity. You can also use Laban's effort qualities to adjust the energy state of the gesture.

3. **Repeat the above exercise several times with different movements.**

4. **With each pattern, note how the emotional and physical center of the body has changed.** What becomes the dominant area? Ask yourself these questions: Where does this character that is you but not you speak from? What is the primary motivation for this person in the world? Prestige? Money? Sexual conquest? A perfect body?

---

[5] The reference to the shadow refers to that aspect of self that we do not feel is socially appropriate and try to keep hidden. It can refer to the miserly person who tries to appear generous to others or vanity hidden under the guise of good manners. The shadow is one aspect of archetype discussed in Stephen Larsen's book *The Mythic Imagination* (New York: Bantam Books, 1990), 264-265.

5.   Verbalize the internal monologue that naturally springs from your imagination as you play within this physical vocabulary.

6.   Return to the day-in-the-life score, incorporating the character's exaggerated gestures. Include as much of the internal monologue as seems relevant. Do not try to create an accurate logic for the character; allow the movement to create its own logic. Part of discovering the comic side of the self mask is to appreciate and even enjoy ourselves in moments when we are completely committed to our excesses while at the same time realizing that they are at odds with our social mask.

7.   Perform day in the life for others.

Journal: Write out the internal monologue for the character. This monologue is the character's response to the situation that he/she does not speak, but only thinks.

NEUTRAL MASK

Self as centered and flowing,
Self as rooted and soaring,
Self where mind, spirit and body are one,
and there is no need to win.

Ze'eva Cohen

When working on a text, our primary challenge is to uncover the subtext below the surface of the dialogue. Two questions we often ask are, "What part of this character is like me, my life, my experiences?" and "How is this character different?" Frequently, we find that we have a difficult time negotiating the boundary between self and character. Sometimes the character becomes so much a part of us on stage that we find we are still playing the role in our offstage life. Understanding neutral or a state of neutrality is a technique that can help you to transition from self to character and back again. Moreover, the potential for neutral to help you as a performer does not stop here. As it releases you from a focus on yourself, the state of neutral is a stimulating starting point from which to unearth ways of moving and speaking that are unique to your creative process.

Figure 24: Neutral Mask

The Mask

There are many different forms of neutral mask. The one supplied by most commercial distributors is white. Although white is not universally thought of as a neutral color, as the presence of all color, white is often considered a blank slate on which to paint. But one might also say that the mask should be black–the presence of all color–and that the performer's task is to bring out the particular color of the mask from situation to situation. I urge you to consider the question of color as neutral and work with the color that for you contains the feeling quality of neutral (see Figure 24).

Working with the Mask

When working with a neutral mask, take time before putting on the mask to arrive at a state of neutral, using the image of the empty suit. This use of the empty suite image prior to putting on the mask prepares you to embody the mask on a deeper level. Once you complete your personal preparation, pick up the mask and spend a few minutes looking at it, letting the neutrality of the mask further bring you to a state of neutral. If you find that you lose your concentration at this stage, do not hesitate to put down the mask and complete some whole body movements such as yoga stretches or body swings and then return to the mask. After you have put on the mask, walk around the space, letting the mask "soak" into your being before taking up an exploration. Two pieces of advice when working with the mask: (1) as you work with the mask, let your first approach be pure experience, without analysis, and (2) work without judgment.

Exploration 49: Routine Tasks

This exercise is an introduction to the basic ideas associated with neutral. It initiates a discussion of the relationship between neutral mind and neutral body. Goals of the exercise are to discover areas of habitual tension used in daily tasks, to develop new methods of incorporating the musculature to make movement more efficient, and to explore and experience yourself in neutral. This exploration also allows you to work with the relationship between the idea of neutral and the mask. The first part of this exploration can be completed on your own or can be brought to a group for discussion. The second part repeats tasks with and without the neutral mask.

1. **Pick a repetitive task. Repeat it over and over again, pausing slightly between each repetition.** In the repetition of the task, you will want to accomplish two things: first, see if you arrive at some economy of movement through the repetition of a gesture; second, see if you can take the task out of the realm of the specific (usually associated with given circumstances and conditioning forces) and place it entirely within the realm of the physical.

2. **Give yourself 10 minutes of repetition of the same task and move on to a different task.**

3. **Give yourself the opportunity to experience between three to five different tasks.**

4. **Write about the experience in your journal.**

Journal: After you have completed the tasks, answer the following questions: What areas of the body did you notice becoming unnecessarily involved in the movement? What techniques, either mental or physical, did you use to change your orientation to the task to release tension in areas of your body? What happened to your breathing over the period? Did your relationship to time and space change or remain the same? How did you maintain a state of open attention throughout the repetition?

Exploration 50:
Discovering through the Concept of Neutral

Once you have finished your warmup, find your mask and lie on your back on the floor.

1. **Imagine that you have been frozen and placed into a holding tank for a long time.**

2. **The doors to the side of the tank fall open and you wake up and have no memory of who or what you are. You begin to discover everything for the first time–the use of your entire body, including your visual, auditory, kinesthetic, and other**

sensory systems. Try to stay in a mode of constant questioning. Try not to move from images of what you think is primitive movement; try to actually allow yourself to question and discover. Notice that in this mode of questioning, there are moments of physical discovery and related stillness that are similar to those of a small child who is exploring a new toy or an animal in a new environment.

3.   **Allow the exploration to continue until it comes to a natural conclusion.**

Journal: What were the causes of the moments of stillness? Using your sensory memory, describe the total experience including the moments of stillness. Use as many descriptive words or details as possible. Based on this and the previous exploration, write your own definition of neutral.

Exploration 51: The Elements

> To us, water is something to drink;
> to a fish, it is a house.
>
> *Unknown*

Crawford, Hurst and Lugering in their text on acting and style suggest that it is only when we are at one with "nature itself that we can fully control our muscles, tense them properly and relax them."[6] These explorations center on elements from nature. Exploring the potential physical life associated with images related to earth elements is one way to expand your imagination, as implied in the man's entering the forest in Figure 25. Through becoming the different elements, you learn to transform from one physical state to another. The explorations operate on two levels of awareness. The first is the discovery of the subjective experience of the image as it fuses with your imagination on a cellular level. The second is an objective or external awareness of the experience that is applied to a movement study.

---

[6]Jerry L. Crawford, Catherine Hurst, and Micahel Lugering, *Acting in Person and in Style* (London: Brown and Benchmark, 1995), 7.

Figure 25: Nature

Within the first stage, you explore the element as a general abstraction followed by a specific form of the element. For instance, a fire is a general image of an element, while a candle flame, forest fire, or camp fire are specific images that can be made even more specific by adding a set of adjectives. A candle flame, for example, can be a steady candle flame, a flickering candle flame, or a gentle candle flame. The specific images can then become metaphors for the psychological, emotional, and physical life of a character. With each element exploration, combine the technique of feel, fuse, and follow with nature images and your breath to discover the kinesthetic aspects of the element.

Beyond expanding the physical imagination, the elements also provide a means to focus on the dramatic principles of stage movement–*phrasing, transitions, intensity, stillness, and development*. *Phrasing* refers to a gesture or series of postures and gestures that are integral to each other. For example, consider two separate actions: walking into a room and sitting into a chair. A performance of these actions could maintain them as two distinct phrases–walking into a room and sitting in a chair. However, these two actions could be connected via a *transition*. A potential transition for these two actions might be a slight moment of pause prior to sitting down. Another possible transition could be brushing something off the chair prior to sitting down. Brushing the chair could be done with a slashing gesture of the hand or foot that would increase the *intensity* of the transition and thus the intensity of the phrase. Once sitting in the chair, the actor could be absolutely *still* or he/she could be very restless. The actor could *develop* the moment of sitting in the chair by working between stillness and activity by using a combination of flicking and dabbing gestures combined with stillness. The initial actions of walking into the room and sitting in a chair have been transformed by the use of the dramatic principles of phrasing, transitions, intensity, stillness, and development to create a short movement scenario with an implied story line. Although each exploration concentrates on one aspect of the dramatic principles, they all apply to each element.

Fire–Phrasing (Beginning, Middle, and End)

1. **Put on the mask. Begin to move slowly around the space and focus on the image of fire. Feel it coming from one of your emotional/chakra centers.** Feel the fire become transformed by

your breath and feel it move outward from this center until it fuses with every cell of your body. Feel the fire energy move through you as you begin to be part of the fire–a small, flickering flame that is in constant threat of being put out by water pouring down upon it; an enormous rush of fire as it is pushed forward by an updraft of air; a steady stream of fire that slowly but methodically burns through everything.

2. **Be aware of engaging your entire self as a unit, from head through arms, torso, legs, and feet.** What movement phrases continue to repeat themselves? Be aware that your physical movements have a place of initiation in the body where your breath and the image have fused, spaces of follow through, and a point of sending the energy beyond the body. The point of initiation, spaces of follow through, and point of sending are the beginning, middle, and end of a gesture.

3. **Once you have completed the exploration, revisit the experience. Catalogue your memory of the experience through sharing it with others or writing about it in your journal.** What parts of your body did you use? What was the phrasing of the energy moving through your body? What Laban's qualities would you use to describe different forms of fire? As you were working, what did you notice about your emotional engagement with different forms of fire?

4. **Write down the adjectives or verbs that flow from your unconscious.** For example, fire adjectives could be passionate, ardent, fervent, intense, irrational. Also write down verbs associated with the action state of fire, such as ignite, inflame, kindle, light, arouse, excite, incite, inspire, discharge, dismiss, terminate. The adjectives represent possible psychological traits of a character and influence a character's internal monologue. The verbs represent the style of a character's physical actions.

Life cycle of a fire (candle flame, forest fire, fireplace fire)

1. **Put on the mask. Using the same process described for the general fire exercise, explore the life cycle of a specific fire.** Begin by picking periods from the life of the fire and then unite them in a series of movements that transform from one movement into the next and have a beginning, middle, and end. For instance,

the initial lighting of the fire, the period during which it is burning (and any factors from the environment that might influence its burning) and, finally, the fire going out. Some questions to consider are related to phrasing and dramatic intensity: Does the fire start instantly or slowly, burn steadily or erratically? Is it put out quickly, or does it take a period of time for it to go out? Are there moments when the flame is burning with such intensity it is still?

2. **Create a name that metaphorically describes your fire piece and perform it for others. Get feedback and revise it to clarify the intentions of the piece as suggested in its name.**

Water–Transitions

1. **Begin as in the previous exercise but this time start with a definite form of water.** Some possibilities are a flowing river, bubbling brook, ocean waves, drop of water from a faucet, water on an umbrella or edge of a building, an ice cube, steam.

2. **Discover the sound associated with the form and incorporate it with the movement.**

3. **Once you feel you have developed one form completely, move onto another until you have a repertoire of movement based on several different forms of water. What Laban qualities are associated with each form of water?**

4. **Create a nonverbal story that uses phrases from each form of water.** What are the possible transitions between one water state and another? Do you find you use sequential or simultaneous movement to transition from one water phrase to another? Add sound or words.

5. **Share this story with others.**

6. **Repeat the process you used for fire of discovering adjectives and verbs for water.** Others have discovered the following adjectives: liquid, graceful, supple, adaptable, adjustable, flexible, accommodating, easygoing, changeable; and the following verbs: alter, transform, vary, adjust, amend, depart, deviate, diverge, clash.

Wind–Intensity

1. **After putting on the mask, walk around the room, being**

aware of the breath moving completely through your body, from your feet up through your legs, torso, arms, and head.

2. **Concentrating both internally and externally, and using the breath as the initiator of the image, allow your body to become a gentle breeze.** Are there sounds associated with the breeze?

3. **Now feel the breeze picking up intensity as it becomes a rushing wind moving quickly around you and pushing itself through and between your arms and legs.** You may find that the wind takes on the shape of a small whirlwind as it pushes and brushes across the earth. The whirlwind may build in intensity and then release back into the rushing wind. Feel the change in intensity of your own breath/energy as it moves with the action of your body.

4. **Allow the rushing wind to transform itself into a steady wind that keeps moving and moving, always pushing along the earth.** Again, feel the change in intensity of your own breath/energy as it moves with the action of your body. What Laban qualities are associated with different forms of wind? *Adjectives for wind might include sly, mischievous, playful, indirect; verbs might be stroke, whip, ruffle, push, fill, propel, surprise, extinguish.*

Earth–Stillness

1. **Put on the mask and make certain that you are released in all your joints from your ankles, knees, hips, spine, shoulders, elbows, wrist, and attachment of the head at the top of the spine.**

2. **Go from walking to a still posture and begin to explore the image of a mountain.** Be aware of the highest point on the mountain and its connection to the molten rock that lies below the surface of the Earth.

3. **Concentrate on the image, allowing yourself to respond to any mental or physical changes related to the image.** Can you answer the question, "Where is the center of stillness in my mountain?"

4. **Start to walk around the room, and as you move allow the mountain to be transformed into a boulder.** Is your boulder moving or still? Rolling? Bouncing? Majestic? Stable?

5. **Using your ability to focus on an image, transform the boulder to a small round rock.** Where is the physical center of the small round rock?
6. **Transform from a small round rock to a grain of sand.** Where is the physical center of the grain of sand?
7. If you are working with others, begin to move as a unit; as grains of sand blown by the wind. What is your experience of weight and flow as a grain of sand? Other possible earth elements to explore are mud, quicksand, clay, lava (molten and solidified) and an avalanche. What Laban qualities do you associate with different kinds of earth? Possible *earth adjectives: solid, earthy, concrete, material, substantial, fixed; possible verbs: support, defense, bolster, brace, sustain, advance, advocate, champion, promote.*

Vegetation–Development

1. **Take time to sit in a park, your back yard, the beach, or other areas with flowers, trees, grass.**
2. **Incorporate all your senses, focus on a particular tree, bush, flower.** Use your eyes to note the shape and varying textures of the plant. Begin to hear the sounds of the plant growing and responding to the wind, earth, and animals that live within its environment. Feel the smell of the plant move through your nose and down into your body as you breathe. Depending on where you are, reach out and touch the plant with different parts of your skin. How is the touch of the skin different when you reach with your hands, or your feet, or your arms?
3. **Extend your imagination into the cellular structure of the plant as if you were inside it, watching it take in carbon dioxide, water, and other nutrients as it makes its reach for the sun.** See the plant at various stages of its development, from a seed, to seedling, to the beginning development of a bloom or leaves, to full development, to slow decay, and disintegration back into the earth.
4. **Returning to the studio, explore the sensory images and experiences from your visit to the park. Try to focus on experiencing movements that are poetic or lyric abstractions of the actual plant and not illustrative or descriptive. Ask what it would feel like to be a tree rather than what does a**

tree look like.
5. Continue to explore them until you have evolved a movement score that poetically depicts the development of the plant from seedling to mature plant.

Essence

You can apply the experience gained from the elements explorations to learn to refine and edit your physical exploration of a text. Some people refer to this as finding the essence or underlying spirit of a text. Although the method described can be applied to any script, including the plays of Shakespeare, a good place to begin to practice the method is with a haiku poem.

Haiku poems are ideal because they combine images of nature and the body. For example, Ono no Komachi's poems:[7]

This night of no moon	So lonely I
There is no way to meet him.	My body is a floating weed
I rise in longing—	Severed at the roots
My breast pounds, a leaping flame,	Were there water under me.
My heart is consumed by fire.	

Each line of the above poems contain separate images of nature and the body that culminate to depict an emotional state. An interpretation of the emotional state of the first haiku could be longing and a potential interpretation for the second might be loneliness. Thus, working with a haiku provides an opportunity to work with nature elements and use them to convey the text's images in relationship to the text's underlying emotional state.

1. Pick a poem or section of script.
2. Read it several times and write down all the images that come to mind.
3. Physically explore the images, creating a movement phrase for each line of a poem.
4. Refine or reduce a movement phrase to discover its essence.

For example, you might create a movement interpretation of the first

---

[7]Poems by Ono no Komachi can be found in Carol Cosman, Joan Kaeefe, and Kathleen Weaver, eds. *The Penguin Book of Women Poets*, (London: Penguin Books, 1988), 74-77.

line of Ono no Komachi's poem "the night of no moon" that includes a gesture that reaches toward the night sky, a turn that includes the entire space, followed by embracing the torso by crossing the arms across the chest. One example of reducing this phrase to one essential gesture would be an upward gesture of the head followed by a partial turn of the body in which the hands grasp each other in front of the body. Another example of the essence of the initial phrase would be a huge turn in space with the hands outstretched as if embracing darkness, followed by a quick stop. There are many possible interpretations.

5. **Give yourself time to explore many different interpretations and from these choose those that reflect your artistic vision of the meaning of the text.**

6. **Once you have created the essential gestures for the separate lines of the poem or phrases of the text, repeat them in sequence.**

7. **Repeat them in combination with the text.** Are there additional adjustments, refinements or edits you need to make of the movement to express the desires of the poet or character or to increase the emotional connection to the movement?

Elements/Essence/Character

While exploring the elements, you have evolved adjectives and playable verbs for each element. Using adjectives and verbs from the different elements, explore the forms of gestures in Chapter 3–social, functional, emotional and motivational. For example, gestures derived from work with the fire element: What is a passionate shake of the hand? What is it to intensely get a drink of water? What is an ardent response to good news? What is a fervent appeal to a group of people? Try more than one solution for any of the gesture categories. From what emotional/chakra centers do these gestures emerge?

Exploring this movement language, a character or characters will begin to emerge. Who are they? What is important to them in the world? What do the characters want from life? What is their internal monologue? Is there a gesture that is typical of the character's movement signature?

Using this information, develop a physical vocabulary related to the character's internal life. How does the character walk, stand and wait, sit, pick up a telephone, run to meet someone, open a door for a friend, feed a pet, present themselves at a cocktail party, or interact with others? Consider the space as a large park in a city. Or a block or apartment building party. Once you have fully developed this character, go back and repeat the process with other elemental forms.

Entrances and Exits

Using the new levels of sensory awareness you have developed through the elemental explorations, create a performance piece for the following open action score. You can perform both in and out of the neutral mask. This score can be used with any environment, including an office, a train or bus station, a doctor's waiting room, etc. It can also be performed with a successive number of people. One person begins the exercise and leaves the room as the second person enters. Before the second person sits down, a third person enters and so on. As more people are included in the exploration, allow yourself to be influenced by their choices.

1. **Enter a room**

    sit down
    see someone else enter
    exit

2. **Repeat, this time picking a character with whom you have some experience from past scenes or production work.**

3. **Moving from the mental/physical embodiment of this character, be aware of incorporating the dramatic principles of phrasing, transitions, intensity, stillness, and development into your actions.** For example:

    Enter the room with the attitude of a gentle wind.
    Become a wind that is developing intensity.
    Build this intensity as you see someone else enter.
    Attempt to contain this intensity by becoming very still.
    Leave the room quickly as if you were a sudden thunderstorm.

Journal: Which elements were the easiest for you to work with? The most difficult? What did you discover about using Laban's effort qualities to transform your experience of different nature images? Using the adjectives related to each element as personality traits, write a character description using each.

ARCHETYPAL MASKS

Myth is the secret opening through which the inexhaustible energies of the cosmos pour into human cultural manifestations. It has always been the prime function of mythology and rite to supply the symbols that move the human spirit forward.

Joseph Campbell

Each community, from family to neighborhood, ethnic group, urban area, and nation, has a history and an associated set of stories. These stories take the form of written, verbal, and visual performance such as poems, novels, plays, television programs, and films. These narratives; combinations of fact and fiction, incorporate characters, themes, and images that are integral to preserving the life of the community. Incorporated into each story is a set of primordial, universal forces or images that psychologist Carl Jung called archetypes. These universal images are unconscious forces that are a result of thousands of years of human evolution. As Jung explains:

> These images are primordial images insofar as they are peculiar to whole species, and if they ever originated their origin must have coincided at least with the beginning of the species. They are the human quality of the human being, the specifically human form his activities take.[8]

Since Jung created his initial concept of the archetype, Joseph Campbell, in a series of books that includes *Hero of a Thousand Faces*, has illustrated the symbolic similarity of archetypes among the myths of various cultural groups. According to Campbell, a primary function of performance is to dramatize these archetypal forces. Edward Whitmont, a proponent of Campbell's ideas, writes, "The profoundly moving cathartic effect which dramatic art continues to exert through all the ages may well be based upon its presenting us with a mirror of soul and life in the theme of men and women against their destinies."[9] As performers we become the means by which these values and ideals achieve embodiment.

---

[8]Carl Jung, *Archetypes of the Collective Unconscious* (New York: Pantheon Books, 1959), 153.
[9]Edward Whitmont in Stephen Larsen, *The Mythic Imagination* (New York: Bantam Books, 1990), 29.

This section continues to investigate the mask as an extension of an internal energy state through exploring the physical dimensions of archetypes. You begin this process by discovering the specific archetypes that influence your life. The archetypal mask explorations continue with the psychophysical dimensions of an archetype, and finally, the archetypal influences on the personality of characters.

Below is a set of twelve archetypes.[10] Each represents a potential aspect of a personality, in as much as the influence of any archetype can be dominant for a period of time, only to be replaced by another. (Similarly, people or characters are influenced not by any single archetype, but by a combination of two or more.) The archetype also blends positive and negative traits. In any situation, the positive or negative aspect of Jung's shadow side of the archetype can influence behavior. Often we prefer to ignore this negative side; what Stanislavski referred to as the "darker" side of nature. It feels safer to perform only the positive side of characters. It is nevertheless important to appreciate the complexity of individual personality and to remember "that hidden behind these phenomena there is beauty, just as in loveliness there is unloveliness. What is truly beautiful has nothing to fear from disfigurement. Indeed, disfigurement often emphasizes and sets off beauty in higher relief."[11] Knowledge of the negative or shadow side of an archetype helps you to appreciate a character's internal obstacles. This knowledge can be an aide to your development of the specific psychological and physical nature of a character.

The short description of each of the twelve archetypes includes aspects of their positive and negative sides and images that represent each. As you read through the descriptions, expand upon them with images from your experience. Two questions to answer are, "What television, film or stage characters would you place in each? What has been the primary archetype of the characters you have played?"

The Twelve Archetypes

Innocent Innocents have completely accepted the values of the group

---

[10]Separate theorists concentrate on distinct sets of archetypes. Those listed here are based on Carol Pearson's, *Awakening the Heroes Within* (San Francisco: Harper, 1991).

[11]Stanislavski, *An Actor Prepares*, 92.

to which they are born. This does not mean innocents are always in a loving and caring environment, only that they accepted the world as experienced without question. This archetype represents people who wear and believe without question the social masks of the group to which they were born. The desire of the innocent is to remain in safety, while the greatest fear is abandonment. *Potential images associated with the archetype*: Newborns of any kind–plant, animal, or human. *Shadow side*: Innocents are often unwilling to accept change in the world, as new experience represents a dissolution of the order of the mask. This may cause them unwittingly to hurt themselves by setting limits to self-growth and inner knowing. This can also be harmful for others, as the innocent refuses to acknowledge difference.

Potential images of shadow side: Objects that are difficult to move, such as a large boulder.

Orphan Orphans respond to society with a level of awareness about different social groups but do not know to which group they belong. Thus, orphans are in a state of conflict, as their lack of belonging to a particular group conflicts with their desire to belong to a group. They fear they will be exploited or victimized by any group to which they belong.

Potential images: An isolated plant, animal, rock or person.

Shadow side: There is a tendency to play the perpetual victim, with a consequent lack of self-responsibility and a tendency to blame others for the circumstances of life.

Potential image of shadow side: A hermit, a homeless person, a refugee.

Warrior This archetype maintains strong boundaries. These characters pursue a desire to serve the community as protector. The desire of warriors is to win and succeed, usually by overcoming a set of obstacles. The warrior's greatest fear is displaying any appearance of weakness or loss of power.

Potential images: Armor, walls, animals of size.

Shadow side: This is the villain who uses the ability to dominate others for personal gain. This domination can include mental and emotional domination.

Potential images of shadow side: All of the above, but in an asymmetrical as opposed to symmetrical face and body. Shakespeare's Richard III is a good example.

Caregiver This is a parent figure who has a love of nature. She/he is Venus, the lover of beauty, receptive, representing a nurturing balance of emotions. The chief desire of the caregiver is to make a difference in the world through helping others. A modern-day version of the caregiver is Mother Theresa. The biggest fear is becoming ruled by his/her own selfishness.

Potential images: Those aspects of nature such as caves, coves, and hidden places that provide refuge, a tree of life.

Shadow side: This is the suffering martyr, whose means of controlling people involves manipulating the feelings of others through guilt.

Potential images: Same as above, but with a continually nagging sound in the background–a quiet pond with a constant drip.

Seeker Seekers are way-showers and wanderers who search life's pathways both in self and the world. There is a constant desire for enlightened transformation and a desire to brave the unknown. Seekers strongly believe in the perfectability of existence and are always searching for a better way of life. A seeker's greatest fear is becoming trapped in the culturally normative.

Potential images: Natural spaces that represent journeys or places of emotional retreat including deserts, woods, oceans, outer space.

Shadow side: This is the perfectionist who can never have the house that is tidy enough, the paper that is well enough written, etc.

Potential image: A person who is obsessive about neatness, organization, dress, etc.

Destroyer Destroyers do away with one situation and replace it with another. They transform themselves and their environment. This personality is closely allied with death and rebirth. Thus, fulfillment for a destroyer is found in those moments of growth and metamorphosis. Destroyers become bored with a routine life, as it feels to them like stagnation.

Potential images: Natural disasters–forest fires, typhoons, whirl-winds, tidal waves.

Shadow side: This is the addictive side of a personality which can lead to self-destruction through undermining relationships, careers, etc.

Potential images: Drug addicts, crisis-oriented people, Jobba the Hut from Star Wars.

Lover The lover archetype expresses a multifaceted passion for all of life's experiences. Lovers embody the gift of perception, extended vision, strength of insight, and intuition caused by the marriage of the masculine and feminine within the self. The aspiration of the lover is the bliss to be found in unity with another. The greatest fear is loss of love and disconnection from the other.

Potential images: Flowers in various stages–buds, unfolding, full bloom.

Shadow side: The use of sexuality to gain emotional control over others for either short- or long-term personal fulfillment.

Potential images: Hidden thorns on a rose bush.

Creator This is someone always focusing on the awakening of new life. Creators need to be involved in the act of conceiving something new. This can be a piece of art, a new company, a new invention, or a new life. The creator's greatest fear is lack of imagination.

Potential image: Birth.

Shadow side: Creation run amuck. The personality that destroys in the act of creation, as in the development of too much of anything–people, technology, food, etc.

Potential image: Rapid technological change, a new word processing program every week.

Ruler This is the mediator, adjuster, or arbitrator who has a deep love of simplicity, fairness, and balance. A ruler feels responsible for creating a life or a government that is harmonious and prosperous. A ruler fears those forces within self, nature, or the group that create chaos.

Potential image: A man or woman standing in perfect symmetry.

Shadow side: This is the unreasonable dictator who indulges his/her whims at the expense of other people.

Potential images: The Mouse King from *The Nutcracker.*

Magician This is one who has an artful sense of flexibility in all aspects of communication and the ability to transform a moment from negative to positive. The intent of the magician is to move reality from lesser to better states. The magician fears that his or her personal power will not be enough to overcome any evil.

Potential images: Constant transformation from one energy construct to another, movement from animal to people, people to inanimate objects, morphs, etc.

Shadow side: The opposite of working for benefit of self or other by lessening options and diminishing what might be possible.
Potential images: Same as the above but used to control or gain power over others.

Sage This is the spiritual teacher who is gifted at imparting information or inspiring others, helping them to make ideas tangible. A teacher, the sage is a sleuth who asks questions about the nature of existence and then imparts the answers to students. The sage's wish is to promote truth and understanding in the population. Fear for the sage rests with the potential that he/she has not found the path to wisdom.

Potential images: Old people, animals, places, or things.

Shadow side: This is a heartless rational judge of knowledge or people.

Potential images: Same as above but frozen in an unyielding attitude.

Fool This personality is filled with mirth, humor, and sexual appetite. Theatrical comic characters are good examples. The fool takes many forms, the wise fools and buffoons of Shakespeare, the outrageous and clumsy fools of farce, and the modern fools of the theatre of the absurd. As an archetypal personality, the fool has been explained as follows:

> The inner fool is never far away from us. . . .The Fool is the aspect of the inner child that knows how to play, to be sensual and in the body. It is at the root of our basic sense of vitality and aliveness, which expresses itself as a primitive, childlike, spontaneous, playful creativity.[12]

The joy of the fool is in pleasure and aliveness; the fear is that pleasure will be taken away.

Potential images: People's actions that make us smile, laugh, guffaw, snicker, chuckle, grin, smirk, leer, sneer. Charlie Chaplin. Bill Irwin.

Shadow side: This is someone entirely defined by lusts and other bodily urges without any self-control.

Potential images: A glass of wine that constantly replenishes itself.

---

[12]Pearson, 221.

Exploration 52: Archetypal Inventory

Mythic images] are pictures that involve us both physiologically in our bodily reactions to them and spiritually in our higher thoughts about them. When a person is aware of living mythically, she or he is experiencing life intensively and reflectively.

David Feinstein and Stanley Krippner

This exercise helps you to better understand the myths and related archetypes that influence your life through considering those incorporated into your life in the past. For your inventory, please answer the following questions:

1. What are the primary stories you remember from your childhood? They can be fairy tales or stories that were read to you often or a book you read for school. Once you have identified the story or stories, describe in detail the personality of the primary characters. Using Laban's terms, describe how you imagine the characters moving. If appropriate, what is a metaphor that you would apply to the character? What are the underlying themes associated with the role of this character and the goals the character is seeking to attain?

2. During your life, have you had real or fictional characters who were heroes for you? Potential examples could come from the television or film industry, novels, and politics. Describe the hero using the same information that you used in question one.

3. What is your family's history? Are there special people or stories that seem central to the family's view of themselves in the world?

4. What is your personal explanation for how the world functions? Do you believe in the Bible, the Koran, karma, a pantheon of gods, or alien beings? Do you have any daily or seasonal rituals associated with this set of beliefs?

5. Note that all these questions could be asked for a particular character.

6. Watch television for two or three hours, channel surfing if possible, and describe the characters you see from different kinds of television programs (talk shows, game shows, newscasts, movies, dramas, situation comedies, etc.). What archetypes are the most

common? What do you rarely see represented? Note the differ-ences in physical representation (you can use Laban description here) of different archetypes.

Exploration 53: Archetypal Masks

This exploration is one way to discover the psychological and physical life of both sides of each archetype. It requires that you maintain a state of relaxed concentration to allow the energy of the image to flow through your body. Choose an archetype to work with, move to some part of the room and assume a position, either lying, sitting, or stand-ing. With your internal eye, review the archetype you want to investi-gate. What are its primary attributes? What are some potential images associated with the archetype?

1. **Once you have taken time to mentally explore the archetype, bring yourself to a neutral or open state.** As in previous explo-rations, place the image in the emotional/chakra center to which your intuitive self suggests it belongs. With each inward breath, begin to feel the breath/energy of the image. Fuse your con-sciousness with the image. Follow each exhalation of breath as the energy of the image moves from the emotional center outward until it inhabits all cells of your body, from the soles of your feet to the palms of your hands and the top of your head. Your entire self becomes a conduit for the archetypal image.

2. **Filled with the energy of the image, start to move around the room as the archetype.** An internal monologue may instantly begin to form–do not be afraid to express it verbally. In fact, the physical personality of the archetype becomes a more rooted and powerful experience if you verbally express these thoughts. From the mind of the archetype, answer the following questions: What is my primary motivation in the world? What is it I need most from other people? What gives me the greatest joy? The great-est pain? What is my most treasured memory?

3. **Once you feel you have thoroughly explored the archetype, stop, gently shake out all parts of your body, and return to neutral.** Give yourself the opportunity to explore all the arche-

types from their positive aspects.

4. **Repeat the exploration from the shadow side of the archetype.** Which chakras dominate each aspect of the archetype?

5. **Apply physical vocabulary for the archetypal character you have discovered to the following action score.**

During the working session you will discover that the image evolves and changes. Do not try to prevent it. It is only necessary to stay kinesthetically connected to the energy of the image through the use of the breath.

Journal: Describe each archetype.

Open Action Score

The following physical score could apply to a variety of situations that respond to the W questions of *who, where, when, what,* and *why.* Allow the archetype you are working with to determine the who of the character; what he/she wants to accomplish and why. A warrior archetype might be a corporate executive of a large computer firm involved in a takeover of a media company. Use the who as the basis for selecting the when (time period) and where (location). Using the previous illustration of the corporate executive, the time period would be contemporary and the location could be a New York City office. Determine a reason or why of the particular media take over. Possible reasons for why might be–a desire for power, to get revenge, to impress a significant other. Take your time selecting, disregarding, and creating new physical possibilities for each of the five W questions. Perform the scenario for others.

An empty space with block and chair

Walk into space.

Sit on chair.

Move to block.

Place hand on block.

Stand.

Place hand on head.

Start toward stage left.......stop.

Turn and return to chair.

Place hand on back of chair.

Turn.............................. look around space.

Start to leave....stop.

Sit.

Look around space.

Journal: Describe your character and related scenario.

Exploration 54: Yin/Yang Energy

Repeat Exploration 53. This time use the archetype to discover its yin qualities (as receptacle of energy) or its yang qualities (as an external producer of energy). Yin and yang are Chinese theories of the body that are sometimes used by western theorists as feminine and masculine. However, in the Taoist system from which they were evolved, they do not specifically signify gender. Instead, they concentrate on style and form of energy. Aspects of yin and yang energy can function in three categories:

> *use of space*
> *quality of movement*
> *method of communication.*

Use of space refers to the size of your bubble. How much space do you command? What is the shape of the bubble? Cross-culturally, theatrical depictions of masculinity in the physical life of characters often show masculine characters projecting themselves into the world with a very large bubble. The opposite is true of classic portrayals of femininity, in which the bubble is smaller. In our contemporary culture, female characters in the classical drama, such as Medea and others who have large bubbles, are often seen as exhibiting male traits. The opposite is true of men who have small bubbles–the scholars of Shakespeare's plays, for example, are often men who wished they had a large bubble, but do not have the personal qualities to project it.

Another aspect of yin and yang energy qualities is *quality of movement.* Both exhibit Laban energy qualities: Yang energy qualities are strong, sudden, bound, and direct; Yin energy qualities are light, sustained, free, and indirect.

The final aspect is *communicational style*. A yang personality is most often described as goal centered. Goal-centered personalities concentrate on quickly and directly accomplishing tasks that they feel will be good for them and their communities. A yin or process style of communication is less direct. Yin personalities try to accomplish the same task but take the same information and reflect on it before taking action.

As you work with the archetypes, observe how focusing on aspects of yin and yang changes the movement quality of different archetypes. What kind of warrior is a receptacle of energy? What kind of caregiver also externalizes energy? A fool who is the receiver of the energy put out by others? A fool who is a source of externalized energy?

During the twentieth century, cross-gender productions of Shakespeare's play challenged previous conceptions of gender.[13] These challenges reflect changing norms and the evolution of relationships between men and women. Your task is to discover the complexity of the character, not to recreate a cultural or dramatic stereotype. Thus, as you work with the opposites of big and small bubbles, energy qualities, or forms of communication, remember that masculine/feminine designations are not binaries; instead, they form a continuum. Staying focused on the continuum rather than the opposition will help you to discover unique physical characters and personalities.

Journal: Describe those people, from personal experience or from the stage and media, who have been gender models for you. What combination of yin and yang did they display in their movement vocabulary? What combination of yin and yang do you incorporate in your movement vocabulary? How did using the concepts of yin and yang change the personality of an archetype you worked with?

---

[13]Peter Lichtenfel's cross-gender production of Romeo and Juliet at the Main Theatre University of California, Davis, 1998 is one example.

Exploration 55: Activating the Imagination

The imagination, according to Stanislavski, is a pivotal component of the actor's craft. "An actor's imagination can draw to itself the life of another person, adapt it, discover mutual and exciting qualities and features."[14] The actor's artistic imagination unites his/her life, experience, and creativity with the inner world of dreams, a world in which:

> We can use our inner eye to see all sorts of visual images, living creatures, human faces, their features, landscapes, the material world of objects, settings, and so forth. With our inner ear we can hear all sorts of melodies, voices, intonations, and so forth. We can feel things in the imagination at the prompting of our sensation and emotion memory.[15]

Stanislavski divided the imagination into two types, *passive* and *active*. In a state of *passive imagination*, the actor is a watcher who observes the details of a setting but does not necessarily interact with it. The actor is literally setting the stage in his/her imagination. In a state of *active imagination*, the actor's imagination actively engages in playing a role within the imagined environment. Each form of imagination–passive and active–necessitates that the actor focus on a set of mental and related sensory images. This requires, on the part of the actor, the ability to concentrate on a set of images for an extended period of time as one might when day dreaming. Carl Jung developed a technique that expands the active imagination by using a passive state similar to day dreaming.

Jung and his followers believe the unconscious to be the realm of the archetype or, as Jung also referred to it, primordial images. Activating the imagination is a simple process in which you engage in a dialogue with images from a state of relaxed concentration. The participation in the imagined event moves the experience from the realm of pure fantasy to what Stanislavski called *active imagination*. This state

---

[14]Constantin Stanslavski. *Creating a Role*, trans. Elizabeth Reynolds Hapgood (New York: Routledge/Theatre Arts, 1989), 19.

[15]Stanislavski, *Creating a Role*, 20.

is the space in which the conscious and unconscious minds meet in a purely symbolic experience of images. When you experience the images, you also experience parts of yourself related to the images. The experience of the symbol is simultaneously the experience of the complex archetype that the symbol represents. For example: a lamb could symbolize the innocent archetype, a staff could symbolize a sage, and a broom could symbolize caregiver.

The process is in three steps: inviting the unconscious, dialoging the experience, and creating a performance based on the experience. Within the scope of this exploration, we are focusing on an actor's rather than a character's archetypal journey. The same process can be used, however, in work with a specific character and script, as discussed in chapter 5.

The Steps

1. **Invite the unconscious.** Provide yourself with a quiet working space in which you can lie or sit and focus on your breath. Maintain this focus until you feel a state of internal quiet. From this state, begin to place yourself in a specific environment; a city park, the redwoods, an ocean beach, or other location. Note the environment in detail, including the color and shape of different parts of it, the smells, quality of light, the sounds associated with it. Notice a path or method, such as a specific mode of transportation, that allows you to navigate through this environment. While traveling on this path, note the changes in the path as you observe it from different positions. You are stopped by someone or something that represents a challenge. Fulfill the requirements of the challenge and continue on the path. Before you complete your journey, you will be stopped two other times. In each case, fulfill the requirements of the challenge. On completing the final challenge, allow yourself to find your final destination.

2. **Dialogue and experience. Write down a detailed description of your experience. From this, create an action score that represents the story of the experience.**

3. **Use the score to create a short movement sketch that tells the story of your journey.**

Journal: This exploration is a good way to begin to discover and extend the parameters of your imagination. Thus, you should write a description of your experience for future reference. Some questions to consider are: What aspects of creating an imaginary world were easy for you? Difficult? For instance, did you find you could see the shapes of things but not the color? Could hear the sounds, but had no awareness of smell? Could concentrate on the environment, but had a difficult time extending your imagination toward a person? Did you find your imagination had a tendency to meet people, animals, objects or a combination of all three as part of the journey?

CHECKLIST OF POINTS TO REMEMBER

This chapter's explorations provided an opportunity to begin to apply the material from the first three chapters to work with masks and texts. The self mask explorations gave you an opportunity to discover more about your unique perspective as an artist. The neutral mask explorations helped to expand your ability to explore neutral and provided additional work in using imagery and metaphor. The archetypal mask explorations provided a method for beginning to consider character types.

Exploration

- Masks are a means to free your creative impulse.
- Understanding the experience of neutral is a lifelong process.
- Following an impulse reveals your unconscious mind.

  The principles of dramatic movement are phrasing, transitions, intensity, stillness, and development.

Breath

- Breath is at the center of stillness.
- Breath is the link between image and action.

Imagery

- Knowing the masks you wear helps you to understand the masks of characters you are playing.
- Archetypes are universal forces that individually and in combination influence behavior.
- Characters have real desires and needs they are trying to keep hidden under a carefully constructed mask.
- The image of neutral is an entrance into and an exit from the physical/emotional world of the character.

Ti Jean and His Brothers Directed by Yvonne Brewster,
Christopher Peak as the Devil

CHAPTER FIVE

PERFORMING AN IDENTITY: CREATING A CHARACTER

An actor must be constantly filling the storehouse of his memory by studying, reading, observing, traveling, keeping in touch with current social, religious, political and other forms of life.

Constantin Stanislavski

Your career as an actor will integrate diverse venues, from stage to television, and a variety of performance styles, from classical to realism to postmodernism. Each venue requires you to generate an internal set of images from which to enact a character. It is this development of a world of inner images that Stanislavski admonishes should be at the center of your preparation for a role: "Forget entirely about the feelings and put all your attention on the inner images. Study them as carefully and describe them as fully, as penetratingly and vividly as you can."[1] Thus far, the application section of the text has focused on your ability to use imagery to explore essence and archetype to create a character. You explored these characters further through an action score. The goal of this chapter is to provide you with a process of creating a character from a written text.

Creating a character is, according to Stanislavski, a three-stage process. It includes a period of study or script analysis, a period of physical embodiment, and a period of emotional engagement. Although each director will have a unique approach to rehearsal, these stages will often overlap and influence each other during the rehearsal process. Regardless, each rehearsal process requires you to combine research on the world of the play with personal experience and your imagination.

---

[1]Stanislavski, *Building A Character,*125.

TEXT ANALYSIS (A PERIOD OF STUDY)

Each script and related production represents a complex system of interrelated communities, with disparate viewpoints that are brought to life on stage through the dramatic imagination of actors, directors, and designers. The world they bring to life is often referred to as the 'world of the play.' Within this world, social groups interact with each other to act out their belief systems, governmental structures, forms of non-organic structures, aesthetic ideals, and modes of communication. The interactions of these elements are expressed physically in the actual movement vocabulary of the social group; from methods of greeting one another to forms of combat. A character's actions are related, therefore, to a specific community's world view, which is influenced by the geographic environment, from rural to urban, from desert to jungle; the manner in which their external environment is internalized as religious beliefs (this has a big influence on which parts of the world have spiritual power; the cathedral or the forest, etc.). All of the latter influence the evolution and development of social groups within a community. This category includes the form of government, the internal dynamics of the family, and the daily physical tasks of the individual.

Regardless of historical period or style, the first step in a text analysis is to establish or define the world of the play. Facts from the script include—location of the story, gender, age, and occupation of the characters, and the event that has brought these characters together. Directors generally describe their interpretation of the parameters of the play's world to the design team. Costume, set, sound, and light designers define the visual dimension of the director's interpretation. Thus, the world of the play is created by combining facts derived from the script with the collaborative imagination of the director, designers, and, finally, actors. The rehearsal process and final production is an ongoing negotiation of the play as written by the playwright, conceived of by the director, and understood by the designers and actors. Often, the world of the play is the topic of the first rehearsal, in which the director, dramaturg, designers, and actors discuss their interpretation of the script's world and the characters that inhabit it.

Whether the script is set in New York City or in historic London, the script's context can be researched for its physical and aesthetic aspects by examining associated art forms. These include paintings, dance, music, literature, and architecture. In the "Analysis" section of Chapter 3 you learned a method of observation that can be applied to these materials. Each form provides information for your imagination on possible clothing styles, body stances, and movement vocabulary. Additionally, in any society there are ritualized physical movements between different social groups according to sex, age, ethnicity, and gender. These may vary within the society between social contexts. From the above sources, you can glean greetings, physical stances, gestural language of verbal and nonverbal communication styles, and the use of spatial distance.

The physical relationships of the script's characters are further defined in rituals that take place at fixed times, within cycles of that society based on climate (fall/winter/spring/summer or wet/dry); on a specific historical event of the community; on celebrations associated with the life cycle (birth, puberty, marriage, death, and potentially others). Information on all of the above can be gathered from acting style texts, books on social manners, biographical material from the period, journals, collected letters, and historical accounts.

The information you collect on the play's world serves as the basis from which you can ask more detailed questions. Use the questions in this section as a guide to create a description of the world of the play, its basic cultural parameters, and, therefore, its movement vocabulary. Different plays focus on different thematic material; concentrate on those questions relevant to the play's major themes. For example, if you are playing Joyce or Marlene in Caryl Churchill's play *Top Girls*, you would want to focus on the political life in England in the 1980s and Margaret Thatcher's role in it. You would also want to understand the historical figures of the restaurant scene and the office environment of the 1980s. If you were to play one of the brothers in Sam Shepherd's *True West*, it would be helpful to understand the arid environment in which the play is set, as well as family dynamics in contemporary America.

Exploration 56: World of the Play

The following chart is used to discover the play's physical style. You begin by identifying the particular aspects of the world of the play followed by considering this world from the standpoint of your character. An initial analysis of *Hamlet* would define the historical time period, location and the social, religious, and aesthetic world view. A second level of analysis would incorporate the character you are playing. For instance, if you were playing the grave digger in *Hamlet*, you would particularize the initial analysis by responding to the questions as a peasant within the social hierarchy. You would have a very different set of answers if you were playing Ophelia or Horatio.

1. **What is the play's physical environment and climate?** Large urban area, suburban community, unpopulated desert, unpopulated rain forest, a community based on agriculture.

2. **Method people use to obtain the necessities:** Community consists primarily of farmers, ranchers, herders, hunters, gatherers of food from the surrounding environment, merchants, some combination of these.

    Housing: Tent, mud hut, large stone buildings, small individual dwellings, caves, leaf-covered houses?

    Clothing: Very little, layers of animal skins, clothes made of fabric? What part of the body is covered or uncovered? What part of the body is accentuated or not accentuated?

3. **What is the status and governing structure of the play's world?** Homogeneous, with all adults sharing equally in the decision-making process? Tribal, organized in family categories? Chiefdoms, in which one person from one family is considered the final decision maker for all other familial groups? City-states or large groups of people, organized by a system of government based on either control of one group over another or some method of participatory government (not necessarily one man one vote), in which the nuclear or extended family is the building block for the rest of society?

4. **The different groups represented in the play:** What is the basic family unit–or, who lives together (nuclear family, extended

family, extended kin system)? What groups exist within this soci-ety–landowners and peasants; royalty, merchants, and peasants; merchants, religious leaders, teachers, etc?

Relationship between men and women: Equal, or one or other dominates?

Relationship between old and young: Equal or, one or other dom-inates? When is one considered an adult male or female? The role of each age-related group?

Relationship between peer groups: Sibling rivalry? Groups of similar generation have relationships based on attendance at a par-ticular school, participation in specific organization, sport, etc.?

5. **What is the religious system or systems inherent in the play?** A religion based on a god/goddess who is a part of or separate from nature? A religion based on one god/goddess or many gods and goddesses; gods who are male or female or both; religion asso-ciated with ancestors or not associated with ancestors? The forces of the world are divided into good and evil; the forces of the world are a constant interplay of evil becoming good and the reverse? What is the human relationship to the god?

Rituals: When do they take place, based on the history of the community, cycles associated with climate, cycles associated with the life cycle, cycles associated with political or historical events, cycles associated with the economy?

6. **What are the primary forms of entertainment/recreation?** Always associated with a ritual occasion, separate from religious rites, take place among all groups of society? Takes place indoors, outdoors, in some special location? Associated with specific places within the community? With sports?

7. **What are the aesthetic values?** What artistic activities are pur-sued and by whom (painting, music, singing, dances, poetry)? What are the time values associated with art?—Primarily located in the past (including mythological time), in the present, in the future? What form of art is important?—Visual, auditory, written? On what occasions would we most likely find this artistic form expressed? Is the visual art representational or nonrepresenta-tional? What is the role of the verbal/written expression? Is it metered or otherwise? What are the poetic forms they rely on?

- **What is the form of the music?** Is it based primarily in solo voice or solo instrument or small ensembles of either? Is it based in an even or uneven meter? Does it rely on an interrelationship between the instruments, and what is that relationship if it does? Is it electronic?
- **What are the values associated with dance?** Do they value large or small movements? Restricted or nonrestricted? Movements that follow a straight line or a curved path? Movements that use the entire body or only a portion in relationship to the other parts? Do people dance together in groups, separately, in some form of combination?
- **What is the relation of aesthetic values/performance styles to religious and social belief systems of a character?** While answering the relevant questions concerning the play's world, you will begin to identify how the character you are playing conforms, adapts, and adjusts to this world. What is his/her position in it? How does he/she go about either maintaining or trying to change this position? Are there people who oppose the character's desires? What would be the worst event that could happen? What would be maintaining the status quo for the character? What would be the character's wildest dream come true?

Once you have answered the questions, return to Activating the Imagination in chapter 4. Use the first stage of this exploration to create detailed mental images of the character's environment. Once you have established the play's world in your imagination, begin to search for sensory images to enhance the mental images. Find costume pieces to help you get the feel of the clothing. Find local groups who are familiar with the music and dance styles and take classes. Visit potential recreational sites where you might find food associated with the script's community. Each of the above will provide a variety of experiences that will add sensory depth to your understanding of the character's world. The combination of mental and sensory images will produce an inner stream of images that represents your interpretation of the character's ambitions, thoughts, and feelings. This inner vision/image/knowledge becomes the beginning of developing a through line of action for your performance.

Journal: As part of your development as an actor, you will want to find some way of documenting the rehearsal. One format for keeping a record is to xerox the script and place it in a three-ring binder with additional pages, either next to each scene/act, or at the end of the script.

SELF, ACTOR, CHARACTER
(A PERIOD OF PHYSICAL EMBODIMENT)

Stanislavski advises actors that they must work with the desires of playwrights and directors but, ultimately the challenge is to discover the complex relationship between themselves and the character:

> An actor can subject himself to the wishes and indication of a playwright or a director and execute them mechanically, but to experience his role he must use his own living desires, engendered and worked over by himself, and he must exercise his own will, not that of another. The director and the playwright can suggest their wishes to the actor, but these wishes must then be reincarnated in the actor's own nature so that he becomes completely possessed by them. For these desires to become living, creative desires on the stage, embodied in the actions of the actor, they must become part of his very self.[2]

This integration of self (actor) and other (character) is a complex process that combines an awareness of your body with the potential physical life of a character. Thus far, you have increased your awareness of your nonverbal language and associated internal images. You have also learned methods of exploring and transforming images though the use of concentration, breath, and the intention of your imagination. This combination of self-knowledge and craft can now be applied to the development of a character.

In creating the general world of the character, you have already completed the first level of analysis. The second step is to read the script, noting the character's specific given circumstances; the who, what, when, and where of age, occupation, family background. Next, read the script and note all the phrases and words that pertain to the character–either said by him/her or by someone else. These phrases provide potential metaphors for movement explorations. For example, a character described as "gentle as a buttercup" can be investigated

---

[2]Stanisalvski, *Creating A Role*, 50.

using the direct image of a buttercup or physical qualities associated with a buttercup, such as light and free. Using the clue words as a base, expand upon the list to incorporate other words with related meanings. From this, write a character biography. Include in this biography answers to following questions. Where was the character born? Who were his/her parents? Where did he/she go to elementary, secondary school or higher education? Who were the significant people in his/her life as a child? As an adult? How does the character describe him/herself physically? What is his/her occupation? What religious system does the character believe in? How does the character feel about the current circumstances of his/her life? Who would the character turn to in time of trouble? Who would the character help if they were in trouble? This can seem like a redundant step, but the act of writing helps to solidify the information in your imagination.

An analysis also needs to consider you, the actor, as a person with a particular personal history and life experience. This personal awareness becomes the center for your understanding the potential physical challenges this character creates for you as an actor. Some of this may have to do with the character's physical personality. You may be playing a character who is physically aggressive with others. In contrast, you are as an individual passive rather than aggressive in your physical interactions. Or the character you are playing may demand you learn a specific skill. For example, it may be necessary for you to know how to juggle, do a somersault, dance a jig, etc.

The following exploration asks you to take a self-reflexive stance concerning yourself as an individual and a character. As you read it, you should consider yourself an artist with a personal history who has learned, through training, a process of creating a character. The chart has been created to help you understand the relationship between your personal history including your movement signature and yourself as a character. The answers provide the information necessary to unite your personal awareness with your technical skills as an actor. Or, as Stanislavski describes the process: "You must still go on developing, correcting, tuning your bodies until every part of them will respond to the complete task of presenting in external form your invisible feelings."[3]

---

[3]Qtd. in Crawford, Hurst and Lugering, *Acting in Person and In Style* (New York: Brown and Benchmark, 1995), 7.

Exploration 57: Self, Actor, Character

The following chart has been designed to be used in conjunction with an analysis of self as discussed in Chapter 1 and Exploration 56: World of the Play. The process you use to answer the questions begins with reading through the questions and coming up with physical answers for both yourself and your character. As you find answers for each question, you will be discovering the extent to which the character you are playing shares your movement vocabulary.

Once you have answered the questions in the following chart start to create the movement signature for the character by exploring potential physical stances, methods of locomotion, and gestures. The initial process for embodying the movement signature of a character is similar to discovering and exploring dynamic alignment. It begins with placing the breath in the pelvis and sending it out through the character's primary emotional centers. Follow the placement of the breath while discovering and centering the character's pelvis. Allow the spine to extend and lengthen to find its connections with the grounding energy of the legs and the balance that comes from the placement of the head. Finally, become aware of the possibilities for communication of the hands and voice. Assembling the physical character in this fashion attunes imagination with dynamic alignment.

1. **Basic Stance:** These questions concern you and your character's basic physical posture in the world.

    What is your (character's) width of stance?
    Are your (character's) feet turned in, out, or forward?
    Where is your (character's) weight held? In pelvis, chest, head?
    What is your (character's) relationship of head to chest?
    Relationship of arms to legs?
    What are some of your (character's) conventional hand positions?
    What is the outline of your (character's) silhouette? Standing? Sitting? Lying?

2. **Social Space:** These questions concern the social mask and interactions with others.

    What size is your (character's) personal bubble?

How does the size of your (character's) bubble change in different social situations?

What is the physical expression of your (character's) status in the world?

How do you (character) greet people? Embrace people?

What is your (character's) expression of yin and yang in your interaction with others?

3. **Emotional Self:** This set of questions begins to establish the difference between you and your character's internal response to the world and how this response is expressed in gesture.

What effort qualities do you (character) use to express yourself?

What is your (character's) primary emotional center (chakra)?

How do you (character) channel energy from the center through your body?

How do you (character) impose will? Restrain will? Join will?

What physical attributes of another attract you (character)?

How do you (character) indicate physical interest in another?

How do you (character) flirt?

How do you (character) physically control obsessions? Or give in to physical desire?

How do you (character) respond to touching? And with whom?

How do you (character) initiate touching? And with whom?

How do you (character) act upon urgency?

How do you (character) engage in positions of power or dominance?

How do you (character) react to situations of fear, loss of control, terror?

How do you (character) physically protect yourself?

4. **Social Self:** This last set of questions concerns the variety of roles or masks with which you and your character interact with the world.

What freedoms does the social mask allow you (character) physically?

Are there different social masks for different situations (self and character)?

How is the information on stance, social space and emotional self transformed with different social masks (self and character)?

What archetypes do you (character) play in similar contexts or situations?

If you were to describe yourself (character) as a metaphor, what would it be?

Journal: On completing this exercise write a physical description of the character's movement signature. Compare it to your movement signature. How are they different? The same? What are the challenges for you? What techniques do you know that will help you unite the two? What movement skills might you have to learn?

Exploration 58: Scoring a Role

The actor must learn how to compose a score of lively physical and psychological objectives; to shape his whole score into one all-embracing supreme objective; to strive toward its attainment. Taken all together the superobjective (desire), through action (striving), and attainment (action) add up to the creative process of living a part emotionally.

Constantin Stanislavski

A segment of the analytic phase is defining the script's action/objective score. An action/objective score for a scene reflects your character's psychological and physical desires with regard to other characters. The action/objective score also needs to incorporate the playwright's expectations as expressed in the stage directions, relationships inherent in the script, the nonverbal physical actions associated with the dialogue and those that take place in conjunction with the dialogue.[4] Some of these actions may be connected to stage business that needs to be accomplished in the scene, such as the constantly moving plates of sardines in *Noises Off*. Sometimes there are script injunctions for physical actions that reveal the playwright's interpretation of the character, as in playwright Jeanne Barroga's expectation that Dee in *Talk Story* would smoke cigarettes. Others involve physical contact related to friendship, family, status, and romantic liaisons. The action/objective score unites the actions indicated by the playwright with the actors

---

[4]The stage directions in the script may or may not have been written by the playwright. Usually, the director, or the teacher if you are doing work within in a class, will indicate whether or not they want you to follow the stage directions as written.

rendition of the character's desires. Below is an example of a score from a short segment of a scene between Martha and Megs, from *Strange Snow* by Steve Metcalfe.[5] Megs, a Vietnam veteran and friend of Martha's brother, has just returned from a fishing trip. Martha invites him to have a bowl of soup. The dialogue is on the left and potential objectives are on the right.

Dialogue		Objectives
Martha:	You are having somsoup	To keep Megs in the room.
Megs:	Soup would be great.	To bolster Martha's confidence.
Martha:	Come on. To the kitchen. Sit. Split pea with ham. Homemade.	To transport him into her world.
Megs:	You're kiddin. By god, if food doesn't come out of can, I usually have a hard time recognizing it.	To assure her he is in need of someone to care for him.
Martha:	I'll have you know I'm a very good cook.	To captivate him with her culinary abilities.

The above action score can be expanded to include a column that allows you to incorporate physical actions related to the objectives. The following score provides a combination of objectives and physical actions (the combination Stanislavski would call physical action) for exploring the set of inner images previously evolved by the actor. The combination of inner imagery and physical score is the means by which the personality, wants, and desires of Megs and Martha are revealed.

---

[5]Steve Metcalfe, *Strange Snow* (New York: Samuel French, 1983), 32.

Dialogue	Physical Actions	Objective
Martha: You are having some soup.	Crosses to kitchen taking off coat.	To keep Megs in the room.
Megs: Soup would be great.	Megs follows Martha and sits in chair.	To bolster Martha's confidence.
Martha: Come on to the kitchen. Sit. Split pea with ham. Homemade.	Martha puts on apron and moves toward refrigerator to remove soup.	To transport him into her world.
Megs: You're kiddin. By god, if food doesn't come out of can, I usually have a hard time recognizing it.	Brushing hand through hair. Stretching and adjusting himself in the chair.	To assure her he needs someone to care for him.
Martha: I'll have you know I'm a very good cook.	Turning to look at him.	To captivate him with her culinary abilities.

Physical actions may change dynamic quality, be eliminated, and or new ones created during the rehearsal process. It is therefore important, throughout the rehearsal process, to remain open and flexible. During the following explorations, you will also continue to refine your character's internal monologue and related images. Precise images help to define the movement language of your character. Stanislavski cautions:

The score for the physical life of a role is only the beginning of our work; the most important part lies ahead–the deepening of this life until it reaches the very depths, where the spiritual life of a role begins to create, which is the main objective of our art.[6]

[6]Stanislavski, *Creating a Role,*154.

EMBODYING A PERFORMANCE:

(A PERIOD OF EMOTIONAL EXPERIENCE)

The spiritual and emotional embodiment of a character is a path of experimentation with different modes of exploration to discover the character's internal impulses. This period of emotional involvement is a refinement of the analytic phases and a unification of yourself as an actor with the physical and emotional life of the character. You are discovering the psychological, emotional, and physical impulse of the character based on your personal past in combination with new impulses created/discovered in the exploration. You are also finding the connections between you and another actor based on visual focus, touch, or other kinesthetic elements. The points of exploration in this section are extensions of previous work in breath, imagery, and energy. Each exploration should begin with a physical warm-up as described in Appendix A.

Exploration 59:
Breath as a Point of Exploration

Beyond being a method of centering and grounding your body, breath is a means to explore the emotional life of a character. An exploration of breath begins with a consideration of the following questions that are derived from your character analysis. The answers to these question serve your basis to physically explore the emotional center and impulsive core of the character's actions.

What emotional/chakra center does the character breathe from and under what circumstances?

Does the character primarily breathe and thus speak from the strong will attached to the solar plexus or from intellectual powers of the head and the sixth chakra?

Is the character sometimes emotionally attached to the strong sexual desire of the second chakra?

Is there a need to survive related to the first or root chakra?

Is the character motivated by a strong love of humanity or of an individual and, thus, is under the influence of the fourth or heart chakra?

Is there a need to express self associated with the fifth chakra?

Is there a connection with a higher power or knowledge affiliated with the sixth and seventh chakra?

Returning to our example of the scene between Megs and Martha, the actor playing Megs wants to bolster Martha's confidence as he follows Martha into the kitchen and says, "Soup would be great." The actor playing Megs may decide that he is speaking from his heart chakra as a compassionate friend. But, the actor could also choose to have Megs speak from his second chakra because of his attraction for Martha.

1. **Using the sounding exploration from chapter 1, explore the sound associated with the primary chakra center for the character.** Begin by placing the breath within a chakra center. Become aware of feeling the breath and fusing with it and the sound affiliated with the charkra and releasing the sound through out your body.

2. **Begin to note the direction of the sound as it flows out of your appendages.**

3. **Begin to note the phrasing of the sound.**

4. **How does the flow of the sound influence the physical action of the legs and arms? Do you find you want to pull in or reach out? Does the flow of the sound cause gestures that slash, punch, press, wring, dab or flick?**

5. **Pick a gesture and repeat it several times.**

6. **Now repeat the gesture, but state the desire or objective of the character.**

7. **Repeat the process, discovering different gestures emerging from the fusion of breath and this emotional center, or another emotional center related to the character, until you feel you have evolved a movement vocabulary for the character.**

8. **Now return to the text, incorporating the movement vocabulary of the character.**

9. **Determine how you would like the other characters in the scene to respond to you.** Will he/she laugh, smile, leave the room, hug you, take your hand, jump up and down, touch your

chin, sign the document, kiss you, pay the bill, or exhibit any number of physical actions related to the scene?

10. **Be prepared to adapt to changes brought about by rehearsal.** During the rehearsal, you may discover that you come to new conclusions about the character. Be prepared to disregard one set of ideas as you come to new realizations.

Exploration 60:
Imagery as a Point of Exploration

Breath, as a point of exploration, can be combined with imagery and the contemporary technology of the holographic image. A hologram is a two dimensional image transformed into 3D. Most of us are familiar with holograms from science fiction films, such as *Star Wars*, that use them as a means for people within the film's world to contact each other. This exploration combines our experience with viewing holograms in the media and uses it to help transform metaphors into characters.

1. **From previous text analysis, determine a metaphor for the character from a scene.** This can be an animal, an earth essence derived from the natural mask work, or an archetype.

2. **Once you have picked a metaphor, see it approximately two feet in front of you, either standing or floating in space.**

3. **Using your imagination, watch the metaphor, if nonhuman, become human by developing an upright position with spine, legs, feet, arms, hands, and head.** Add details to the image, such as color of hair, position of head, spine, legs, and arms.

4. **Once you have flushed out all the aspects of the image take a breath in. And as you breathe out, step into the image.**

5. **Continue to focus on the breath and the related image using the technique of feel, fuse, and follow. Feel the image transforming your body on a cellular level, realigning your pelvis, spine, arms, hands and face as well as legs and feet.**

6. **Once you have aligned yourself with the image, begin to explore different gestures, postures, and forms of locomotion. See the environment around you with the character's**

eyes, hear with their ears, smell with their nose, touch with their skin.

During rehearsal, you may find that the image changes. Such a change is a natural evolution of your unconscious playing with the potential of an image. If this occurs, permit yourself, just as you did during the work with dynamic alignment in Chapter 2, to become this new image. In the process, you may discover that there is really more than one image that is important to your understanding of the character. For example, the actor playing Jim in the "Gentlemen Caller" scene from Tennessee William's *Glass Menagerie* could approach the scene as if he were a steady wind and the actor playing Laura as if she were a delicate flower. Or, they could approach the scene with Jim as a giant bear and Laura as a lap dog. Or, they could approach the scene with Jim as a warrior and Laura as an orphan. Using any of these metaphors as a points of exploration, they would discover new choices for the characters.

Exploration 61:
Space as a Point of Exploration

An element of nonverbal communication is the space with which we surround ourselves (as in the bubble discussed earlier) and related aspect of touch. In acting terms, this space is an aspect of the "where" of a character's life that can be divided into personal and public space. Our experience of personal space is situational and culturally specific. Edward Hall has documented the spatial or bubble preferences for different cultural groups. He divides space into intimate, personal, social, and public. His research suggests that northern Europeans prefer a large spatial distance between themselves and others, while people from the Mediterranean area are comfortable with closer physical contact.[7] Space and the degree of touch, appropriate or inappropriate, is related to social station and gender status as well as cultural upbringing. For instance, in a university setting there are spatial distances considered appropriate for faculty and students and for faculty and mem

---

[7] Edward Hall, *The Hidden Dimension* (New York: Doubleday, 1966).

bers of the administration. There are also distinctive spatial relationships between genders—males/males, females/females, and females/males. According to performance theorist Richard Schechner, space is alive with potential in the interaction of individual sensory systems and the environment. It is a communication from within the spaces of the body to the spaces within the environment.[8]

1. **While in the process of exploring space, consider the activity in terms of words with associative meaning, such as investigate, search, and venture.** Note how much you can observe about the space by first focusing on the use of your eyes, followed by closing your eyes and concentrating on what you hear, then what you smell and, finally, what you feel. Each of these sensory states particularizes the initial state of exploration.

2. **Next you can began to consider how your character moves through space. For example, you can use Laban's effort qualities to consider whether he/she moves directly, attempting to penetrate, invade, or puncture people, furniture, or the space itself as he/she moves through it.** Or is his/her attitude toward space constantly shifting in a series of indirect choices? When the character enters a room or sits in a chair does he/she fill the room with his/her presence or take over a chair? Characters who fill the space are attempting to project themselves into an entire area. Adjectives that describe methods of filling an area include spreading, sprawling, draping, permeating, and expanding. What is the statement you make about your personal boundary by how you fill the space? Characters can also surround objects and people or repulse them. In surrounding something or someone, you are literally attempting to encircle, envelop, enclose or embrace them or it with your arms, legs, trunk and head. Characters can also move through settings by crossing a space/person (ford, span, traverse), advancing through a space/person (promote, progress, exalt), or retreating from a space/person (escape, withdraw, retire).

Each of these approaches to space can influence the action/objective score you have created. Which seem like choices the character might make? Which are completely outside the realm of your charac

[8]Richard Schechner, *Performative Circumstances: From the Avant garde to Ramlila* (Calcutta: Seagull, 1983), 67.

ter? Which might be something they might do under certain circumstances? What are those circumstances?

Exploration 62:
Tempo/Rhythm as a Point of Exploration

Everything–mechanical, animal, plant, and inorganic–has an innate pulse. This is often referred to as a *tempo/rhythm*. Stanislavski considered tempo/rhythm to be one of the most powerful components in an actor's performance. He believed it suggested appropriate feeling and, accordingly, had the power to suggest the emotional life of characters. He claimed an actor using the appropriate tempo/rhythm would captivate the audience's attention.

Tempo/rhythm is the result of the interplay between *duration* (the amount of time a particular moment lasts), *accent* (the emphasis given to a particular moment), and *phrasing* (the repetition of the same elements). For example, the following would be a tempo/rhythm phrase: ,,,* **,, ,**,. The commas represent a simple duration of similar length and the boldfaced stars the accent. A vocalization of the phrase would sound like this: da, da, da, **dum**; **dum, dum**, da da; da, **dum, dum**, da.

Our internal tempo/rhythm is a combination of our heartbeat and breath phrasing. You can discover your internal rhythm by using previous methods for quieting your body and listening for the beat of your heart. If you cannot hear it easily, put your middle finger on a pulse point on the wrist and feel its tempo/rhythm.

1. **Concentrating on this rhythm, begin to allow your body to respond to it.**
2. **Continue to be aware of your heartbeat but begin to note the phrasing of your breath as you inhale and exhale.** How does the heartbeat interact with the phrasing of your breath? What are the number of heartbeats for the inhalation and exhalation?
3. **Keeping your attention on both your heartbeat and your breath phrasing, explore a variety of methods of walking, sitting, and standing.**
4. **Explore the tempo/rhythm of a movement by modifying the**

duration and accent of the breath. For example, duration can be altered if you breathe in quickly and out very slowly. You can breathe out very quickly and hold the breath before you breathe in again. You can breathe in slowly and accent the breath by breathing out in a series of small explosions that can either become a laugh or cause you to cry. Except in cases of physical duress, your heart continues to maintain a constant rhythm regardless of the breath's phrasing. In its capacity to provide the underlying beat, the heart is the equivalent to the bass guitar in a jazz ensemble.

5. **The tempo/rhythm of characters also can be investigated through music.** Bring together a selection of music that represents a particular time period, geographical area, or style/genre that is related to the world of the character. Use the music to underscore your exploration of the action/objective score. How does it influence, enhance, or expand the score? For instance, what is the impact on your movement of the underlying lyrical quality and phrasing of a melodic instrument or the rhythmic underpinning of a drum? The short segment of the script between Megs and Martha is very different if the background music is Mozart or the Grateful Dead.

> ### Exploration 63:
> ### Character's Journey as a Point of

Most characters in scripts are on a narrative journey in which they achieve some of their objectives and overcome some of the challenges or obstacles with which they are confronted and not others. As part of your character analysis, note the major shifts in the character's desires or approaches to the situation. Do these shifts represent different aspects of an archetype; for instance, the positive and shadow sides of a warrior? Or do these shifts represent the play of a completely different archetype? You can use the archetype explorations in Chapter 4 to identify the physical qualities of archetypes associated with different moments in the script. The previously created physical score can be rehearsed using the archetype as a point of exploration.

Exploration 64: Exploring with Others

Although many explorations in this text take you, the actor, as the initial point of exploration, in truth, acting is (re)acting. Just as we understand ourselves through our relationships, actors must understand that their character is acting, as Katherine Cornell points out, "in relation not only to itself but to the other characters in the play."[9] Communication among characters in a scene exists on several levels: the other characters you are talking to at any particular moment, the other characters on stage who you might not be addressing at that moment but could be in the future, and the formal audience. This complex combination of audiences requires you to listen and respond to multiple sets of information. This relationship between yourself and others on stage is comparable to situations from everyday life, from being at a sports event to an opening-night party. At each of these events, you are listening and responding to those in your immediate presence, as well as those on the other side of the room. The stage adds an audience to these scenarios.

The acting skills necessary to interact on multiple levels fall into two categories; *listening* and *responding*. Although we often consider listening primarily in terms of the aural system, listening requires the concentration of all one's senses. Listening is a way of attempting to feel the sensory state of another person. The information perceived from them is consolidated with past experience in order to formulate a response. Since the actual act of being in an exploratory mode incorporates the technique of feel, fuse, and follow, you are in rehearsal continually developing your listening skills.

Responding is the other element in communication. Whether quick or deliberate, the response will be in two phases; a moment of *evaluation,* that comes out of listening, that includes the *formulation* of a response, and the *actual* response itself. The technique of feel, fuse, and follow can be modified to feel, fuse, and send to represent this interaction sequence. In this use of the technique, you feel the impact

---

[9]Katherine Cornell in Morton Eustis, *Players at Work: Acting, According to the Actors* (New York: Theatre Arts Books, 1937), 65.

of the intention of an action executed by the other character. You fuse with this intention through a process of integration and evaluation. Finally, you send a response that represents your reaction to their desires/objectives and their relationship to your desires/objectives.

You can use this approach of feel, fuse, and send with a text and previous explorations in the text. These include:

Chapter 2–Exploration 18 (Seesaw), Exploration 23 (Breathing through the Joints), Exploration 27 (Gravity and Movement), Exploration 30 (Partner Balancing)

Chapter 3–Exploration 36 (Imitations), Exploration 39 (Properties Improvisation).

Each of these explorations establishes a nonverbal communication that could be expanded to include dialogue. This combination of dialogue and specific action can be used to comprehend characters and their relationships. Partner balancing, for instance, in which two people attempt to find the balance point between them, investigates physical balance and power. Breathing through the joints, on the other hand, focuses on the physical dynamics of touch between two people. Either of these initial explorations could serve as a point of exploration from which you evolve other improvisations based on the dynamic of the characters.

To determine which exploration to use, ask yourself the question, "What is the fundamental conflict between these two people?" An answer for the Megs and Martha segment might be Megs' desire to help Martha overcome her shyness, which is in opposition to Martha's desire to keep men at a distance. A rehearsal for this scene could begin with Exploration 18 (Seesaw) and a playful tug of war that is the early stages of their attraction for each other. Continued rehearsals could incorporate imitations of each other, methods of touching; both actual touch and with the eyes, that are extensions of Exploration 36. Regardless of rehearsal method, you can return to a state of listening and responding to other actors in the scene by remembering to focus your sensory capacities–aural, visual, and kinesthetic–on feeling the other actors/characters, fusing with their intention, transforming it, and acting on your character's desires.

FINAL THOUGHTS

The more often I re-live the physical life the more definite and firm will the line of the spiritual life become. The more often I feel the merging of these two lines, the more strongly will I believe in the psycho-physical truth of this state and the more firmly will I feel the two levels of my part. The physical being of a part is good ground for the seed of the spiritual being to grow in.

Constantin Stanislavski

The three-part evolution of a character described by Stanislavski is analogous to the development of your body as a performer. Initially, there is a period of study or a period of evolving awareness, in which you expand your understanding of internal and external states of being. Next, there is a period of physical embodiment. During this phase of training, you practice the somatic skills associated with the processes of breath, exploration, and imagery in the evolution of a performer's body. In the final stage, emotional embodiment, you combine this awareness of your performer's body with skills for creating a persona, and you apply these to bringing a text to life on stage. All of this is revealed in rehearsal. As Stanislavski suggests, "the more often I repeat the scene the stronger the line becomes, the more powerful the movement, the life, its truthfulness, and my faith in it. Remember, that we call this unbroken line of physical actions the line of physical being."[10]

In the end, your job is to create potential physical actions for any moment of performance. The choices you make are part of the building blocks the director uses to shape the production. The creative body from which you discover these choices is relaxed, filled with potential, and open to possibility. It is a body prepared to become a conduit for the character's world. Your ultimate task is the ongoing care and development of this instrument. This requires a lifetime of study and an acknowledgment of the necessity of daily practice. Furthermore, it dictates a commitment to the of study of different historical periods, music, visual art, literature, film, and politics to constantly expand the imagination. This expanded imagination seeks diverse ways to express itself. This diversity comes from recognizing the uniqueness of your particular artistic vision and constantly enlarging that vision through experience. Ultimately, you will constantly be discovering new ways of expressing your artistic gift.

---

[10]Stanislavski, *Creating a Role*, 227.

APPENDIX

DAILY PRACTICE

Daily practice is a means of continuing to deepen awareness and to work with the somatic tools of your imagination–breath, exploration, and imagery. It is also an opportunity to stretch and strengthen your skeletal muscles as well as (through aerobic activity) your heart muscle. In doing all of the above, you will get an opportunity to explore your alignment, balance, grounding, and internal connections between body parts. The goal of this outline is to give you an approach to warming up that moves from internal to external awareness, from what Stanislavski would refer to as one's internal energy system to external expression.

WARMING UP THE BODY

Coming to Attention and Internal/External focus: This is bringing yourself into focus on the practice. Ideally, you should find a quiet place where you will not be disturbed by the telephone, television, or other distractions. Move progressively through the following, being aware of the internal connections between different body parts.

> Body Scan (Chapter 1: Exploration 1)
> Sounding (Chapter 1: Exploration 7)
> Empty Suit (Chapter 2: Exploration 29)

Placing the Breath: This focus on the breath prepares and focuses your body for the practice. It can include any combination of the following or other breath exercises with which you are familiar.

> Breath Explorations (Chapter 1: Explorations 2-6 and Chapter 2: Exploration 13)

Discovering the Pelvis: This extends awareness from the breath in the abdominal cavity to the pelvis as the center of physical balance. You can combine awareness and the imaging work suggested in Chapter 2 (Explorations 15-17) with strength building exercises such as sit-ups and yoga and other stretches for the pelvic region. Below is a description of an efficient method of doing sit-ups.

To Strengthen Pelvis and Release Lower Back: One of the best exercises to strengthen the lower back is crunches, or what some people refer to as sit-ups. There is, however, a right and a wrong way to do them. The right way uses correct form, concentrating the contraction in the lower abdomen, not in upper abdomen and lower back. This method also incorporates the breath into the movement by breathing out on the effort and breathing in on the release. Lie down on your back with your feet in parallel and a comfortable distance from the buttocks, arms across the chest. Lift your upper back and shoulders off the floor as you exhale and release down as you inhale. Take your time with each movement, being certain that:

- Your back is released against the floor. Arching your back puts a strain on the lower part of your spine and doesnot place enough effort on the abdominal muscles.

- Rest your arms across your chest with your elbow com fortably at you sides, keeping them relaxed. They should not lift of your chest as you lift.

- Keep your neck relaxed, your chin tucked in toward your chest. Your eyes should maintain the same position and be looking over your knees at the top of the sit-up.

- Feet should be flat and grounded into the floor rather than pulled up, as you do the sit-up. Toes should be flat on the floor and not pulling back, as this pushes your heel into the floor and causes tension in the buttocks and tightening in the calves.

Many variations on the basic sit-up can be used to strengthen the entire abdominal group of muscles. Many of these variations are the result of different placement of the legs with regard to the torso or a change in direction of the upward reach from straight up to the diagonal.

Lengthening the Spine: The spine is the extension of your pelvis and connects the communication centers of your upper torso with your legs dance, or other physical disciplines that allows you to stretch the spine in all its possible planes–saggital, lateral, and diagonal. Stretches in all directions will insure that you are balancing all the muscle groups of the torso. You can also use images for lengthening the spine downward by releasing the tail bone to the spot between your heels and the head up toward the sky.

Connecting with the Appendages: The following is a set of exercises that uses a variety of circular movements to "oil the joints." Before starting you want to link up and let go. Take a moment and place your feet in a comfortable parallel position approximately shoulder width apart. With your heels firmly reaching into the floor, start a gentle up and down bounce that reverberates through your entire joint structure. Using your internal eye, move from the joints of your feet, to your ankles, knees, hips, coccyx, sacrum, vertebrae, ribs, shoulders, elbows, wrists, and joints between head and spine. As you gently bounce, begin to see each joint as an accordion and begin to feel the spaces in the interior of each joint. Trace a path from your heels, through each joint, feeling the reverberating connection with each joint from your feet to your head. Once this connection is established, allow the bounce to slowly disappear, as waves in the water do after a pebble has fallen into it.

Now consider yourself to be a giant pencil with the bottom of the pencil (the eraser) in the space between your legs and the top (the tip) of the pencil coming out of the top of your head. Start to make circles that you initiate in your feet and involve your entire body. Imagine the top of the pencil is drawing a circle on the ceiling. Make the circle larger and note the adjustment that takes place in each one of your joints. Coil the circle inward so that it becomes smaller and smaller until you finally come to the center of the circle. Stand a moment and take in the feeling of being linked through your joint structure before starting the following exercises.

All of the following exercises use the circular and spiral energy systems of the body. As you complete each circle, use your internal eye to note places in the circle that may not be as fluid as others. (This is a similar approach to work you did with the pelvic circle on the floor.) When you discover an area of the circle that feels stiff or flat, go back and forth over that area and adjust your approach to the circle, not only in that joint but in all the joints of your body. What you want to experience is the fluid quality of your body's energy through its interconnecting links of the joints. Also, be sure to allow the circles to move from large to small so that you can experience the concentration of energy that is associated with the motion of coiling.

Head circles

Drop your head to the front, releasing the muscles of your shoulders. Slowly allow your head to roll to the right and then stretch up to the ceiling as you bring it to the back and over to the left side before it comes to the front again. As you do this, release the jaw and allow the mouth to open when the head goes back. Repeat to the other side. Shift your head horizontally to the right, then bring it to the front, left, and back, drawing a horizontal circle with your chin. Repeat on the other side.

Shoulders

Lift and drop shoulders up and down several times, allowing the muscles between the shoulder blades to release a little more with each drop. One at a time, lift one shoulder, dropping it first in place, then forward of the joint, back in place, and then behind. Repeat with the other shoulder. Now with a large circle and starting from center, connect all the edges of a large circle, moving the shoulders first in a forward circle and then in a backward circle. Alternate shoulders by moving one shoulder back, followed by the other, and then forward, followed by the other. Try to feel the point between the circles when one shoulder is moving forward and the other back.

Circles from the ankle to the knee to the hip

With the weight on your left foot, place the ball of your right foot on the floor and begin circles that move from inside to out with your right foot, all the time thinking of "oiling the joints" of your ankle. While still circling with your ankle, add a circle with your knee and then finally with your hip. Repeat each circle at each joint enough times so that the joint begins to feel loose and relaxed. Reversing the direction of the circle, begin with the hip and move to the knee and ankle. Repeat the process on the left side.

Pelvic circles

With the weight distributed evenly over both feet and knees in a relaxed position, shift the pelvis horizontally to the right, front, left, and back so that the pelvis makes a circle that is separate from the upper torso. Repeat in the opposite direction.

Upper torso circles

With weight distributed evenly over both feet and knees in a relaxed position, shift the upper torso horizontally to the right, front, left, and back so that it makes a circle that is separate from the pelvis. Repeat in the opposite direction.

Leg circles

Standing balanced over both feet, swing your right leg forward and back twice, all the while releasing in the femoral joint; then step onto your right foot. Repeat on the other side. Standing balanced over both feet, swing the right leg in a semi-circle diagonally left, forward and diagonally right, before placing it next to you. Make this into a circle. Repeat on the other side.

Integrated oiling

Shoulder, elbows, bend and stretch–circle shoulders to the back four times. Add the elbows to the movement. Follow this by swinging the arms up and around to the back while bending your knees. Allow the arms to come to the bottom of the circle at your waist and then release to a standing posture. To reverse this swing, allow your shoulders to come forward, add elbows, and reach arms back to forward. When arms reach the top of circle, stretch up with right arm, then left. Your hands touch each other to form a circle above the body and open to the sides and come down as your knees bend and release.

Body swings

Begin with the arms hanging from the sides of the body. Swing your arms up toward the front and around to the back. As they come front again the body rises so that you are balancing on the balls of your feet. Reverse the process with the arms swinging down and around and back and over the head so that the body curves over as the arms come over the head. A verbal phrase for remembering this sequence is "around and up and around and down."

Grounding the Energy and Exploring Connections

Walking around the space, become aware of the breath reaching into your pelvic bowl and out through the bottom of your feet. You are in the center of an energy sphere in which the energy is engaged on all sides as well as the front and back. Feel the warm flow of the energy through your body and on the outside of your skin as it moves up the front and drifts down the back. Or you can visualize yourself standing in a warm waterfall that moves with you; the steam rises in the front of you caressing your legs, belly, and chest and moving past your face as it goes over your head and becomes part of the waterfall than sends water rolling down your back, dropping off your buttocks and the sides of your legs until in runs off the floor at your feet and becomes steam which rises up the front of your body.

Begin moving around the space through different locomotive patterns and styles of locomotion–walk, stride, run, creep, crawl, hop, jump, dash, dart, float, glide, penetrate, retreat, fall, drop and any other movements that gurgle to the surface of your body's imagination. Begin moving and stop. Creating a posture/attitude, find the center or stillness of the posture, keep the energy alive in the stillness and return to moving around the space. Repeat several times.

Come to a quiet standing position. Complete a quick standing body scan, any final stretches your internal eye indicates is necessary, and start today's exploration or rehearsal.

AEROBIC ENDURANCE

Aerobic endurance is a function of how well and efficiently you use oxygen. To determine your level of endurance you need information provided by the three following heart rates. Take your pulse rate by locating the pulse either on your wrist or neck artery. Count the pulse for six seconds and add a zero to get your pulse rate.

Resting Heart Rate

Many factors can influence resting heart rate, including temperature, humidity, previous activity, emotions, time since eating, fatigue, and illness. People who have high levels of aerobic fitness have a lower resting heart rate and a quicker recovery time than people with less aerobic fitness. The best time to determine your resting heart rate is to take your pulse before you get out of bed in the morning.

Working Heart Rate

There are various rates: 60 to 90 beats per minute is an extremely light to a very light level of exertion that is associated with the warm-up or cool down phase of aerobic activity. 100 to150 beats per minute is the training zone for your heart. At 100 to 150 beats per minute, you still burn fat; and, yet you can breathe and speak easily. As your heart rate moves into the 140 to150 zone, you are moving toward the training zone and as a consequence you are sweating more and starting to have trouble carrying on a conversation. At 160 to 200 beats per minute your body reverses the aerobic process to protect itself from stress. This approximates the endurance of a competitive athlete. Your breathing is labored (you can't talk) and the muscles are burning. For the high end, imagine sprinting as hard as you can in the 100 yard dash.

Recovery Heart Rate

This measurement is taken five minutes after you have slowed the activity. After five minutes, your pulse should not exceed 120. If it does, you know you are overextending yourself, so simply continue to walk slowly and stretch until the rate is 120 or less. Ten minutes after exercising it should be below 100. If not, you should cut back on the intensity with which you exercise. At your next workout, move less vigorously by walking more, running less, and using your arms less energetically.

Rate of Perceived Exertion

This is a way of becoming involved in the experience of your heart rate to determine your aerobic level. Instead of focusing on your pulse rate, you concentrate on the experience of your activity. You will want to note your reaction to different types of activity and to different amounts of exertion.

Know Your Capacity

The first rule of aerobics is: Never get ahead of yourself. Rushing just doesn't work and only invites trouble. Work up to your goals gradually. This is important not only to accustom the heart to new demands but also to let tendons and muscles adjust themselves to the new activity.

Indications that you are overdoing your exercise are: a feeling of tightness or pain in your chest, severe breathlessness, dizziness, losing control of your muscles, and nausea. Any one of these symptoms is a clear signal to stop exercising immediately. Shortness of breath an hour and a half later is another indication of overexertion. By comparison, the normal breathing rate at rest ranges from 12 to 16 breaths per minute.

SELECTED REFERENCES

The texts listed in this section reflect a cross-section of background information in the areas of acting, somatic therapy, martial arts, Laban, and physical style. They have been selected based on their prevalent use among practitioners. The goal is to provide a beginning reference list for you.

General Texts

The references identified in this section include texts in the areas of actor training, anthropology of the body, health and fitness research, somatic awareness, and brain research.

Balk, Wesley. *The Radiant Performer*. Minneapolis: University of Minnesota Press, 1991.

Barnes, Clive. *Theatre Games*. London: Methuen, 1977.

Bates, Brian. *The Way of the Actor*. Boston: Shambhala, 1987.

Bateson, Mary Catherine. *Peripheral Visions*. New York: Harper and Row, 1994.

Benedetti, Robert. *The Actor at Work*, 6th ed. New Jersey: Simon and Simon, 1994.

Blacking, John. *The Anthropology of the Body*. London: Academic Press, 1977.

Bliss, Shepherd, ed. *The New Holistic Health Handbook*. New York: Penguin, 1985.

Block, Susana, and Pedro Orthous, Guy Santibanez. "Effector Patterns of Basic Emotions: A Psychological Method for Training Actors," *Journal of Social Biological Structure* (10) 1987.

Brook, Peter. *The Empty Space*. London: Pelican, 1972.

Calais-Germain, Blandine. *Anatomy of Movement*. Seattle: Eastland Press, 1993.

Calais-Germain, Blandine and Andree Lamotte. *Anatomy of Movement: Exercises*. Seattle: Eastland Press, 1996.

Cooper, Robert K. *Health and Fitness Excellence*. Boston, Mass.: Houghton Mifflin, 1989.

Crawford, Jerry L. and Catherine Hurst and Michael Lugering. *Acting in Person and in Style*. London: Brown and Benchmark, 1995.

Czikszentmihalyi, Mihalyi. *Flow*. New York: Harper and Row, 1990.

Damasio, Antonio. *The Feeling of What Happens*. New York: Harcourt Brace, 1999.

Davis, Martha, Elizabeth Robbins Eshelman, and Matthew McKay. *The Relaxation and Stress Reduction Workbook*. Oakland, Calif.: New Harbinger, 1988.

Donnelly, Joseph. *Living Anatomy*. Illinois: Human Kinetics, Pub., 1990.

Elison, Lawrence M., and Wynn Kapit. *The Anatomy Coloring Book*. New York: Harper and Row, 1977.

Eustis, Morton. *Players at Work: Acting According to the Actors*. New York: Theatre Arts Books, 1937.

Fleshman, Bob, ed. *Theatrical Movement*. London: Scarecrow Press, 1986.

Fitt, Sally Sevey. *Dance Kinesiology*. New York: Schirmer Books, 1988.

Franklin, Eric. *Dynamic Alignment Through Imagery*. Illinois: Human Kinetics, 1996.

Hanna, Judith Lynne. *Dance, Sex and Gender*. Chicago: University of Chicago Press, 1988.

Heller, Joseph. *Bodywise*. New York: Jeremy Tarcher, 1986.

Johnson, Mark. *The Mind in the Body*. Chicago: University of Chicago Press, 1987.

Juhan, Deane. *Job's Body*. New York: Station Hill Press, 1987.

Jung, Carl. *Archetypes of the Collective Unconscious*. New York: Pantheon Books, 1959.

Kagan, Gerald. *Your Body Works: A Guide to Health, Energy, and Balance*. Berkeley, Calif.: Transformations Press, 1980.

Keleman, Stanley. *Embodying Experience*. Berkeley, Calif.: Center Press, 1989.

Kern, Stephen. *Anatomy and Destiny*. New York: Bobbs-Merrill, 1975.

Loehr, J. E. and P. J. McLaughlin. *Mentally Tough*. New York: M. Evans, 1986.

Masters, Robert, and Jean Houston. *Listening to the Body*. New York: Delta Books, 1978.

Murphy, Michael. *The Future of the Body*. Los Angeles: Jeremy Tarcher, 1992.

Nagrin, Daniel. *Dance and the Specific Image*. Pittsburgh: University of Pittsburgh Press, 1994.

Oida, Yoshi. *An Actor Adrift*. London: Methuen, 1993.

Olsen, Andrea. *Body Stories*. Barrytown, New York: Station Hill Press, 1991.

Pierce, Alexandra, and Roger Pierce *Expressive Movement*. New York: Insight Books, 1989.

_____. Generous Movement. Redlands, California: Center of Balance Press, 1991.

Schechner, Richard. *Performative Circumstances: From the Avant Garde to Ramlila*. Calcutta: Seagull, 1983.

Spence, Alexander. *Basic Human Anatomy*. Menlo Park, Calif.: Benjamin/Cummings, 1982.

Vlahos, Olivia. *Body: The Ultimate Symbol*. New York: Lippincott, 1979.

Yuasa, Yasuo. *The Body: Toward an Eastern Mind-Body Theory*. trans. Shigenori Nagatomo and Thomas Kasulis. New York: SUNY Press, 1987.

Acting

There are many texts on acting, but I have chosen to include three by the primary acting theorist of the twentieth century, Constantin Stanislavski and his biographer, Jean Benedetti. They are a source of reflection and inspiration.

Benedetti, Jean. *Stanislavski and the Actor*. New York: Routledge/ Theatre Arts, 1998.

Stanislavski, Constantin. *An Actor Prepares*. New York: Routledge/Theatre Arts, 1989.

_____. *Building a Character*. New York: Routledge/Theatre Arts, 1989.

_____. *Creating a Role*. New York: Routledge/Theatre Arts, 1989.

Alexander Technique

The Alexander technique is a method of body work developed by F. Matthias Alexander (1869-1955). The practitioners, who call themselves teachers, work with people in individual sessions to teach them the proper use of self through the alignment of the head, neck, and torso. The technique is often the basis for movement and voice training. The following texts represent some of Alexander's writing and those by contemporary teachers.

Alexander, Matthias. *The Universal Constant in Living*. London: Chaterson Ltd., 1946.

_____. *The Use of Self*. Long Beach, California: Centerline Press, 1985.

_____. *Constructive Conscious Control of the Individual.* Long Beach, Calif.: Centerline Press, 1985.

Barlow, Wilfried, M.D. *The Alexander Technique.* Rochester, Vermont: Healing Arts Press, 1973.

Gelb, Michael. *Body Learning: An Introduction to the Alexander Technique.* New York: Delilah Books, 1981.

Jones, Frank Pierce. *Body Awareness in Action: The Alexander Technique.* New York: Schocken Books, 1979.

Krantz, Judith, and Robert B. Stone. *The Alexander Technique: Joy in the Life of the Body.* New York: Beaufort Books, 1980.

Leibowitz, Judith, and Bill Connington. *Alexander Technique.* New York: Harper and Row, 1990.

Maisel, Edward, ed. *The Alexander Technique: The Essential Writings of F. Matthias Alexander.* New York: University Books, 1989.

Sanfilippo, Phyllis. *The Reader's Guide to the Alexander Technique: A Selected Annotated Bibliography.* Long Beach, Calif.: Centerline Press, 1987.

Bioenergetics

Bioenergetics is a system based on Reichian therapy developed by Alexander Lowen. The goal is to develop self-awareness, assertion, and possession. This is achieved by restoring the body to its natural state through a series of exercises to ground the body by releasing tension, thus creating spontaneity, or what performers refer to as impulse.

Lowen, Alexander. *Physical Dynamics of Character Structure.* New York: Grune and Stratton, 1958.

_____. *Bioenergetics.* New York: Penguin Books, 1976.

_____. *Betrayal of the Body.* New York: Collier, 1976.

Reich, William. *Character Analysis.* New York: Orgone Institute Press, 1949.

Breath

The study of breath is a fundamental part of performance training. Early proponents of the study of breath as fundamental to understanding the body include two authors listed here, Elsa Gindler and Ilse Middendorf.

Freid, Robert. *The Breath Connection.* New York: Plenum Press, 1990.

Gindler, Elsa. "Gymnastik for Everyone." *Somatics*. 6 (1987): 35-39.

Middendork, Ilse. *The Perceptible Breath*. Trans. Gudula Floeren and Dieter Eule. Paderborn, Germany: Junfermann Verlag, 1990.

Speads, Carola. *Ways to Better Breathing*. Rutland, Vermont: Healing Arts Press, 1992.

Eastern Movement and Martial Arts

Since the discovery of Zen by the Beat Generation in the 1950s, Asian physical disciplines have been incorporated into performance curricula to teach students methods of concentration, techniques of breathing, and forms of mind/body integration. The following texts provide introductions to these disciplines.

Chia, Mantak. *Chi Self-Massage*. Huntington, N Y.: Healing Tao Books, 1986.

_____. *Awaken Healing Energy Through the Tao*. New York: Aurora Press, 1983.

Chia Siew Pang, and Goh ewe Hock. *Tai Chi: Ten Minutes to Health*. Sebastopol, Calif.: CRCS Books, 1985.

Crompton, Paul. *The T'ai Chi Workbook*. Boston: Shambhala, 1987.

Egami, Shigeru. *The Way of Karate: Beyond Technique*. Tokyo: Kodansha, 1976.

Feldshuh, David. "Zen and the Actor." *The Drama Review* 20 (1976) 79-89.

Franck, Frederick. *The Zen of Seeing*. New York: Vintage, 1973.

Gach, Michael. *Acu-Yoga*. Tokyo: Japan Pub., 1981.

Judith, Anodea. *Wheels of Life*. St. Paul, Minn.: Llewellyn, 1990.

_____. and Selene Vega. *The Sevenfold Journey*. Berkeley, CA.: The Crossing Press, 1993.

Karagulla, Shafica, and Dora van Gelder Kunz. *The Chakras and the Human Energy Fields*. Wheaton, Ill.: Theosophical Publishing House, 1989.

Kleiman, Seymour, ed. *Mind and Body: East Meets West*. Champaign, Ill.: Human Kinetics, 1986.

Kobayaski, Kiyoshi. *The Sport of Judo*. Rutland, Vt.: C.E. Tuttle, 1956.

Leadbeater, C.W. *Man Visible and Invisible*. Wheaton, Ill.: Quest Books, 1971.

Li Po. *Wave Hands Like Clouds*. New York: Harper and Row, 1975.

Master Lam Kan Chuen. *The Way of Energy*. London: Gaia, 1991.

Masunaga, Shizuto. *Zen Imagery Exercises*. Tokyo: Japan Pub., 1991.

Namikoshi, Toru. *Shiatsu and Stretching*. Tokyo: Japan Pub., 1990.

Olsen, Mark. *The Golden Buddha Changing Masks*. Nevada City, Calif.: Gateways, 1989.

Palmer, Wendy. *The Intuitive Body*. Berkeley, CA.: North Atlantic Books, 1994.

Reid, Howard. *The Way of Harmony*. London: Gaia, 1988.

Teeguarden, I. M. *The Joy of Feeling: Bodymind Acupressure Jin Shin Do*. Tokyo: Japan Pub., 1987.

Vishnudevananda, Swami. *The Complete Illustrated Book of Yoga*. New York: Julian Press, 1972.

Yamamoto, Shizuko and Patrick Mc Carty. *The Shiatsu Handbook*. Eureka, California: Turning Point, 1986.

Yang Jwaing-Ming. *Advanced Yang Style T'ai Chi Chuan: Volume 1 and 2*. Jamaica Plain, Mass.: Yang's Martial Arts Assoc., 1988.

Feldenkrais

The Feldenkrais method is another popular basis for movement training. This method was developed by Russian-born Israeli physicist and engineer, Moshe Feldenkrais (1904-1984). The goal of the approach is to establish new connections between brain and body through the complementary methods of awareness through movement classes and individual sessions in functional integration.

Feldenkrais, Moshe. *Body and Mature Behavior: A Study of Anxiety, Sex, Gravitation, and Learning*. New York: International University Press, 1970.

_____. *The Case of Nora: Body Awareness as Healing Therapy*. New York: Harper and Row, 1977.

_____. *Awareness Through Movement*. New York: Harper and Row, 1977.

_____. *The Potent Self*. San Francisco: Harper and Row, 1985.

Laban and Interpreters

Rudolf von Laban was a dancer, choreographer and movement observer who created two complementary systems of analysis. One system describes the exact location of the body in time and space while the other describes the body's dynamic qualities. Together, these systems provide a method of dance notation. In performance programs, Laban's effort qualities have been used as the basis for self-study and the creation of characters.

Bartenieff, Irmgard, and Martha Davis. "Effort Shape Analysis of Movement: The Unity of Expression and Function." *Research Approaches to Movement and Personality*. New York: Arno Press, 1972.

Bartenieff, Irmgard, and Dori Lewis. *Body Movement: Coping with the Environment*. New York: Gordon and Breach, 1980.

Hutchinson, A. *Labanotation*. New York: Theatre Arts Books, 1970.

Laban, Rudolph von. *Laban's Principles of Dance and Movement Notation*. Boston: Plays, Inc., 1975.

_____. *Modern Educational Dance*. Boston: Plays, Inc., 1963.

_____. *The Mastery of Movement*. Boston: Plays, Inc., 1971.

_____. *The Language of Movement*. Boston: Plays, Inc., 1974.

_____ with Lawrence F. C. *Effort: Economy in Body Movement*. Boston: Plays, Inc., 1974.

Lamb, Warren and Elizabeth Watson. *Body Code*. London: Routledge, 1979.

Moore, Carol-Lynne and Kaoru Yamamoto. *Beyond Words*. New York: Gordon and Breach, 1988.

Preston-Dunlop, Valerie. *A Handbook for Modern Educational Dance*. Boston: Plays, Inc., 1980.

Thornton, Samuel. *Laban's Theory of Movement*. Boston: Plays, Inc. 1974.

Meditation

Although meditation is not taught as a practice in theatre programs, mediation techniques are often integrated into training programs to help performers gain concentration skills. The texts below are general guides to meditation and do not necessarily encourage a particular religious viewpoint.

Carrington, Patricia. *Freedom in Meditation*. Garden City, N. Y.: Anchor, 1977.

LeShan, Lawrence. *How to Meditate*. Boston: Little Brown, 1974.

Johnston, William. *Silent Music: The Science of Meditation*. New York: Harper and Row, 1974.

Steinbrecher, Edwin. *The Inner Guide to Meditation*. Santa Fe, N. M.: Blue Feather Press, 1978.

The Mythic Dimension

In his numerous publications and television programs, Joseph Campbell described in detail the relationship between myth, art, and popular culture. The texts in this section include some by Campbell and others by people who combined his ideas with those of Jung to work with the creative process.

Campbell, Joseph. *Myths to Live By*. New York: Bantam Books, 1972.
_____. *The Hero with a Thousand Faces*. New Jersey: Princeton University Press, 1968.
_____. *The Mythic Image*. New Jersey: Princeton University Press, 1974.
_____. *The Inner Reaches of Outer Space*. New York: Harper and Row, 1986.
Feinstein, David, and Stanley Krippner. *Personal Mythology*. Los Angeles: Jeremy Tarcher, 1988.
Harner, Michael. *The Way of the Shaman*. New York: Harper and Row, 1990.
Johnson, Robert A. *Innerwork*. New York: Harper and Row, 1986.
Larsen, Stephen. *The Mythic Imagination*. New York: Bantam, 1990.
Lorler, Marie-lu. *Shamanic Healing*. N. M.: Brotherhood of Life, 1990.
Pearson, Carol S. *Awakening the Heroes Within*. San Francisco: Harper, 1991.

Neutral Mask

French mime and theatre artist Jacques Le Coq developed an approach to performance training popularly referred to as neutral mask work. While not all training programs incorporate this work, most programs do include some concept of neutral or a state of relaxed readiness that is free from habitual patterns of movement.

Eldredge, Sears A. "Jacques Copeau and the Mask in Actor Training." *Mime, Mask and Marionette II*, 3 and 4 (1979-80): 187-230.
_____. "Masks: Their Use and Effectiveness in Actor Training Programs." Doctoral Dissertation, Michigan State University, 1975.
Eldredge, Sears A., with Holly Hudson. "Actor Training in the Neutral Mask." *TDR* 22 (1980) 19-28.
Pitt, Leonard. "Mask Technique for the Actor." *San Francisco Theatre I*, 2 1977) 81-83.
Rolfe, Bari. *Behind the Mask*. Oakland, Calif.: Personna Books, 1977.

Non-verbal Communication

Referred to either as kinesics or proxemics, nonverbal communication is the study of the culturally specific nature of movement. Studies in this area help performers appreciate the diversity of communication styles.

Birdwhistell, Ray. *Kinesics and Context*. Philadelphia: University of Pennsylvania Press, 1970.

Davis, Martha, ed. *Interaction Rhythms*. New York: Human Sciences Press, 1982.

Hall, Edward. *The Silent Language*. New York: Doubleday, 1959.

_____. *The Hidden Dimension*. New York: Doubleday, 1966.

_____. *Beyond Culture*. New York: Doubleday, 1976.

Holding, Dennis. *Human Skills*. New York: John Wiley and Sons, 1989.

Lamb, Warren, and Elizabeth Watson. *Body Code*. London: Routledge, 1979.

Lustig, Myron, and Jolene Koester. *Intercultural Competence*. New York: Harper/Collins Collete, 1992.

Wolfgang, Aron, ed. *Non-verbal Behavior: Application and Cultural Implications*. New York: Academic Press, 1979.

Rolfing

Rolfing, or structural integration, is named for its founder, Ida P. Rolf (1876-1979). It shares a philosophy similar to that of other somatic therapies in that it assumes that structure determines function. Through a set of ten deep tissue massage sessions, Rolfing breaks up old patterns of the muscle and connective tissue.

Fetis, Rosemary. *What in the World is Rolfing*. Santa Monica, Calif.: Institute for Structural Integration, 1975.

Rolf, Ida. *Rolfing: The Integration of Human Structures*. New York: Harper and Row, 1977.

_____. *Ida Rolf talks about Rolfing and Physical Reality*. New York: Harper and Row, 1978.

Sensory Awareness

The following texts represent the work of such early sensory awareness advocates as Charlotte Selver and of contemporary work in the constructed nature of perception, such as the writings of Constance Classen. The former are inspirational reading concerning the body; the latter offer valuable insights into the formation of identity and thus of character.

Ackerman, Diane. *The Natural History of the Senses*. New York: Vintage Books, 1990.
Brooks, Charles. *Sensory Awareness: The Rediscovery of Experiencing*. New York: Viking, 1974.
Classen, Constance. *The Color of Angels: Cosmology, Gender and the Aesthetic Imagination*, London: Routledge, 1998.
Lidell, Lucy. *The Sensual Body*. London: Gaia Books, 1987.
Liguerer, Annick. *Scent: The Essential and Mysterious Powers of Smell*. Tokyo: Kodansha, 1992.
Montagu, Ashley. *Touching*. New York: Columbia University Press, 1971.
Selver, Charlotte, with V. W. Brooks. "Report on Work in Sensory Awareness and Total Functioning." *Explorations in Human Movement Potential*. Springfield. Ill.: Charles C. Thomas, 1966.

Style and Period Dance

The books in this section are reference materials for period style plays. They fall primarily into two categories, books that describe Renaissance and Restoration dance styles and acting texts that focus on Western acting styles.

Arbeau, Thoinot. *Orchesography*. New York: Dover, 1967.
Barton, Robert. *Style for Actors*. New York: Mayfield, 1993.
Brissenden, Alan. *Shakespeare and the Dance*. New Jersey: Humanities Press, 1981.
Crawford, Jerry L., and Joan Snyder. *Acting in Person and in Style*. Iowa, City, Iowa: William C. Brown, 1976.
Harrop, John, and Sabin R. Epstein. *Acting with Style*. New Jersey: Prentice Hall, 1982.
Hilton, Wendy. *Dance of the Court and Theatre: 1690-1725*. New Jersey: Princeton Book Company, 1981.

Russel, Douglas A. *Period Style for the Theatre*: Mass.: Alleyn and Bacon, 1980.

Schreck, Everett M. *Principles and Styles of Acting*. Mass.: Addison-Wesley, 1970.

Silver, Fred. *Auditioning for the Musical Theatre*. New York: Newmarket Press, 1985.

Spencer, Paul. *Society and the Dance*. Cambridge: Cambridge University Press, 1985.

Stayn, J. L. *Restoration Comedy in Performance*. Cambridge: Cambridge University Press, 1986.

Theatre Movement Theorists

This list combines references to the nineteenth century system of movement developed by Delsarte with the thoughts of designers, Gordon Craig, mimes, Samuel Avital, and directors such as Myerhold, Grotowski, and Suzuki. Each represents a distinctive aesthetic with respect to the performer and the visual elements of the stage space.

Boal, Augusto. *Games for Actors and Non-actors*. London: Routledge, 1992.

Delaumosne, Abbe. *Delsarte System of Oratory*. New York: E. S. Werner, 1893.

Chekhov, Michael. *Lessons for the Professional Actor*. New York: PAJ, 1985.

Craig, Edward Gordon. *Books and Theatre*. London: Dent, 1925.

_____. *Gordon Craig on Movement and Dance*. New York: Dance Horizons, 1977.

_____. *Craig on Theatre*. London: Methuen, 1983.

Grotowski, Jerzy. *Towards a Poor Theatre*. New York: Simon and Schuster, 1968.

Meyerhold, V. E. *Meyerhold on Theatre*. New York: Hill and Wang, 1969.

Stebbins, Genevieve. *Delsarte System of Expression*. New York: E. S. Werner, 1884.

Suzuki, Tadashi. *The Way of the Acting*. New York: Theatre Communications Group, 1986.

Zorn, John W. *The Essential Delsarte*. New Jersey: Scarecrow Press, 1968.

Todd-Sweigard "Psychophysiology/Ideokinesis":

Mabel Todd's *The Thinking Body* revolutionized dance training in the United States. Her ideas have been continued through her students Clark,

Dowd, and others. Her primary premise was the evolution of a released body. Lulu Sweigard's method of uniting mind and muscle through imagery is evolved from Todd's initial work.

Clark, Barbara. *Body Proportional Needs Depth*. Tempe, Ariz.: Clark Manuals, 1975.
_____. *How to Live in Your Axis*. Tempe, Arizona: Clark Manuals, 1968.
_____. *Let's Enjoy Sitting, Standing, and Walking*. Tempe, Arizona, Clark Manuals, 1963.
Dowd, Irene. *Taking Root to Fly*. New York: Contact Collaborations, 1981.
Sweigard, Lulu. *Human Movement Potential: Its Ideokinetic Facilitation*. New York: Harper and Row, 1974.
Todd, Mabel Elsworth. *Early Writings, 1929-1934*. Brooklyn: Dance Horizons, 1977.
_____. *The Thinking Body*. Brooklyn: Dance Horizons, 1968.

Visualization and Imagery

The process of visualization is derived from Asian meditation techniques that were introduced into the United States by Asian immigrants. Currently, this process has become both a means to enhance performance in sports and an aspect of the self-cultivation component of New Age philosophy.

Berendt, Joachim-Ernst. *The World is Sound Nada Brahma: Music and the Landscape of Consciousness*. Destiny Books: Rochester, Vt., 1983.
Halpern, Steven. *Tuning the Human Instrument*. Belmont, Calif.: Spectrum Research Institute, 1978.
Gardner, Kay. *Sounding the Inner Landscape*. Maine: Caduceus, 1990.
Gendlin, Eugene T., *Focusing*. New York: Bantam, 1982.
Leppert, Richard. *Art and the Committed Eye*. Denver, Co.: Westview, 1996.
McKim, R. *Experiences in Visual Thinking*. Belmont, Calif.: Wadsworth, 1972.
Pavio, A. *Imagery and Verbal Processes*. New York: Holt and Rinehart, 1971.
Richardson, A. *Mental Imagery*. New York: Springer, 1969.
Samuels, Mike, and Nancy Samuels. *Seeing with the Mind's Eye*. New York: Random House, 1975.
Singer, J. *Daydreaming*. New York: Random House, 1966.
Wiehl, A. *Creative Visualization*. Los Angeles: Peach Pub., 1972.

INDEX